determination that a particular treatment method is suitable for a given patient should be based on a comparative evaluation of the diverse approaches available in terms of specific parameters. The essential differences and interfaces between individual and group therapy form the theme of Dr. Anthony's second contribution to this book.

Regardless of the group therapist's therapeutic orientation—whether he emphasizes the here-and-now or the historical antecedents of the patient's behavior—and whatever his goals are, a careful evaluation and diagnosis help determine whether the patient is suited to group treatment and, if so, what type of treatment he can benefit from. Therefore, the sections by the editors on clinical diagnosis and the selection of patients and the organization of the group present a detailed discussion of the diagnostic process and of the classification of psychiatric disorders as set forth in the second edition of the American Psychiatric Association's Diagnostic and Statistical Manual of Mental Disorders.

CONTENTS

MODERN GROUP BOOK II

The Evolution of
Group Therapy

BOOKS BY DRS. KAPLAN AND SADOCK

Comprehensive Textbook of Psychiatry
Alfred M. Freedman and Harold I. Kaplan, Editors

Studies in Human Behavior
Alfred M. Freedman and Harold I. Kaplan, General Editors

Modern Synopsis of Comprehensive Textbook of Psychiatry
Harold I. Kaplan, Benjamin J. Sadock, and Alfred M. Freedman

Comprehensive Group Psychotherapy
Harold I. Kaplan and Benjamin J. Sadock, Editors

Modern Group Books
Harold I. Kaplan and Benjamin J. Sadock, Editors

HAROLD I. KAPLAN

Harold I. Kaplan received an undergraduate degree from Columbia University and an M.D. from the New York Medical College. He trained in psychiatry at the Kingsbridge Veterans Hospital and Mount Sinai Hospital in New York and became a Diplomate of the American Board of Psychiatry and Neurology in 1957; presently he is an Associate Examiner of the American Board. He began the practice and teaching of psychiatry and was certified in psychoanalytic medicine at the New York Medical College in 1954 where he became Professor of Psychiatry and Director of Psychiatric Training and Education in 1961. He is Attending Psychiatrist at Metropolitan Hospital Center, Flower and Fifth Avenue Hospitals and Bird S. Coler Hospital. He is the Principal Investigator of ten National Institute of Mental Health training programs, specializing in the areas of undergraduate and graduate psychiatric education as well as the training of women in medicine. He is the author of over seventy scientific papers and co-author and co-editor of the books listed on this page.

BENJAMIN J. SADOCK

Benjamin J. Sadock received his A.B. from Union College and his M.D. from New York Medical College. He trained at Bellevue Psychiatric Hospital. During his military service as an Air Force psychiatrist he was also on the faculty of Southwestern Medical School. Dr. Sadock became a Diplomate of the American Board of Psychiatry and Neurology in 1966 and is an Assistant Examiner for the American Board. Currently Associate Professor of Psychiatry and Director of the Division of Group Process at New York Medical College, Dr. Sadock directs the training program for group therapists and is Chief of Continuing Education in Psychiatry, Chief Psychiatric Consultant to the student health service and co-director of the Sexual Therapy Center. He is on staff of Flower and Fifth Avenue Hospitals, Metropolitan Hospital, and the New York State Psychiatric Institute. Dr. Sadock is active in numerous psychiatric organizations, an officer of the New York County District Branch of the American Psychiatric Association, a Fellow of the New York Academy of Medicine, and has written and lectured extensively in general psychiatry and group psychotherapy. He is co-editor with Dr. Harold I. Kaplan of *Comprehensive Group Psychotherapy* (1971) and co-author with Drs. Alfred M. Freedman and Harold I. Kaplan of *Modern Synopsis of Comprehensive Textbook of Psychiatry* (1972).

The Evolution of
Group Therapy

Edited by

HAROLD I. KAPLAN, M.D.

Professor of Psychiatry and Director of Psychiatric Education,
New York Medical College, New York, New York

and

BENJAMIN J. SADOCK, M.D.

Associate Professor of Psychiatry and Director,
Division of Group Process, New York Medical College,
New York, New York

Jason Aronson, Inc.
New York, New York

Library of Congress Catalog Card Number: 72-96927

Standard Book Number: 0-87668-078-3

The editors express their appreciation to the following persons, publishers and publications for permission to reprint portions of the works cited.

Aldine-Atherton, Inc. for "The Marathon Group," by G. R. Bach, reprinted from Hendrik M. Ruitenbeek, editor, *Group Therapy Today* (New York: Atherton Press, 1969); copyright © 1969 by Atherton Press. Reprinted by permission of the author and Aldine-Atherton, Inc.

Bruner/Mazel, Inc. for "The Use of Videotape in the Integrated Treatment of Individuals, Couples, Families, and Groups in Private Practice," by Milton M. Berger, M.D., reprinted from *Videotape Techniques in Psychiatric Training and Treatment*, Milton M. Berger, M.D., editor. Bruner/Mazel, Inc., New York, 1970.

Dr. Herbert Holt for the unpublished essay, "Existential Group Therapy: A Phenomenological Methodology for Psychiatry."

International Journal of Group Psychotherapy for "Sexual Acting Out in Groups," by the members of the Workshop in Group Psychoanalysis of New York: A. Wolf, R. Bross, S. Flowerman, J. Greene, A. Kadis, H. Leopold, N. Locke, I. Milburg, H. Mullan, S. Obers, and H. Rosenbaum. *International Journal of Group Psychotherapy*, Vol. 4, pp. 369-380, 1954.

for "Accelerated Interaction: A Time Limited Approach on the Brief Intensive Approach," by Frederick H. Stoller. *International Journal of Group Psychotherapy*, Vol. 18, pp. 220-235, 1968.

for "Group Therapy and the Small Group Field: An Encounter," by Morris Parloff. *International Journal of Group Psychotherapy*, Vol. 20, pp. 267-304, 1970.

International Universities Press for "Group Therapy with Alcoholics," by A. Stein, M.D. and Eugene Friedman, Ph.D., Chapter III of *Fields of Group Psychotherapy*, S. R. Slavson, editor. International Universities Press, 1956.

American Psychiatric Association for "Phoenix House: Therapeutic Communities for Drug Addicts," by M. S. Rosenthal and D. V. Biase, *Hospital and Community Psychiatry*, Vol. 20, p. 27, 1969.

W. W. Norton & Co., Inc., and the Hogarth Press Ltd. for an excerpt from *An Outline of Psycho-Analysis*, Volume XXIII of Standard Edition of Sigmund Freud, revised and edited by James Strachey. Copyright 1949 by W. W. Norton & Co., Inc., and copyright © 1969 by the Institute of Psychoanalysis and Alix Strachey.

The Williams & Wilkins Co. for an excerpt from "Group Therapy in Married Couples," by Helen Papanek, M.D., reprinted from *Comprehensive Group Psychotherapy*, Harold I. Kaplan and Benjamin J. Sadock, editors. Copyright © 1971 by The Williams & Wilkins Co.

for an excerpt from "Videotape Feedback in Group Setting," by F. Stoller. *Journal of Nervous and Mental Disorders*, Vol. 148, No. 4, pp. 457-466.

Seymour Lawrence/Delacorte Press for an excerpt from *Cat's Cradle* by Kurt Vonnegut, Jr. Copyright © 1963 by Kurt Vonnegut, Jr. A Seymour Lawrence Book/Delacorte Press. Reprinted by permission of the publisher.

Contents

Preface

The emergence of group psychotherapy within the past two decades constitutes one of the most significant and extraordinary developments in the field of psychiatry. Gradually during this period, but particularly within the past five years, group therapy has come to be chosen for the treatment of a widening range of patients with highly diverse problems. Concurrently, professionals and laymen alike see a growing interest in the relationship of group therapy to sociocultural and educational concepts, processes, and systems. Predictably, these theoretical developments are accompanied by the development of myriad therapeutic approaches which vary with respect not only to their underlying philosophy but also to the planning and conduct of treatment.

Psychotherapy is an art as well as a science. What is taught via the lecture hall or seminar room constitutes just one aspect of the teaching curriculum. Training in psychotherapy must also include clinical exercises performed under the supervision of an experienced clinician who acts as a model for the student. The editors' commitment to this project, and its concomitant goals, evolved from their extensive experience as both educators and clinicians. The editors' special interest in group psychotherapy as a treatment technique, and an awareness of the need for more intensive training in this discipline to ensure its continued growth and development, led to the establishment, at the New York Medical College, of the first medical-school-affiliated postgraduate certification program in group psychotherapy. In addition, they have participated in the organization of training programs in group therapy for workers in other mental health disciplines —psychology, psychiatric social work, and psychiatric nursing.

The stated goal of this series—to provide a survey of current theoretical and therapeutic trends in this field—carries with it the obligation to pursue an eclectic orientation and to present as comprehensive an account of events at every level of its development as is possible. The organization and orientation of this series attempts to provide a comprehensive survey of the theories, hypotheses, and therapeutic techniques which dominate contemporary group practice. There are no final answers, as yet, to the problems and issues which currently face group psychotherapy. But we may help to identify these problems and issues and place them in proper perspective.

This book is one of a series of paperback volumes based on *Comprehensive Group Psychotherapy,* which we previously edited. New articles have been written for each of these volumes and certain subjects have been updated or eliminated in an effort to reach a wider audience. Invitations to participate were extended to those workers who have made major and original contributions to the field of group psychotherapy and who are acknowledged experts in a particular area of theory and/or practice. Thus the preparation of this series afforded the editors a unique opportunity to engage in a stimulating interchange of ideas and to form many rewarding personal relationships. As a result, what would appear to have been an ardous undertaking has in fact been a most gratifying experience.

The editors have received dedicated and valuable help from many people to whom they wish to express their appreciation. For their secretarial and editorial help, we would like to thank Robert Gelfand, Sylvia Houzell, Mercedes Paul, Paulene Demarco, Louise Marshall, and in particular Lois Baken, who coordinated these efforts. Spe-

cial thanks are extended to our publishers, E. P. Dutton, and to our outstanding editor, Robert Zenowich.

Finally, the editors wish to express their appreciation to Virginia Sadock, M.D., who acted in the capacity of assistant to the editors and assumed the multitudinous tasks of that office with grace and charm.

HAROLD I. KAPLAN, M.D.

BENJAMIN J. SADOCK, M.D.

Introduction

There is a wide array of group therapy techniques currently available. Not only do the planning and conduct of treatment vary but also the theoretical model on which they are based. Today, every school of personality theory and psychopathology—Freudian, Sullivanian, Horneyan, and others is represented in group practice, although in certain approaches the relationship between treatment technique and a specific theoretical model is a tenuous one.

HISTORY OF GROUPS

Despite the extensive differences in technique and theoretical orientation, all therapy groups share the same historical roots. It follows, then, that an understanding of the evolution of group psychotherapy as a treatment modality is a prerequisite for the understanding of the current status of groups. This essential background material is provided in the chapter by Anthony, which is an overview of the history of treatment in groups. His writing extends well beyond the traditional chronological account of events that led to the emergence of group therapy. Rather, he synthesizes these events, forming a cohesive whole, describing and placing in proper perspective the innovative contributions of behavioral scientists to a variety of disciplines.

BASIC CONCEPTS

Apart from their historical origins, all present-day group therapy approaches share certain basic principles in common. The goal of this book is to elucidate these principles, which can be subsumed under the term *group dynamics*.

Just as the term *individual dynamics* refers to the property of individual behavior, so group dynamics refers to the properties of group behavior. But the distinction between the two must be clearly understood. Kurt Lewin emphasized the fact that the group is an organic whole psychologically, not just a collection of individual persons. The whole is different from the sum of its parts; it has definite properties of its own. Fried in her chapter, summarizes those properties that are intrinsic to the field and that are present in every therapy group, regardless of the therapist's technique or theoretical orientation.

COMPARING GROUPS

Spotnitz then compares the different types of group therapy. The fact that so many group techniques are available suggests that no one approach is superior to the others. Yet, in determining that a particular treatment method is suitable for a given patient, the therapist should base his judgment on a comparative evaluation of the diverse approaches available. He must consider the goals he hopes to achieve for the patient, that is, his optimal level of functioning consonant with his level of ego strength; his motivations for treatment; and such practical considerations as the patient's financial resources and current life situation, and most significant, the depth of personality exploration desired. The goal of certain psychoanalytic groups is to produce meaningful personality changes in much the same way that individual psychoanalysis does. Other methods —such as the behavioral or transactional group therapies—place emphasis on symptom removal and do not stress the relationship of these symptoms to past events in the patient's life.

Some patients may not be eligible for group psychotherapy at all and can best be treated on an individual basis. To make such a determination, the therapist must understand the essential differences between these modalities as well as their interfaces. These differences and similarities form the theme of Anthony's second contribution to this book. Many clinicians believe, for example, that patients in the early stages of depression should be treated individually, because the depressed patient's dependent needs are best gratified in the one-to-one relationship. However, group treatment may be recommended after these needs have been gratified and the patient has recovered from the acute depressive phase.

COMPOSITION OF GROUPS

Even if the patient is a suitable candidate for group therapy, the therapy may not be successful if he is assigned to the wrong group or if the composition of the group is not conducive to therapeutic progress. Therapists differ in their opinions about group composition, but the great majority agree that most desirable groups are heterogeneous; they include male and female patients in many diagnostic categories whose behavioral patterns and ages vary, and who are drawn from different socioeconomic levels. Mirror image patients who present complementary psychological problems—such as a son who competes with his father and a father who is in competition with his son—are frequently placed in the same group.

There is consensus that therapy groups function most effectively when membership is limited to eight to ten patients. Most therapists believe that this number ensures sufficient interaction among group members yet permits them to remain aware of the personal dynamics of each patient. However, optimal group size varies, depending on the approach used and the therapist's biases. Apart from theoretical and therapeutic considerations, some clinicians feel that they are better able to monitor a larger group of patients. These variations in group size and in group composition and their underlying rationale are elucidated in this volume.

BASIC CONCEPTS

Historically, psychotherapy evolved from psychoanalytic treatment, and group psychotherapy, in the initial stages of its development, was based on the psychoanalytic theory of personality and psychopathology. Newer approaches notwithstanding, the majority of group therapies are still governed by psychoanalytic concepts, which are outlined by the editors in their chapter on clinical diagnosis. Although certain methods, such as those that attempt symptomatic improvement, do not necessarily require an understanding of the individual patient in genetic-dynamic terms, the therapist's knowledge of psychoanalytic concepts is nonetheless important for his understanding of the patient's behavior within the group. Therefore, an outline of the basic principles of group psychotherapy must include the significant details of the psychoanalytic theory of personality.

CLINICAL DIAGNOSIS

The editors' decision to include a section on clinical diagnosis was based on similar considerations. The importance of diagnosis in group treatment has long been a source of disagreement among therapists. The editors hold to the firm conviction that careful evaluation and diagnosis of the individual patient is essential to the efficacy of group therapy. Moreover, it has become evident, in the light of recent therapeutic developments, that diagnosis is essential if casualties resulting from group experience are to be avoided. Regardless of the group therapist's orientation—whatever his goals are—careful evaluation and diagnosis will help him determine whether the patient is suited to group treatment and, if so, what type of treatment will benefit him. In addition, the psychiatric interview, the major tool of diagnosis, can also serve an important function, for it underscores the nature of the therapist's attitude toward and perception of the patient. This plays a crucial role in treatment. Therefore, the chapter by the editors on clinical diagnosis presents a detailed discussion of the diagnostic process and the classification of psychiatric disorders as set forth in the second edition of the American Psychiatric Association's *Diagnostic and Statistical Manual of Mental Disorders.*

PATIENT SELECTION

When the group is used as the psychotherapeutic vehicle for change in personality functioning, careful selection of patients and careful group organization are essential clinical responsibilities. Group psychotherapy cannot be applied as a blanket form of psychiatric treatment, suitable for all types of emotional disorders, even though a great variety of patients have been exposed to the method.

Clinical experience shows that patients who have done poorly in group psychotherapy may do well in individual psychotherapy. The reverse is also true; patients who have not made gains during individual treatment have done so in group. This makes it difficult to predict with accuracy which patient will do well in which form of therapy, although certain guidelines can be offered and are included in the chapter by the editors on the selection of patients and organization of the group.

It should be emphasized, however, that even if an accurate determination is made about a particular patient's suitability for group therapy, the success or failure of treatment may depend on the group into which he is placed. Each therapy group develops its own configuration, network of interpersonal relationships, standards, and values.

The goal of all is to foster a group atmosphere where therapy will flourish, thus enabling the patient to learn new ways to cope more effectively with internal and external conflict and to fulfill his potential, to the highest degree possible.

1

The History of Group Psychotherapy

E. James Anthony, M.D.

INTRODUCTION

History can be written in at least two distinctly different ways. The historian can choose to tell it as it really happened (*wie es geschehen ist*, in Ranke's famous phrase) or to reconstruct it in the context of present-day theory and practice. The first method has little dynamic value for the clinical historian, and there is no convincing reason why one should have to contemplate past ideas solely in terms of the *Zeitgeist* prevailing at the time. Moreover, it tends to place history firmly and disjunctively in the past, with little or no bearing on the present except as interest or illustration.

The second historical approach was first opened up by Nietzsche in his *Unseasonable Reflexions* and carried, as so much of his work did, psychoanalytic undertones. According to him, the reconstruction of the past should not be an end in itself but the means of relating the past to the present in a meaningful and operational way. This process could be understood as the historian's equivalent to the transference. This approach assumed that the historian could and should live contemporaneously in the two worlds of the past and the present. In fact, only by linking these two together dynamically could the historical past be made to have both relevance and value in the present. Sometimes surprisingly, the apparently demoded insights of the past could be refurbished for current use. The student of history frequently sees how the present unconsciously plagiarizes the past.

This dynamic viewpoint ensures that

history becomes an indispensable handmaiden of on-going life rather than remaining monolithically isolated as a monument to the past. It allows what is now to transact with what was then, and it finds an equal place for both within the continuous historical process. In this crucial scientific dialogue between past and present, the present must take and keep the initiative. The present should in no way become a slave to the past in the manner of tradition; it must be free to make full use of the past for its own evolving purposes.

The essence of the dynamic historical method is to select the significant facts of history and arrange them within a temporal sequence. Inevitably, some manipulation is involved in this selection and arrangement, but there must be no distortion of the facts. The clinical historian must be ready to admit that, although he may have a bias in his arrangement of facts, he is still able to recognize other perspectives, even when they contradict his own thesis. Like the good therapist, he should be able to see in this multiplicity of incompatible perspectives not failure or foolishness but the very richness of life.

The never-ending discovery and rediscovery of past developments by present-day workers are the expression of a dialectic that will last as long as the particular discipline concerned remains viable and growing. On the other hand, the workers who disconnect themselves from the past not only miss out on the enrichment and self-revelation provided by the past but are also fated, if Freud and Santayana are right, to repeat compulsively the past while deluding themselves that they are breaking new theoretical or technical ground. An attentive awareness of past modes of feeling, thinking, and doing—what Meinecke refers to as historicism—helps to safeguard against this proclivity.

It would be a naive conceit on the part of the historian to suppose that he can reduce the conglomerated past to a unified and linear development. In this discipline, as in all other disciplines, there is always an irreducible plurality of operating systems. It is, therefore, important to preserve a wide-angled viewpoint on all the global conspectuses that have existed within the historical evolution—whether actual, factual, mythological, or fantasied—granting to each the recognition of its particularity.

There is another reason for mapping out the topology of the historical field. By doing so, the worker can develop what Whitehead, in a different context, aptly termed graded envisagement. He can become aware of a system of kinship within the general population of ideas belonging to his discipline. For example, the group worker can begin to realize that the disparate concepts of Gestalt therapy and analytic group therapy not only have antecedents in common but are often in close theoretical relationship, separated only by semantic confusion. Since all these ideas fall more or less within the same family system, it is not altogether surprising that intellectual totems and taboos are set up, so that it seems to become something horrendous to mate what are apparently neighboring ideas. Many theorists, having swallowed their own intellectual totems, react to closely related ideas as if they were incestuous.

The ultimate lesson from history, therefore, is that for coherent, logical development in a discipline, one must constantly and consistently remember where he came from and where he is going. The past is conglomerate, complex, confabulatory, and conflictual, but it is incumbent on every worker to resolve these perplexities and complexities for himself and, by so doing, discover his own professional identity and ultimate purpose. Each group psychotherapist must become his own historian and

thread his way with open-mindedness and relative impartiality through the shoals of psychobiologically improbable, mythological, mystical, and paralogical ideas of the past and present, asking his own questions and seeking his own answers within the totality of what is known or imagined. He has to undertake this job for himself, since no one can do it for him.

The scientific mind that is brought up and nurtured on history obtains an equanimity and objectivity that becomes characteristic of the scientist in all his dealings. Bronowski, in describing how scientists communicate, has this to say:

They do not make wild claims, they do not cheat, they do not try to persuade at any cost, they appeal neither to prejudice nor to authority, they are often frank about their ignorance, their disputes are fairly decorous, they do not confuse what is being argued with race, politics, sex or age, and they listen patiently to the young and to the old who both know everything.

Patience, that essential scientific virtue, can come not only from listening to patients but also from listening to history.

GROUP PSYCHOLOGY

The beginning is always difficult, wrote Schopenhauer. This is true for birth, for writing history, and for history itself. Once, however, one recognizes that the beginning is never really the beginning and that there is always a prehistory antedating every start, the conflict of inertia can be solved. One can deal with group psychology and, by means of it, find his way imperceptibly, if the historical development holds true, into the field of group psychotherapy.

World War I proved to be a great impetus to the development of group psychology and World War II, to the development of group psychotherapy. This relationship to war cannot be regarded as entirely accidental. In war, individual man is forced into groups of all sizes and structures for reasons of survival. In war, he loses much of his identity and becomes better known for fighting, rationing, and security purposes as a number. The understanding and maintenance of group morale becomes a critical factor in the country's struggle for existence. In World War I, various group psychologists stepped forward to meet this pressing need.

A pioneer in this field, and one of the most scintillating intellects of his time, was Wilfred Trotter, a neurosurgeon who, in the middle of World War I, published a remarkable document on the herd instinct in peace and war. Whether there is such an organizing instinct in man has been much debated and is still in dispute, but Trotter developed the insight that it is both logical and biological for human groups to form if one regards the group as a continuation of the multicellular character of all higher organisms. The instinct to come together and develop multifunctional skills for the sake of individual and group survival would be in keeping with evolutionary trends. Later authors also pointed to needs for pairing and fighting as basic elements in group formation, but they gave psychodynamic reasons.

Le Bon and the Popular Mind

It was Le Bon who inadvertently gave the group a bad name to begin with, in 1920. He cannot be blamed for this, since he was careful to specify that his descriptions applied to large groups or crowds that are essentially unorganized or under the mysterious and irresistible influence of charismatic leadership. The capacity of a leader to sway a crowd in the direction of his own purpose— playing on its suggestibility, its exaggerated emotionalism, and its credulity—has never been as subtly portrayed as in Mark Antony's brilliant display of demagoguery in Shakespeare's *Julius Caesar*.

According to Le Bon, the person who joins a group, especially a large group, sacrifices something of his precious individuality. He becomes more suggestible and, therefore, more susceptible to the contagion of neighboring minds. Le Bon's description of the group mind has many of the characteristics of the child, the primitive, and the impulse-ridden psychopath. The group mind is illogical, intolerant, prejudiced, rigid, uninhibited, and submissive to any dominant force that exerts its authority.

If this were even partly true, it would follow that the group is more susceptible to therapeutic influence than the individual and, therefore, a better bet with regard to treatment. Freud, however, pointed out that this detrimental and depreciatory appraisal of the group mind reflects the contempt with which certain thinkers view the masses. This appraisal is certainly not very different from prejudices characteristic of the aristocratic elements of society at all times.

Other critics, such as Kraskovic, held the view that group enthusiasm would bring about the most splendid achievements. The question of who was right gave place, with further consideration, to the view that perhaps both could be right and that the group contained within itself the seeds of both success and failure.

McDougall and the Group Mind

In 1920, McDougall started out from this apparent contradiction and found a solution for it in the factor of organization. In his understanding, there are two psychologies of the group, the one dealing with an unorganized group and the other with a group that is organized.

McDougall's judgment of the unorganized group is as severe as Le Bon's. He, too, saw it as emotional, impulsive, violent, fickle, inconsistent, irresolute, suggestible, irresponsible, and at times almost like a wild beast. But this is not the whole story. A marked change occurs when the group is organized and task-oriented. The collective mental life is then raised to a higher level, and some of the psychological disadvantages of group formation are removed. In addition, the exaltation or intensification of emotion that takes place in every group member and that stirs each one to a degree that they seldom attained under any other conditions can now be used for great achievement.

The "primitive sympathetic response," which is somewhat similar to Le Bon's "contagion," can be harnessed for better purpose if five main organizational conditions are established: group continuity, a system of group relationships, the stimulus of intergroup rivalries, the development of traditions, and the differentiation and specialization of functions. A sixth condition that can be added to these five is the emergence of leadership, a phenomenon that later workers have tended to focus on, since it has special bearing on the therapist's role in group psychotherapy.

The problem for the group psychotherapist using McDougall's frame of reference is how to further the organization desirable for optimal collective life and at the same time make therapeutic use of the primitive sympathetic response that brings with it the mutative affective experience. Throughout the subsequent history of group psychotherapy, workers would be torn between the therapeutic potential of the group mind and the group emotion.

Freud and the Group Leader

In 1921, Freud first outlined a group psychology that was and still is meaningful to the group psychotherapist. One can only conjecture, with regret, what extraordinary developments could have occurred had he been able to follow up on his group psychology and do for group psychotherapy what he did for psychoanalysis. He himself did not feel that the two psychologies are as different as they seem on first glance. He felt that it does not make sense to consider the individual psychologically except in relation to other individuals, so that in a way all psychology is essentially group psychology, and group psychology is the original and older psychology. He was thus able to speak of a group of two, by which means he was able to link individual and group psychology together.

The repercussions of this viewpoint still haunt group psychotherapy. The question of treating the individual through the group or the group through the individual is a perennial one, and one might conclude, in agreement with Freud, that it is largely a pseudoquestion and that the therapist always does a bit of both.

Freud addressed himself to three problems. These are crucial not only for the understanding of group psychology but also for the practice of group psychotherapy: (1) What is a group? (2) How does the group come to exercise such a strong influence over the mental life of the individual? (3) What changes does the group bring about in the mental life of the individual?

Freud indicated that a collection of people is not a group but, given the proper conditions, can develop into a group. A major condition for this to happen is the development of leadership, but to what extent this is dispensable depends on the nature of the group and on the presence of strong group bonds. A leading idea can substitute for an actual leader, especially if it occasions the same strong feeling tones and identifications.

Morphologically, Freud distinguished between transient and permanent groups, homogeneous and heterogeneous ones, natural and artificial ones, and organized and unorganized ones, but his major differentiation was undoubtedly between leadered and leaderless groups.

All these distinctions are still of great importance to the field of group psychotherapy. Therapists are still wondering whether they do better with short-term groups than with long-term groups, whether heterogeneous groups are less therapeutic than homogeneous ones, and whether natural groups, such as families, start off with a stronger therapeutic advantage than artificial stranger groups.

It was Freud's opinion that the mechanism of identification is a basic one in group formations. The group members identify with the leader, whom they view as a father surrogate, and they identify with one another and relate to one another through their common tie to the leader.

A second important mechanism at work in the group is that of empathy, which enables the group members to experience their group life through one another.

By means of these two powerful mechanisms, the one leading to the other, the individual patients in the group are able to obtain an inward experience of another's mental life. Identification not only helps to further positive feeling within the group but also helps in limiting aggressiveness, since there is a general tendency to spare those with whom one is identified.

The psychological cement responsible for group ties is, according to Freud, a composite of cohering elements, such as imitation, identification, empathy, relatedness, sympathy, common purpose, mutual interests, and, more fundamentally, a recognition of something common that is incorporated and shared by all the membership. In its most concrete form, the cohesive element would be eating together; on a more psychological level, it would be taking in and sharing a leader. In the therapeutic group, the feeling of having similar problems, sharing the same therapist, and being together in the same group makes for unification. Some of the narcissism of the members is projected onto the group, so that it becomes something very special, and some of it is projected onto the leader, making him an ego ideal. Under conditions of charismatic leadership, the group may become, as it were, hypnotized, surrendering to the superior power of the leader. The members may then show a marked dependency and submissiveness, a set of circumstances frequently seen in psychotherapeutic groups.

Freud's perception of group formations as being cardinal to the life of the group was indeed an accurate one. To the extent that the members develop into a real group, there is less need for dominant leadership. The more leader-centered the group is, the more regressive does its organization tend to become. For group psychotherapists, the paradox has long been a familiar one. In the words of Lao-tse, the best leader is he who knows how to follow.

When a group with a strong leader loses its leadership, a dissolution of ties rapidly occurs, and, as a result, panic ensues. The members cease to relate to one another in an integrated way, cease to listen to orders, cease to have any concern except self-concern, and become susceptible to the sudden emergence of a gigantic and senseless dread that spreads through them like contagion. Later psychotherapists have substantiated Freud's original observation and have attempted to account for its occurrence. How Freud could develop so much insight into the workings of a group without systematic group experience or experience in a group psychotherapy group remains as much a mystery as how he acquired so much insight into intrapsychic matters

without undergoing a training analysis.

Having coped brilliantly with the questions that he himself raised, Freud confronted himself with still another perplexing problem: What brings the group together?

It has always been recognized that man is a social animal born into a group, living within a group, and usually dying supported by a group. In some religions, it is alleged that he rejoins the group in the afterlife. The instinct theorists, from Trotter on, have postulated some kind of herd instinct that makes the human animal, like other gregarious animals, feel incomplete when he is alone. There is also some sense of security that comes from being with individuals like one's self, the corollary being the sense of threat when associating with individuals unlike one's self.

Freud, although an instinct man, was inclined to reject the theory of a social instinct. For him, man is not a herd animal but a horde animal—that is, an individual brought together with other individuals into a group by a leader. The group is a revival of the primal horde conjectured by Darwin— the herd that is ruled over despotically by a powerful male. What brings the individual members together into the group is the leader, but this is essentially different from what brings the leader into the group. There were thus two basic psychologies within group psychology: the psychology of the individual members of the group and the psychology of the leader of the group. It is these two psychologies, operating in every group psychotherapy group, that makes group psychotherapy twice as complicated as individual psychotherapy.

Deeper forces that keep a group together concerns the erotic impulse, but Freud had less to say about these ties, chiefly because it could not have been possible for him to analyze them without the help of a therapeutic group. However, his hunch was that homosexual love was far more compatible with the maintenance of group ties than was heterosexual love. Both love and neurosis he saw as having a disintegrating effect on the group.

At this point, Freud made one of his most important pronouncements regarding group psychology and group psychotherapy. He pointed out that, where there is a powerful impetus to group formation, neurosis tends to diminish and eventually to disappear, and he felt that it is justifiable to turn this inverse relationship between neurosis and group formation to therapeutic account. He observed that well-organized groups are a powerful protection against the development of neurosis and that, when the individual is excluded from the group, he is compelled to replace group formations with neurotic formations. If Freud had followed up this lead to its logical conclusion, he would have created a complete system of group psychotherapy.

Why did Freud stop at that point? Curiously enough, he did the same thing with the natural group of the family as he did with the artificial stranger group. In his book *Totem and Taboo*, he set out three postulates that could have laid the foundation of systematic family theory and therapy: first, that there is a family psyche whose psychological processes correspond fairly closely to those of the individual; second, that there is a continuity of emotional life in the family psyche from one generation to the next; and third, that the mysterious transmission of attitudes and feelings through the generations is the result of unconscious understanding that makes the latent psychic life of one generation accessible to the succeeding one.

These three postulates could have become the cornerstone of a dynamic and developmental family psychopathology. They presumed a collective psychological life for the family, a process of intergenerational transmission of neurosis, and an unconscious understanding that assimilates neurotic disturbances and generates family pathology.

Why did he stop at these critical points? Who can tell? It is possible that his intense interest in individual intrapsychic conflicts—his own—superseded everything else.

Burrow and Group Analysis

Trigant Burrow gave the name group analysis to the type of behavior analysis first conducted in groups. Since this name

led to a great deal of misunderstanding as to what he was doing, he dropped the term and spoke instead of phyloanalysis, which indicated that his interest was in man in his evolutionary status. Although he had a background of psychoanalytic knowledge and working in groups, he did not strongly affect the field of current group psychotherapy. Essentially, he does not belong to the history of group psychotherapy, but one might consider some of his ideas in the light of present-day knowledge. In the first place, he refused to polarize the therapeutic situation into a sick patient needing help on the one side and a well physician giving him help on the other hand. Burrow saw both as elements in a sick society, with both needing to understand the social aberration from which they were suffering. This abdication of the therapist from the leader's role has its current counterpart. In the second place, Burrow stressed the importance of the here-and-now and paid scant attention to genetic aspects. Third, his concern was not with words but with the visible somatic manifestations of stress as they are subjectively or objectively experienced.

What Burrow was searching for was some undiscovered factor within the sphere of man's behavior that belonged to the biophysical bedrock. This factor was observable, physiological, and concrete, with definite localization, and was most manifest in a group setting. To study it, he set up, with his associate, what almost amounted to prolonged sensitivity training groups conducted over many years. Within these groups, he made use of a series of laboratory exercises in an effort to make subjective man objectively appreciative of his own subjective processes. All this sounds as if he were a precursor of the National Training Laboratories at Bethel except for the fact that his frame of reference was radically different.

Since his terminology is often needlessly difficult, it may be helpful to quote a lucid discussion of his approach given in his book *The Social Basis of Consciousness:*

I was led to the idea of an analysis which should take place in a group of persons in which no one individual would hold an authoritative position in relation to the others except in the measure in which his thoughtfulness and intelligence automatically qualified him to act in a responsible capacity. My idea was that each participant would seek to discover the nature of the motivation to the customary expression of his thought and feeling as well as test for himself the nature of the motives to the reactions socially stimulated by him. At the same time he was to register and, in as far as possible, determine in turn the motive to whatever reserve or hesitation or distortion might occur in the spontaneous expression of himself and of others. There was not the slightest interest in hearing about the individual's ideas or opinions as such, or in knowing what he might at any time have thought, said or done. Such reminiscent preoccupations were neither here nor there. Nor was there any concern to know what he planned at some future time to do. *The effort was to reach the organism's immediate motivation in relation to the situation at hand.*

Here is a group in which spontaneity, immediacy, and process are at the heart of things. What Burrow tried to accomplish was a bridging of the gap between words and feelings and a recognition by all the group members that verbal expression is incorrigibly false. He discovered that people in groups exist in a general state of repression and that there is a covert covenant to present one's self in the most acceptable light.

Burrow's training labs discouraged self-consciousness and secrecy and were conducted, as far as possible, nonjudgmentally. The social image or what encounter theorists would call a mask came under close scrutiny in the group experiments. Behind the social image lie Freudian resistances, and behind these resistances lie the bedrock physiological factors continuous through the phylum. Once the group penetrates behind the artificial personality that the individual member created verbally for himself, he is able to function at a more preconscious level that gains expression in a quiet, self-possessed mood.

Burrow can be considered a pioneer of training groups, of the laboratory approach to social neurosis, and of recent work dealing with psychophysiological responses within the group. He progressed from psychoanalysis through group analysis to phylo-analysis, and somewhere along the line, perhaps because of his medical preconceptions, he appeared to take a wrong turn and ended up with an inflated evolutionary theory in which both the individual and the small group were totally lost.

Lewin and Field Theory

Strong primitive forces emanate from groups before they become domesticated by organization. But the controls are never complete, so the life of any group can be plotted in terms of both progressive and regressive outputs.

According to Kurt Lewin, conflict is inherent and inevitable in the group. As he put it, every group contains within it the seeds of its own destruction. In terms of his topological or field theory, each individual member of a group struggles for adequate life space in the way that animals struggle for territory, and it is inevitable that the needs of any particular member conflict in this respect with the needs of the group as a whole. The group situation always demands some sacrifice on the part of the individual member and some limitation on his space for free movement. The amount of conflict generated varies with the amount of restriction imposed by the group as compared with the amount of mutual support and involvement that it gives in exchange.

What the membership does with such group tension depends partly on the structure of the group and partly on its leadership. Two group prototypes in this respect can be described. In the one, the group is poorly organized, weakly integrated, and leaderless; as a result, tension is poorly distributed and tends to rise to disruptive levels. In the contrasting type, the group is well-organized, well-integrated, and well-led; the tension is more evenly distributed, and communications flow more smoothly. Here again, in quite a different conceptual framework, are the two types described by McDougall.

Almost all group behavior may be said to lie somewhere between the two extreme types described. In every group, there is a balance of cohesive and disruptive forces, and the level of tension depends on which factor is paramount. Under benign leadership, the tension within the group remains optimal, allowing for constructive group activity.

As a function of group structure, group leadership, and group interaction, every group develops an atmosphere characteristic of it. The leader may be potent in creating this atmosphere, but the atmosphere, in turn, may create the leader, so that leaders tend to emerge spontaneously from different group situations.

The members of the group also bring into the group with them the status that they habitually occupy and the roles that they normally play. Unless new roles are assigned to them in the group, they will attempt to affirm their usual roles and manipulate other group members into supporting such role activity.

The leadership role is perhaps the most complex of the different roles open to group members and may take different forms. The leader, for example, may be required to coordinate the group's activities, control its internal relationships, symbolize its unity and integration, take the blame for its failures, assume the place of the father in the lives of the members, act as arbitrator in their conflicts, display expertise on all matters, and serve as a model for appropriate attitudes and behavior. In addition to all this, he is expected to take full responsibility for the present and future life of the group, gaining praise for its successes and censure for its failures.

Lewin, despite his profound involvement in social issues and his dedication to action research, had neither the wish nor the capacity to contribute directly to group psychotherapy. He was too much of an experimentalist to be a therapist himself. However, his system of group dynamics and his ahistoric conception of group tensions have been incorporated into several systems, even those with a psychoanalytic structure. The here-and-now is prominent in the encounter groups, but it is also a feature of every group-oriented group where the developmental aspects of the individual are left in abeyance. The psychoanalytic concept of transference has the advantage of

linking past and present into a coherent whole and is a more useful tool for the group psychotherapist. The delineation of the leadership role covers most of the functions assumed by the group psychotherapist but omits his representation within the unconscious minds of the group participants. Field theory may complement but never substitute for the more complex and analytic theories.

Bion and the Basic Assumptions

Once the group is civilized and organized, the more primitive elements are largely underground and tend to show themselves only in situations of panic, disrupting tension, and disorganization. The group, like the individual member, functions on both a latent level and a manifest level. Le Bon and McDougall visualized the latent forces as primitive to the point of psychopathy, whereas Bion sees them as psychotic. This latent layer is covered over by the organization that allows the group to become task-oriented. At this manifest level, the group gets to work and occupies itself in ways that are conscious, rational, constructive, and busy. And at this level it needs a leader who can drive the group and direct it. When, however, the group has nothing to do and no leader to lead it, the inner irrational feelings and fantasies become mobilized and rise to the surface, where their presence is felt by a marked increase in tension.

Like Freud, Bion poses some interesting questions and offers some even more interesting answers. He, too, asks why the group comes together in the first place and what keeps it together once it has formed. In addition, he wonders how it deals with its inner tensions, especially when it has been deprived of its leader, and in what way the members get in touch with one another.

At the overt level, the group members are brought together and held together by anything they they have to do together, and, when this is ended, they may disband. They may also continue to work together without a leader, but after a while, unless someone emerges to fulfill this function, the work they do begins to suffer. While they are engaged in legitimate work, the level of interaction rarely deepens. The members communicate mostly in verbal terms and dissipate their tensions in a number of social ways, so that the level of tension never gets to the point of disruption.

Below this overt level, the life of the group is entirely different and has little relationship to reality The group members come together and stay together because of strong basic needs. They want to find and keep a leader who will meet all their dependency needs, assist them in finding a sexual partner, and direct them into fight or flight when danger becomes threatening. The search for a leader, therefore, brings the group members together, and, once they find him, they cannot do without him. If rendered leaderless, they invent a leader in the shape of some predominant idea around which they can coalesce. A leaderless group, consequently, spends a large part of its time searching for a leader, and, depending on the state of the basic assumptions within the group, some kind of leader eventually emerges.

The student of history is intrigued by the fact that similar ideas keep recurring and are always treated as if they were something quite novel. It was once said that there are only seven basic story plots and that storytellers manipulate these with considerable skill to produce new stories for each new generation. The world of ideas may well be similarly impoverished, but theorists become so skillful at putting old ideas into new language that an exhilarating sense of progress is produced. Therefore, the two-group concept has dominated the history of group psychology from the very beginning and is an outcome of the manifest and latent, the conscious and unconscious postulates put forward by psychoanalysis. The two groups within the group perform different activities, have different needs, and speak essentially a different language, since the basic assumption group can communicate nonverbally, empathically, intuitively, and by contagion.

Nevertheless, Bion has created, even if only in a limited form, a group psychology of the unconscious and, by linking this psychology with Kleinian metapsychology, has made it directly available to the group psychotherapist. Furthermore, Bion has raised the important question of how the manifest and latent groups interact. The manifest and latent layers of the mind, as described by psychoanalysis, are in continuous transaction, and one's personality is to a great extent determined by what happens at the interface. Although it may be confounding to extrapolate from the individual member to the group, there is no doubt that the personality of the group may also be a product of a similar interplay. The manifest group tries in all sorts of devious ways to manipulate the latent group, although it keeps an eye on its realistic aims and purposes. If the manifest group becomes disorganized in any way, there is the immediate danger that the basic assumptions will return from the unconscious and take control of the situation, leading to a rise in tension followed by the appearance of primitive drives and feelings.

On the basis of this model, Bion has been able to describe different types of group culture in which some of the basic assumptions are gratified and some frustrated. These cultures represent a transient ascendancy, so that a pairing state may be prominent on one occasion and a fight-flight state on another. This means that one can follow cultural variations over time in the same way as in Lewinian groups; the climate may undergo alteration with any change in leadership.

One can invent a group psychology and not follow it up by making it applicable to group psychotherapy. This happened with Freud and, to some extent, with Bion. He sees himself not as a group psychotherapist but rather as a group investigator.

Whitaker and Lieberman and Focal-Conflict Theory

Focal-conflict theory, thought up by Thomas French, attempts to explain the current behavior of a person as an expression of his method of solving currently experienced personality conflicts that originated very early in his life. The person is constantly resonating to these early focal conflicts. The original solutions and the original feelings are modified by the altered circumstances of later life. The conflicts and their attempted solutions are so much part of the person's way of life that he can hardly do without them, however much he may want to rid himself of them.

In the context of the group situation, Whitaker and Lieberman suggest that each member of the group is affected by some group-focal conflict, as a result of which he tends to behave in a particular stereotyped way. The group conflicts are a threat to the individual member, since they expose him to personal conflicts. The individual member sticks to his pathological solutions because they protect him from the anxiety stemming from unconscious conflicts, and the other group members may respond helpfully or unhelpfully to these lifelong solutions. As the group progresses, the hidden conflict begins to emerge both as a wish and as a fear, and the group may act to reduce the fear and maximize the wish-fulfillment.

This type of group psychology has an artificial ring about it. In the first place, it is an oversimplified adaptation of an individual psychological approach that itself has never gained much general acceptance because of its somewhat schematic nature. The propensity to use borrowed theories has certain pitfalls. As Freud was first to point out, a group does not occur simply by putting a number of people together. Why it comes together and why it stays together are integral parts of how it functions together. Focal-conflict theory has nothing to say about these parts; as a consequence, it lacks the appeal of the conceptual framework put forward by Freud and Bion.

Ezriel and the Common Group Tension

Ezriel, as a psychoanalyst working with groups, also became interested in the interaction between the manifest and latent levels of the group. In the place of Bion's basic assumptions, he postulated an underlying common group problem that gives rise to tension and is a common denominator of the dominant unconscious fantasies of all the group members. In addition, each member projects his unconscious fantasy-objects upon various other group members and then tries to manipulate them accordingly.

This theory is not so difficult to accept. The idea of a collective fantasy may sound Jungian, but then group psychotherapists and group psychologists are always skirting the Jungian unconscious without acknowledging it in any way. The manipulation of the group members in terms of the internal object society is simply an example of group transference and the tendency everyone has of manipulating transference figures.

The emphasis put on insight as an experience leading to change is generally in keeping with the psychoanalytic approach. Others have tended to depreciate the value of insight as an essential therapeutic factor and to accord the leading position to experience.

Foulkes and the Network

What happens in the other 22 or 23 hours of a patient's life when he is not engaged in a psychotherapeutic situation is becoming increasingly important, even to the psychotherapist. Community psychiatry attempts to follow the patient out of the clinic into his world to arrange helpful contacts for him outside of his hour. The more one considers the social orbit of a patient in the framework of the newer ecological approach, the more one becomes aware of the many pathogenic and therapeutic influences at work within it. The idea of a network—that is, the natural group in which the patient lives at the time of his illness and his treatment—was formulated by Foulkes as an adjunct to the fuller understanding of the group analytic situation that he refers to as the group matrix. The matrix and the network together can help to illuminate the understanding of illness as a social process. The matrix is the frame of reference for the interactional context of the group as expressed manifestly, symbolically, symptomatically, effectively, behaviorally, and verbally.

The dynamically interacting network of the patient has, according to Foulkes, a fundamental significance in the production of illness in the patient. And when a significant change occurs in a patient, particularly a change toward greater independence, the other members of the network become active. The network covers not only the nuclear but also the extended family group and can involve friends as well. (It is interesting, in this context, to note that Post found more psychiatric illness within the social orbit of psychiatric patients than one would expect from the distribution of psychiatric illness in the general population.)

The thesis put forward by Foulkes is that illness and related disturbances are due in part to psychopathological processes that involve a number of interacting persons. In the psychoneuroses this multipersonal network of interaction is of central significance, and change in any member of such a network is linked to corresponding changes in other members. Even the nature of individual symptoms may rest on this interdependence. Therefore, the emotional disturbance can no longer be regarded in a vacuum, limited to one individual personality; it is always a function of relationships involving many people. The disturbance is an expression of a disturbed equilibrium in a total field of interaction. The patient is more or less unaware of this fact and may expect changes in himself without concomitant changes in the rest of the network. But it is impossible to change the patient without changing his network. There are, therefore, two important crises in the patient's life. The first period of disequilibrium occurs in the network with the onset of the original disturbance, and the second period of disequilibrium takes place at the cessation of the emotional disturbance. There may be a final re-equilibrium after an enforced readjustment of roles in the various members of the network.

The concept of the network certainly extends the understanding of the group, since each participant enters the group as a representative of his more or less sick network. No doubt the psychotherapist enlarges the scope of his understanding through these twin concepts, but it is difficult to say to what extent the psychotherapy itself gains from this extended viewpoint. Like the researcher, the therapist can easily get bogged down when his variables are multiplied beyond necessity. The psychoanalyst achieves his goal by focusing intensively on the intrapsychic processes. He can widen his focus to include nonverbal behavior. But once he brings in extra-analytic factors, not only does his field of therapy become contaminated, but he may lose his way within the multiplicity of influences at work. Whether the matrix-plus-network perspective is too wide for focused and intensive therapy remains to be investigated.

Moreno and Acting Out

The end of man, said Goethe, lies not in thought but in action, and Moreno has always been action-oriented. This action includes acting, drama, catharsis, spontaneity, creativity. Moreno is essentially an actor who became a therapist, and the role he has set for himself in therapeutic life is to help produce Everyman's drama. He has taken the Shakespearean lines to heart:

All the world's a stage,
And all the men and women merely players.

And he has made use of Aristotle's proposition that the task of tragedy is to produce, through the exercise of fear and pity, a liberation from such emotions; the audience is purged and absolved from the necessity of expressing these emotions in their own lives. Moreno extends this theory. According to him, the playwright, the actor, and the spectators all undergo catharsis.

Moreno coined the term acting out more than 40 years ago, and, oddly enough, it is one of the few things that psychoanalysts have borrowed from him. Psychoanalysts and psychoanalytic group therapists are not generally dramatic men and are not given to dramatizing the emotional struggles going on within their patients. They are more voyeuristic than exhibitionistic, whereas the reverse may be true of the psychodramatist. Furthermore, the individual psychoanalyst and the group analyst are apparently satisfied to reconstruct the conflictual situation presented to them by in feelings, irritability, or difficulty in concentration. The depression is clearly evident, however, in the expressions of futility, hopelessness, self-depreciation, shame, and thinly veiled hostility.

During the interview the therapist should investigate the depressed patient's suicidal tendencies by asking about his interest in life, whether life seems to be worth living, and whether he has thoughts about dying or taking his own life. If the patient has already tried to commit suicide, he should be asked how others reacted and how they would react to his death. If he admits to contemplating suicide, he should be asked what method he would use.

With a delusional patient, the psychiatrist should demonstrate his interest, understanding, and acceptance and should try to convince the patient that he realizes he is expressing thoughts and feelings with a significant meaning, although the meaning may not be clear at the time. But he must not give the impression that he subscribes to the patient's delusions. He should neither agree with nor contradict the patient. A skeptical attitude may help to raise doubts in the patient's mind and make him more receptive to the psychiatrist's efforts to find out more about the delusional thoughts and who he feels is responsible for them.

A withdrawn patient may be so absorbed with his inner world of fantasy that he is unable to talk spontaneously about his feelings, and so the psychiatrist must ask him questions. But the therapist should change the subject when he sees that he has touched on an area of conflict. Shifting to less disturbing subjects helps the patient accept the psychiatrist. If the patient does not respond to any questions, the psychiatrist may express an interest in talking to him again later, emphasize that he is always available, and plan frequent, brief visits.

A manic patient may be so highly excited that the therapist cannot establish rapport with him. The psychiatrist should remain calm and receptive, paying particular attention to the content of what the patient says. Overtalkative, disturbed patients often reveal underlying conflicts that they conceal when they regain control.

Evaluation of Interviewing Techniques. The therapist's interviewing techniques can be considered effective if the patient reacts in certain ways during the interview: He becomes less tense and anxious, more relaxed. His speech becomes more spontaneous and natural, less inhibited and defensive. He shows increased interest in his feelings and in the origins of his symptoms and illness, and he accepts more responsibility for his condition. His feelings of guilt, self-blame, self-contempt, self-hate, and hostility decrease. His despair gives way to hopefulness. He expresses an interest in further diagnostic procedures or in treatment.

Improvement in the patient's symptoms between the initial interview and later interviews may indicate the effectiveness of the therapist's interviewing techniques, or it may be just still another manifestation of the patient's psychopathology. Contact with the therapist may have temporarily satisfied the patient's irrational dependency needs or given rise to unrealistic expectation about treatment. He may have been temporarily removed from external stress and relieved of responsibility, or he may feel relieved of the obligation to try to help himself. Or symptomatic improvement may be a natural evolution of the illness.

The Psychiatric Report

The patient does not usually present diagnostic information in a logical, orderly fashion. But if the therapist prepares a report—whether for his personal use or as a source of information for others—he is compelled to collate and organize the information so that he gets a picture of the patient and a sequential, logical account of the development of his illness. Properly evaluated, this information then enables him to arrive at a preliminary diagnosis, make a prognostic statement, and recommend an appropriate course of therapy.

There is no single correct form for recording the information gathered during the psychiatric interview. But the therapist should follow a prescribed outline, such as the one used below, to make sure important developmental areas are covered and to point up any contradictions in the material presented.

the hospital by means of loudspeakers. In 1940 Snowden actually gave a course of lectures in which he described the causes of different mental illnesses and then had the patients discuss the lecture in the context of their own illness.

The methods began to grow in sophistication. In 1941 Low and in 1946 Klapman put aside the lecture format and began to use the group as a group.

Burrow. Parallel to these developments in general psychiatry, certain psychoanalysts became interested in group treatment and the possible application of psychoanalysis to it. Trigant Burrow was psychoanalytically minded, but what he did could not really be called group psychotherapy. However, Burrow did note that many of the characteristics of a psychoanalysis could be found in the group. The patients were able to verbalize actual fantasies and family conflicts and even to manifest defense and transference mechanisms—a discovery that has been replicated many times since. Freud had hinted at the same things earlier. Today, it is accepted that groups do have many of the psychological qualities of the individual, although therapists are now as much interested in the differences as in the similarities in the two approaches.

Burrow treated patients in groups because he felt that a patient is less resistant to the treatment process in a group than in individual therapy. Within the setting of the group, the patient becomes aware that he shares many things with others, good things as well as abnormalities. He is no longer alone, his problems are no longer unique, he no longer feels the need for isolation and secrecy, and he is increasingly appreciative of the group support. Burrow felt that, whereas Freud was treating the individual, he was dealing with the human race, but both were using psychoanalytic methods and insights. But Freud put the major emphasis on the past; Burrow stressed the present and eschewed personal reminiscences.

Wender. Wender was probably the first to conduct psychoanalytically oriented groups, and he did so in a hospital setting. In 1936 he combined the group method with individual interviews and made the discovery—also replicated by many others—

that patients involved in group psychotherapy move much more freely and more productively than in the individual situation. However, like the general psychiatrists, he took a didactic line and started each group session with a lecture on the dynamics of behavior and the significance of dreams. Wender, like Burrow, also found that transference relationships develop within the group in relation to both the therapist and other patients. He further found that patients in groups appear to be better motivated than patients in individual psychotherapy.

Wender's work represented a fairly straightforward application of early psychoanalytic theory within a group setting. His observations that the groups themselves did helpful things to patients, apart from lowering their resistances and increasing their spontaneity, were almost incidental to the fact that he was applying his knowledge of psychoanalysis. But psychoanalysts at that time were not well-read in group dynamics (they are not so well-read in group dynamics today), so the significance of the group by itself and in itself did not get any profound consideration.

Schilder. During the same decade of the 1930's, Paul Schilder began to work psychotherapeutically with groups. From every point of view, Schilder was an extraordinary person. With his encyclopedic mind and his tremendous scientific drive, he was the one person who might have become the Freud of group psychotherapy, had he given it his whole attention. He also possessed the flexibility of the genuine scientist, in that he was not bound by any dogmatic adherence to rules. Not only was he a first-class theoretician, but he was well-grounded in the theories of others. He was not only interested in individual patients but deeply interested in their various conglomerates in society; he was interested not only in adults but also in children. His range of interests was extremely wide. As a psychiatrist, a psychoanalyst, and a phenomenologist, he could draw on physiology, neurology, and general psychiatry to serve his purpose as an investigator. His influence on Rapaport and through Rapaport on psychoanalysis was appreciable. Rapaport referred to him as an unsystematic genius who sowed scientific seeds without any thought of the harvest that others might be able to reap.

Schilder, like Burrow, began his group interest with the body, more specifically with the body image. It was Schilder's conviction that the system of ideologies a patient develops around his body and the self associated with his body plays a major part in his psychopathology. Any injury to the body, no matter how slight, has an effect on the patient's body image, on the ideology that goes with it, and on his way of life. The exploration of ideologies is especially attuned to the group situation. The patient shares with others the basic tenets that govern his life and faces the criticism that they provoke. The group discussion often starts on an intellectual level but gradually becomes more personal and emotional. When others are able to identify with the particular ideology, the patient professing it is better able to work through it.

One rather surprising fact regarding Schilder as a group psychotherapist is his willingness to reveal his own ideology and to justify it before the group. He was, therefore, very much a member of the group in a way that therapists before him were not.

In response to a direct question, Freud once remarked that he was not a good psychoanalyst because he was too interested in finding out original facts about the patient and tying these facts to his developing theories. The same is probably true of Schilder. His encyclopedic mind ranged over so many interests in such depth that he may have experienced some difficulty in dealing with the everyday problems of everyday patients in a way that was immediately meaningful to them. He was, perhaps, a little too cognitive to be therapeutic and too theoretical to be practical.

The technique of analyzing ideologies has not really caught on in group psychotherapy, although most group psychotherapists from time to time have to deal with the ideologies put forward by their patients. But therapists are more inclined to treat these ideologies as resistances than as illuminating psychological material to be investigated in their own right.

World War II Efforts

The major impact of emigrating psychoanalysts from Germany and Austria on American psychiatry and psychotherapy has only recently begun to subside. In Britain, the effect was less marked, chiefly because psychoanalysis never managed to get a strong foothold into academic medical circles.

In Britain as in America, psychoanalysts were drafted into the Army, and they eventually congregated at centers for the treatment of psychiatric casualties. The main center in Britain was at Northfield, and Northfield's main claim to fame was that it provided a setting for the application of analytic ideas to groups and communities.

The Northfield experiment gathered together a group of analysts or analysts in the making—Freudian, Kleinian, and Adlerian. The roll call included Anthony, Bierer, Bion, Bridger, Foulkes, Main, and Rickman—all of whom later made contributions to group psychotherapy. The first phase of the Northfield experiment was sparked by Bion and Rickman. In a revolutionary way, they attempted to cut Army red tape and treat a whole ward of soldiers almost as if they were civilian patients with rights and responsibilities of their own. Ward discipline was maintained through free discussion with the soldier patients. Not surprisingly, this revolution was brought to a sudden end, but the two venturesome analysts, so far away from their private offices and couches, had made their point and had facilitated the development of the second phase at Northfield.

During this second phase, Foulkes, who at the start of the war in civilian practice had been undertaking analytic group psychotherapy, introduced his method into Northfield. In so doing, he established a milieu that was highly propitious to group psychotherapy. At the time, Foulkes looked beyond the group to the community as a whole, regarding the group instrument as a crucial one for dealing with the individual patient's network of relationships within the community.

The Northfield experiment was the training ground for group theorists, group activists, and group practitioners. There, both group psychotherapy and community psychotherapy received the vital stimulus and momentum that carried them through the unsettled postwar years. The author has described Northfield's significance this way:

To some, it presented an unrivaled opportunity to apply their analytic knowledge to a challenging new field, while for others, it carried the hope that this new method of exploring the human mind might add significant chapters to psychopathology. In many respects, it had something about it of the Vienna of early psychoanalysis, when almost everyone was a contributor of some sort because almost everything was so new. We talked, then as now, about field theory, leaderless groups, group dynamics, group tensions, the analytic approach, etc., but already group styles were beginning to separate out, and one could detect growing differences between the group-analytic groups, the Bion-type groups, Adlerian groups and Tavistock-type groups. With the dissolution of Northfield after the war, each went his own way and more or less lost contact with the others. The war had been the great harmonizer and integrator; with peace came rivalry, dissension and disruption. I do think, however, even though some of us may be reluctant to admit it, that we learned a great deal from one another in those early, encapsulated days and that, perhaps, more cross-fertilization took place than subsequent published acknowledgments admit.

Something of the same quality was noted by Main:

It was a time of freshness, activity and high morale but it would be wrong to suppose that there were no strains at Northfield. We were, after all, like any other group. There was quarreling and dissension on theory, and, as well as friendship, personal malice and rivalry, not less than in any other fiercely active organization .... The first Northfield Experiment fathered by Rickman and carried out by Bion produced some ideas about groups which have had their own developmental life ever since. Foulkes' work with groups had precedence, but it was of a different order and went in a different direction. The two developments were each legitimate, novel, brilliant; but because they concerned the newly entered area of group work the excitement and vehemence of argument tended to set them up as rival systems and for dissensions to take on personal forms.

What is apparent from these comments is that engagement in group work carries with it no immunity from group dissension and strife. In fact, at times group therapists seem to bring their group skills strategically into the polemical battle with them.

It is also apparent that the dialectics of controversy had a marked creative influence on British group psychotherapy. One seems to need the impact of thesis and antithesis to spark off new levels of theory and practice.

A third conclusion is that theorists who are loved and admired within their immediate circle but are treated outside with criticism and even hostility often appear to thrive on such a situation. Freud was a striking example, and so today is Moreno.

Foulkes and the Group Analytic Approach

Foulkes has always been an innovator, and at no time during his long career has he ceased to make original observations and contributions. As Main remarked of him:

Anyone can be a pioneer for a short time by accident, but it takes the patience and doggedness of a Foulkes to make the most of a chance setting and to become an innovator: to study, criticize, check, correct, gain colleagues, undertake experiments, erect, criticize and refine theory and grow bodies of ideas for further examination.

Foulkes was, as Main remarked, at the center of all the group treatment at Northfield,

interested, puzzled, inspiring, enjoying his work and infectiously formulating ideas about the nature of group process.

The author, as a close collaborator of Foulkes, feels that the puzzlement was the most creative thing about Foulkes. Many leading group theorists present a clear, concise, positivistic, and optimistic statement of their theoretical ideas, almost as if the ideas were all cut and dried and ready to be served out, shaped forever. With Foulkes, on the other hand, one always felt a groping toward some profound insight that was never immediately manifest but always several fathoms below in the depths. This habit of groping was sometimes mystifying, often nebulous, and almost always exasperatingly slow for those in search of immediate answers, however glib these might be. One soon learned, however, either in a dyadic or group relationship with him, that behind chiaroscuro was a subtle and steady mind at work. A personal comment from a group member, Abercrombie, is perhaps the nearest one can get to this style, which is so hard to describe, so difficult to imitate, and so effective, not only in theory but also in therapy.

It is extraordinarily difficult to communicate to one who has never been there the subtle, rich and profound experiences of being in a group conducted by Dr. Foulkes. Superficially, the group has no obvious structure or palpable texture; it may seem formless, embedded in an intangible, floating vagueness. At Dr. Foulkes' treatment of the group, or rather, one should say, his participation in it, he is in fact highly disciplined, dictated by a sure perception of strong and rigorous, but changing, patterns of relationships. What may seem to the other group participants a serene, withdrawn passivity is one manifestation of his intense involvement and of his sensitive and steely mastery of technique.

With Foulkes, more than anyone else in the field, one can say that the style is the man, and the man is his theory, so that there is a completeness about him that comes through when one is sitting with him in a therapeutic group.

His contribution on the group matrix and its ambient social network furnish the practitioner with a triple perspective on the individual patient, on the group, and on the interpersonal environment from which the group members come. The intrapsychic, the intragroup, and the intranetwork provide a comprehensive frame of reference to bolster the confidence of any beginning group psychotherapist. Technically, the advantages for the therapist are considerable. The approach enables him, as Foulkes says, to apply a figure-ground orientation to events, to locate the configuration of disturbances in all their variety within the group, and to envisage each member in a more intensive and extensive way.

The group analytic psychotherapist sees the group analytic situation rather the way the psychoanalyst perceives the psychoanalytic situation. The therapist establishes and maintains the arrangements, the setting, the fees, and the total culture in a dynamic way as essential elements for the initiation of the therapeutic process. The therapist is passive in the sense that he puts himself at the service of the group and follows it wherever it goes; but on the other side, he actively analyzes defenses and resistances. His accepting attitude embraces all communication, from both the here-and-now and the there-and-then. The atmosphere generated is one of perpetual attentiveness, tolerance, and patience. With Foulkes, as a co-therapist in the group, one gets the feeling that he is always waiting for something to happen but is in no way discomforted when nothing happens. There is no pressure on the patients to perform for his benefit, as there sometimes is with other group therapists. Occasionally, reading the protocols given by certain authors, one is left with the impression that the members are putting on a show to keep the therapist happy and interested and totally absorbed with them.

As a psychoanalyst, he inevitably focused on the transference situation—between the members and the therapist, between the members themselves, and between the members and the group as a whole. This array of reference has excited many group psychoanalysts, but the group analytic psychotherapist observes it as one aspect of the total phenomena occurring in a group. He often works through it and with it but not in the genetic sense of the psychoanalyst.

The influence of Kurt Lewin and his group dynamics is also obvious in the conduct of analytic group psychotherapy, although Foulkes himself has concentrated on the interpersonal rather than on the group as a whole. The field and its boundaries are well-delineated, and the incidents at the interface between group and outside are easy to detect. Within the field, the temporal perspective is very much on what is happening now in the field and within the individual life space of each member. The network is an important extension of the concept of life space. The current life situation and the current life network remind the therapist that the patient is only the top of the iceberg and that, to know him fully, one has to know him, as Freud once said, both from the inside and from the outside.

The intrapsychic life of the patient takes

second place to his life as a group member. In this permissive, neutral, nondirective situation, it is not surprising that a fully formed transference neurosis can often be clearly recognized in the group and, to some extent, analyzed. But the group analytic psychotherapist realizes that the transference does not develop in pure form and cannot be worked through in quite the same detail as in psychoanalysis. Some group analysts, such as Durkin, feel that the fundamental character of the transference neurosis is not affected by the group context and that it can be effectively analyzed for the purpose of achieving structural change in the personality of the patient. Durkin is fairly convinced that a systematic analysis of the resistance inherent in the defensive transferences can be carried out, that infantile conflicts can be resolved, and that working through does occur in group therapy.

The group analytic approach also takes note of the patient's development in his early family setting as it reappears in the transference.

Very little work has been done on the development of the ego's capacity to create and to maintain a group relationship. A conceptual model that is also developmental could be very useful in group psychotherapy. There is an implicit assumption in psychosexual development that a person passes from a one-body to a two-body to a three-body and finally to a multibody situation, using Rickman's terminology. In the theoretical development proposed by Talcott Parsons, these external groups are internalized in terms of the role played by the individual members. Susan Isaacs also described early group developments in nursery school children, pointing out that group relationships at this stage of life are evanescent and vivid and that hostility is often the factor that draws the children together, either in attacking or in defending their rights and areas.

Foulkes and Anthony have described in detail the construction of the group situation, the material arrangements for conducting a group, the natural history of group development, and the phenomenology associated with the group situation, such as resonance, mirroring, chain phenomena—all indicating the reactivity of the members to one another.

Bion and the Leaderless Group

Bion is tentative about describing himself as a group psychotherapist, as are many analysts on both sides of the Atlantic. Perhaps such work is beneath their dignity, or they do not wish to be labeled unorthodox, but one is left with the conclusion that there is something peculiar about working therapeutically with more than one patient at a time. Bion admits to little more than that he had an experience of trying to persuade a number of patients to make the study of their tensions a group task. It is, perhaps, permissible for a psychoanalyst to be interested in group psychology, since Freud had that interest, but group psychotherapy is not for analysts, and it is true that Freud never attempted to practice it.

The best way to describe what Bion does in a therapeutic group is to use his own words:

At the appointed time members of the group begin to arrive; individuals engage each other in conversation for a short time, and then when a certain number has collected, a silence falls on the group. After a while desultory conversation breaks out again, and then another silence falls. It becomes clear to me that I am, in some sense, the focus of attention in the group. Furthermore, I am aware of feeling uneasily that I am expected to do something. At this point I confide my anxieties to the group, remarking that, however mistaken my attitude might be, I feel just this. I soon find that my confidence is not very well received. Indeed, there is some indignation that I should express such feelings without seeming to appreciate that the group is entitled to expect something from me. I do not dispute this but content myself with pointing out that clearly the group cannot be getting from me what they feel they are entitled to expect. I wonder what these expectations are and what has aroused them.

The effect of this type of group management is almost predictable. The group comes with the high expectation that they will be treated, and the therapist does nothing about it at all. He simply wants to discuss their expectations. The group does not like what he does with them, and they see his behavior as provocative and deliberately disappointing. They feel that he is perverse, that he could behave differently if he wanted to, that he has chosen to behave in this peculiar way out of spite.

Bion then points out that it must be hard for the group to admit that this could be his way of taking groups, that perhaps he should be allowed to take them in his own way, and that there is no reason why he should take groups in the way expected by the patients.

The group members, of course, know that he is a very clever and well-known clinician, so that he cannot be doing what he does for want of knowledge or technique. They are inclined to interpret his attitude as artificially naive and egotistical.

It becomes clear after a while that—because of Bion's tentative, evasive, and noncommittal attitude and behavior—the group cannot stop themselves from being preoccupied with him. Eventually, they can stand it no longer, and one of the members begins to take over and repair the iatrogenic damage. This deputy leader wonders why Bion cannot give a straightforward explanation of his behavior. Bion can only apologize and state that he, too, feels that his explanation that he is in the group to study group tensions is really inadequate, but he confesses that he is unable to throw any light on the matter. The group seems determined to find out what *his* motives are for coming to the group, not what their own motives are. The group situation seems about to break down because of the inability of the group to tolerate the therapist's behavior, and a movement gets under way to exclude the therapist from the group or, if exclusion is not possible, to ignore his presence.

Eventually, a member speaks up on behalf of the therapist, only to state that the therapist must have some good reason for taking the line he does. This statement relaxes the tension in the group immediately, and a more friendly attitude toward the therapist becomes apparent.

A lesson is slowly emerging in the group, and this lesson is pointed out to them—namely, that it is difficult for an individual member to convey meanings to the group that are different from the meanings the group wishes to entertain. This lesson

annoys the group, but they are then informed that they have every right to be annoyed. Nobody ever explained to them what it means to be in a group in which Bion is present, and nobody ever explained to Bion what it is like to be in a group in which all these individual members are present.

The only disagreeable member of the group at this point is the therapist, and he points out that he thinks his interpretations are disturbing the group. A crisis is now reached. Certain members may well have discovered that membership in a group run by Bion happens to be an experience that they do not wish to have. The group has to face the fact that some of the members may want to leave.

Bion then tells the group that he considers the emotional forces underlying this situation to be very powerful. He is, he says, merely one member of a group possessing some degree of specialized knowledge. Although he is no different from any other member of the group, they are quite unable to face the emotional tensions in the group without believing that the therapist is some sort of god who is fully responsible for all that takes place. When the group turns resentfully and somewhat anxiously to another member, Bion sees them as looking to this other member to be leader but without any real conviction that he could be the leader.

The conversation dies down. For most members the experience is becoming painful and boring, so a fresh thought occurs to Bion, and he passes it on to the group. He tells them that they seem determined to have a leader and, moreover, a leader with certain characteristics that are not easy to describe. Why should they have any leader at all?

Both Foulkes and Bion seem on superficial inspection to be like corks floating on the sea of group turmoil, never sinking under the fury, and apparently drifting aimlessly at the mercy of the group. As the Bion and Abercrombie accounts illustrate, this impression is highly illusional. Both Foulkes and Bion, while seeming to follow the group, are subtly leading it to a resolution of its tensions and other problems.

Slavson and Analytic Group Psychotherapy

Slavson, although not a qualified psycho-analyst, stays close to the psychoanalytic model. He refers to his method as analytic group psychotherapy, which contrasts in more than name with the title used by Foulkes of group analytic psychotherapy. With Slavson, the prime emphasis is on the analytic; with Foulkes, the emphasis is on the group. This is not to say that Slavson is not aware of the group process, but he has battled constantly and vigorously for the autonomy of the individual patient in the group. Each patient, he insists, must remain a detached entity in whom intrapsychic changes must occur.

In the therapeutic group, according to Slavson, it is each patient for himself, and the therapist should, therefore, concentrate on the individual rather than on the group as a whole. Slavson recognizes that the individual members affect one another in a variety of ways, including sibling and identification transferences and mutual empathies that make for a collective experience based on the integration of the individual member into the group. The group tends to catalyze the dynamics of the individual patient, accelerating regression, weakening defenses, and at least transiently impairing individuation.

Slavson differentiates between transference and what he calls the basic solidity of the therapeutic relation—what psychoanalysts refer to as the therapeutic alliance. He recognizes that the transference is modified both quantitatively and qualitatively in the group, where he perceives levels of transference.

Slavson has been prolific in his group writing, and his influence on American group psychotherapy has been enormous. He has instigated its development as a profession, its recognition as a therapeutic discipline, and its acceptance as an area of worthwhile research by behavioral scientists. He has also appointed himself as a watchdog who can be depended on to bark at strangers and bite the wild men who haunt the fringes of group psychotherapy. Because of him, group psychotherapy in the United States operated for many years as a branch of applied psychoanalysis, which had two effects: This arrangement was a powerful impetus to the development of group psychotherapy; at the same time, the arrangement set limitations to the further growth of group therapy as a form of treatment in its own right. Slavson has introduced a number of terms and phrases, some of which have become incorporated into general use. Because of his didactic skills, this tentative branch of therapeutics can now be codified into textbooks. As a theoretician, he is more categorical than creative, and there is a positiveness about his position that the state of the art hardly merits.

Perhaps his greatest contribution has been the development of group therapy with children—in its play form with preschoolers and in its activity form with those in the latency phase. The psychological treatment of children in any form poses a number of technical problems, largely because children at different stages of development are almost different species. They think differently, feel differently, and act differently. These differences necessitate treating them differently, which is what Slavson set out to do. Perhaps because he was not a developmental psychologist, his conclusions about what children could or could not do and could or could not understand were essentially faulty. As a consequence, his group work with children, although novel and interesting, is lacking in a rich developmental background. Nevertheless, his expectation that children prefer to act out rather than speak out is confirmed by his protocols. His patients do abreact physically in groups. The group analytic approach to children makes no such assumption. As a result, the patients undergo conversational catharsis, which goes to show that children in therapy have a habit of living up or living down to the expectations of the therapist. What the analytic group and group analytic approaches have both established beyond question is that group psychotherapy can be applied naturally to children. As Slavson says:

Group experience holds limitless growth possibilities for children.

This is true not because children are limited in their understanding but because children, like adults, can learn to make use of people according to their therapeutic needs.

Today, the activity-interview method sounds a little old-fashioned in the light of modern ego psychology. For Slavson, the child is a function-mechanism whose psychological development results not from thought but from action, not from knowledge and ideas but pragmatically through experience and association. Because the child is immature and cognitively deficient, he must be treated through action and by action, using controls and affectionate guidance rather than interpretations. To child psychoanalysts, this type of release and ego-strengthening therapy rings a familiar bell. For a long time the child was considered unanalyzable because he was allegedly unable to free-associate, develop transference, handle deep-going tensions, or work through resistances. Today, an interpretative form of psychoanalysis can be carried out with quite young children. Likewise, today interpretative forms of group analytic psychotherapy can be carried out with quite young children, and acting out is treated as a defense in children, as it is in adults. In fact, what Socrates described as the remedy of sweet words is effective with all human beings at all stages of life, since words specifically separate them absolutely from the dumb brutes.

There is much argument in the literature as to who began group psychotherapy and where. Various claims have been made involving different therapists and different countries. But the group idea was really part of a *Zeitgeist*, as a result of which there was a gradual convergence of ideas that characteristically led to the plethora of approaches that usually antedate the evolution of any unified theory. Slavson felt that, unlike many other techniques in psychiatry that had their beginnings in Europe, group psychotherapy originated in the United States—and quite understandably so, since American culture is essentially a free group culture. It is probably truer to say that the United States is a place where things catch on because there is more freedom for them to develop. And this is as true for an individual therapy such as psychoanalysis as it is for group psychotherapy.

Wolf and Psychoanalytic Group Psychotherapy

In the two decades of the 1930's and 1940's, several psychoanalysts began to carry out therapeutic work with groups based on the psychoanalytic model. They followed the free-associative technique and attempted some degree of psychoanalysis with each patient. Schilder and Wender were two of these psychoanalysts, and Weininger was another. Weininger's method was essentially different in that he confined the entire treatment session to one patient, with the others in the group playing the part of spectators. The psychoanalytic approach came to fruition in the hands of Alexander Wolf, who began to develop psychoanalysis in groups in the first place to offset the burden imposed on many patients by the cost of individual psychoanalysis.

For Wolf, the group situation is not essentially unfavorable to the type of psychic work carried out in ordinary psychoanalysis, such as the uncovering of infantile amnesia, the interpretation of transference, the analysis of dreams, and genetic reconstruction. He assumes that the patient's unconscious is as accessible in the group situation as it is in the individual psychoanalytic one and is explorable by identical techniques. The group situation is thus conceived of as a set of interlocking psychoanalytic situations.

Whereas Slavson has continued to believe that transference cannot be as intense in groups as in individual treatment and that interpretations in groups cannot penetrate into areas of personality as deeply as in psychoanalysis, Wolf believes that the group situation often allows for deeper analytic exploration than is possible in individual psychoanalysis. The reason he gives is that the group ego, with which each member gradually comes to identify himself, offers the necessary support for more radical probing. The tolerance for anxiety, which is the limiting factor in all psychological analysis, is upgraded by the group. Not only is each member a source of support for other members, but he is also an ancillary therapist in his own right—capable, after a certain amount of group experience, of a well-high professional analysis of the material.

One of the most debatable practices inculcated by Wolf has been his attempt to direct the course of treatment in a series of preconceived stages. Since Freud's early suggestion that the period of treatment be portioned off, like a game of chess, into an opening gambit, a middle phase, and an end game, various therapists have attempted to distinguish a natural historical development in the course of therapy. Group therapists have also succumbed to this evolutionary exercise, and some have built up elaborate stratified models of therapeutic development. A few, like Wolf, have gone even further and have tried to impose a dynamically logical sequence leading to a programming of therapeutic tasks for the group.

In view of these psychoanalytic and quasi-analytic approaches to group psychotherapy, one can only wonder what course Freud himself would have taken had he followed through from group psychology to group psychotherapy. No doubt, his preoccupation with group leadership would have led him to concentrate particularly on the functions of the group therapist and on the relationship between the therapist and the group membership. Although well-aware of the individual mechanisms of identification operating within the group, his closely argued discussion of Le Bon and McDougall would have led him eventually to the concept of the group functioning as a whole.

Whether Freud would have created a group dynamics out of the workings of the nuclear Oedipus complex seems less easy to conceive. However, Foulkes has pointed out that the Sophoclean tragedy could without distortion be considered in group terms, as the hero and the chorus interact in the working out of the plot. The same inescapable emotional tie unites all the people on the stage; at any one time, some are active, and some are passive, and at moments of high tension the conflicting tendencies in the group also find their spokesmen, who voice feelings common to all. The group's defensive mechanisms, operating to preserve an ignorance of its own wishes and projecting them instead onto some individual scapegoat, are very much like the driving demand of the chorus that the hero fulfill its group expectations. The scapegoat is frequently the conductor, who is called on to know the things that the group does not as yet dare to know. The re-enactment of the drama of a conflict under the guidance of the conductor can lead to a re-evaluation and re-integration of feelings, which finally make the presence of the conductor unnecessary.

Freud might have accepted this transposition. He would most certainly have reached the conclusion that any event in a group must be regarded as something that potentially involves the group as a whole and that, like the Oedipus complex in the individual patient, can express itself in a wide variety of configurations. The therapist's task is to examine this matrix and locate—to use the language of Foulkes—the crucial disturbance. It is hardly likely that Freud would have been content to make a simple extrapolation from the psychoanalysis of the individual patient to the psychoanalysis of the group without considering the nature of the transformation involved. He was too aware that something fairly radical took place when what he termed the group of two was extended to encompass a much larger number of persons. He was a group psychologist on his way to becoming a group psychotherapist but was deflected by pressing intrapsychic considerations.

It was left to others to follow his lead, and group psychotherapy has undoubtedly profited from the fact that a number of dedicated people have made it their life work to carry on where Freud left off and to pursue the path to its logical conclusion. Every discipline must be explored to its very edge of non-sense and beyond, so that practitioners can learn from recountable experience where the impossible lies. It is fairly certain that Freud himself would have soon recognized that the group is not the most suitable place to analyze a transference neurosis, and he would then have focused on group formations as the nub of therapy in the group situation. (It is one of the historian's prerogatives to speak for the dead, who can no longer speak for themselves!)

Powdermaker and Frank and the Eclectic Approach

By 1953, the literature on group psychotherapy was already voluminous, although the body of established knowledge was still small. There was a wide range of group practice from simple exhortation to profound psychoanalysis. The gamut, according to Slavson, ran from

the authoritarian approach of Low, the confessional-inspirational method of Pratt and his followers, the didactic technique of Klapman, the aesthetic activation of Altschuler, the drama forms of Moreno, the social-educational method of Bierer, and the quasi-analytical approach of Wender and Foulkes, to the psychoanalytic method of Schilder.

Therefore, Powdermaker and Frank thought it necessary to carry out some studies on how group psychotherapy works. To observe and study the therapeutic process, however, they had to decide on some form of group psychotherapy. Their choice fell on the analytic for two reasons: They thought that it would be of greater help to their patients, and they thought that the analytic approach offered considerable promise of adding to the understanding of group dynamics in relation to therapy. The next question was: What choice of analytic? Here they decided on an eclectic compromise that tries to draw from the best of everyone while eschewing their faults.

Their eclectic treatment is of importance in the history of group psychotherapy because it induced a large number of therapists to practice it. Even today, many American group psychotherapists continue to use the method without being aware of its origins. This composite technique is best summarized by Powdermaker and Frank themselves:

Our approach to group therapy with neurotic patients had points in common with that of Foulkes, Ackerman, Slavson, and Wolf, and we were influenced in our thinking by Schilder's analytic concept and Trigant Burrow's emphasis on the study of group interaction. We were stimulated by Bion's descriptions of the group process but avoided his exclusive attention to it. Although our groups were not social groups as were Bierer's, the leadership was completely informal. We differed from Schilder in not using questionnaires

and set tasks, and from Wender, Klapman, and Lazell in that in no case did the psychiatrist in charge give case histories or systematic presentation of psychiatric concepts. We encouraged interaction among the patients. We helped them to examine their attitudes and behavior toward one another (*process*) as well as the personal material which they presented (*content*).

The striking and unique thing about this venture is that it was simultaneously engaged in treating the patient and studying the process. This dual approach is, unfortunately, unusual in the history of group psychotherapy. The attitude toward research, nevertheless, was essentially clinical, and the patient's needs were always put before the investigation. Both the individual patient and the group were brought under scrutiny, although the examination of process was organismic rather than elementaristic. Their method was to single out and describe patterns of change involving individual patients, the group, and the therapist, and these descriptions were termed situation analyses based on running accounts.

An illustration of a situation analysis will help to clarify the way in which significant developments within a session can be delineated and stored for later examination in relation to previous and subsequent sessions. The example given is abstracted from a first meeting and demonstrates the rallying of the group after a typical sticky beginning.

Doctor	Nonsupportive, passive, silent.
Group	Patients seemed to know they should be discussing personal matters; afraid to reveal themselves to others; talked on impersonal subjects. Tension rose.
Central patient	X, dominating member; repeatedly tried to get focus of attention.
Situation preceding rally	Group talked on impersonal subjects.
Precipitating event	Doctor intervened: "Have you any idea of the trend of the discussion?" Tension rose sharply. X, after trying in vain to question others, introduced rallying topic.

Event   Rally round topic: feelings about psychoanalysis and resistance to therapy.

Effects   Intimate discussion of illness. Relief of tension.

On several occasions over the next seven sessions, the crucial role of the therapist in precipitating a rally was nicely brought out. He precipitated a rally mainly by indicating to the group, in an uncritical way, that he was aware of their difficulty and that he was not at all anxious or uncomfortable about it.

If more such careful investigations had been carried out over the last two decades, the history of group psychotherapy as a branch of scientific medicine would be completely different, and therapists would be less confused by the confusions and the wild uncertainties that pervade the field today. Of even greater interest: The follow-up evaluation was included in the study and underscored the advantage of constantly monitoring work in this way. It cannot be emphasized too strongly that the lack of such basic procedures is a serious handicap. True, evaluation of therapy is a major methodological problem, but even tentative efforts in this direction are better than none and would certainly help to maintain a vigilant self-critical posture, without which therapists are at the mercy of every passing therapeutic whimsy.

If good or even acceptable evaluative techniques had been available, the Powdermaker and Frank investigation would have been a great and epoch-making one instead of simply an interesting and unusual attempt. For example, changes were assessed somewhat loosely in terms of symptoms, social adjustments, and characteristic responses to such stimuli as the Rorschach test. Such assessments were good enough for the time but would demand more rigorous application today.

From a conceptual point of view, the study was curiously barren, as if the authors were frozen in their methodology and unable to go beyond the observed facts. In their defense, however, it should be emphasized that, at the present time, group psychotherapy stands more in need of facts than of concepts, and there is much need for another such detailed study.

New Developments

The term "new" has a serious limitation when it is applied to a rapidly growing field in which anything new soon changes into something old. However, the beginnings of group psychotherapy are still near enough to have the term "new" simply denote something not there from the start. There are new developments by the pioneers Moreno, Slavson, Foulkes, Bion, Bierer, Dreikurs, and others who are still with us and still actively developing; and there are new developments by those who have invaded the field within the last two decades.

Moreno, although practicing a particular form of group treatment that is different from classical group psychotherapy in the way it is set up and structured, has generated a number of important theoretical concepts that have become part of group psychotherapy and are acknowledged by both analytic and nonanalytic schools. He has claimed, with some justification, to have fathered many of the new movements, such as encounter groups, training groups, and existential approaches. His warming up procedures have been incorporated into laboratory exercises used by most of the new methods, and his sociometric tests have been widely employed, not only by sociologists and social psychologists but also by group therapists desirous of sampling group characteristics during the on-going life of the group.

Within recent times, a cascade of experimental approaches has inundated the group arena, so that the more conventional procedures have been transiently swamped by fresh waves of novel and largely untried techniques to which the public has oriented itself because of the novelty, the implicit seductiveness, and the promise of quick change. Often there is a pursuit of the unusual for its own sake on the part of the therapist and a craving for new experiences in human relatedness on the part of the patients. It is difficult to say whether the bewildering situation today in the field of group psychotherapy reflects the primitive phase of its development or the disturbing nature of the world. Perhaps both.

If anxiety was the menace to our patients 20 years and more ago, alienation has emerged as the imperative concern now. The multiple and miasmic urgencies of life today have brought about an impatience with slower historical procedures, and immediate existence in all its calamitous ramifications has become the focus of therapeutic concern. Anything outside the here-and-now is poorly tolerated by the driven inhibitants of this nuclear age. The situation—first postulated by Trigant Burrow many years ago, when he saw therapists and patients in the same predicament—has been incorporated into the existential group movement.

The group therapist is no longer the most psychologically knowledgeable member of the group, the recognized and revered expert in theory and practice; instead, he stands out only by virtue of being the most honest, the most sincere, the most authentic, and the most accepting, both in his commitment to life and to the group. In fulfilling this role, he is obliged to be as open and as honest about himself as he expects the group members to be about themselves. He is offered no special privileges, no diplomatic immunity, no special status. He is a human being among other human beings, a patient among other patients—but perhaps a little more aware of what is implied than are the others in the group.

The development has been a fascinating one. Although it was Freud who first talked of the leaderless group and the deep anxieties that this situation aroused, it was Bion who put these theoretical ideas to the clinical test and examined the panic that ensued at the deepest levels. The group analytic approach, on the other hand, keeps the therapist in the background but sees him as indispensable to the therapeutic life of the group; he does not have to prove his indispensability by defaulting. Today, in some circles, the therapist has become the model of the good patient. He lays on the table not only all his counter-transference cards but also his self-recognized human failings, so that he can no longer claim differentiation from his fellow members because of his mental health or superior clinical insights. He is no longer an alarming model of conventional normality. As a consequence, the group can get closer to one another without guilt or shame, since there is apparently no conscience figure to watch over them like the eye of God.

This godlessness has been much exploited by encounter groups. Under the highly emotional impact deliberately fostered by such settings, an exhilarating sense of freedom from prohibitions and inhibitions is rapidly generated. To the uncritical and naive observer, the internal censors seem to have been eradicated or at least put to sleep. Unfortunately, the vacation from conscience is more apparent than real and more short-lasting than claimed. The return to conventional circumstances soon reactivates the dormant conscience and may even intensify its more punitive and primitive qualities. Fenichel wrote that the superego is soluble in alcohol; it is also soluble—as Le Bon, McDougall, and Freud pointed out—in the ecstasies occasioned by close group interaction, but there is always a hang-over when reality once again asserts itself. This is, in fact, the oldest lesson in psychotherapy: The internal structures of the mind were not built in a day and cannot be reconstituted over a weekend.

American vs. European Group Psychotherapy

Psychotherapy, like other social institutions, is extraordinarily sensitive to cultural influences. The organizational competence of American group psychotherapists has fast brought about a professionalization of group psychotherapy in the United States. What is gained by annual and regional meetings, with their opportunity for scientific interchange, is to some extent lost by the conforming influences of the Establishment. It is here that the experimentalists have a necessary role to play. Every movement is both embarrassed and vivified by its lunatic fringe; heresy, as St. Augustine once pointed out, can be both a threat and a stimulus to progress. The recent rash of experimental approaches has led to some understandable alarm in established circles but also to a surprising willingness to consider these approaches as potential contributions awaiting the test of time and experience. Although American group psychotherapy at times gives the impression of originating from committee work, there are enough unpsychotic and unpsychopathic experimentalists in the field to ensure a measure of vitality to the group movement. What is not acceptable and what can be incorporated into the body of knowledge must engage in a running battle if the field is to advance.

The criterion for acceptance has been laid down in somewhat categorical fashion by Slavson. According to him, all sound psychotherapies have five elements in common: relation or transference, catharsis, insight or ego-strengthening or both, reality-testing, and sublimation. In an acceptable technique, at least the first three of these five criteria should be present. These canons are too much in some respects and insufficient in others. The criteria refer to group psychotherapy solely as a treatment and not as a scientific practice, so that blatantly nonscientific techniques could find acceptance. Many of these nonscientific techniques, especially the cathartic variety, are put forward in Messianic fashion, advertised with Madison Avenue skills, and practiced with a complete absence of discrimination. Their proponents seem singularly blind to all shortcomings and tend to respond to the enthusiasm of their patients rather than to the considered criticisms of their colleagues.

The situation in Europe, especially in Britain, is somewhat different, with the disequilibrium on the other side. There is a striking absence of professional government. The field is small, the practitioners are few, and the handful of theoreticians wend their own lonely ways far from the clamor of conventions. They behave, in all respects, like gifted amateurs, seeking an internal consistency in their systems and failing to respond to outside comment. By American standards, the approach in Britain is less dramatic, less positive, more ambiguous, and given to understatement. There is something peculiarly reticent about the procedures employed, reflective of the culture as a whole. Here, for example, is a comment by Foulkes and Anthony:

The group-analytic approach is complex but not spectacular. It lays stress on under-emphasis and sees merit in the minimum. It recognizes the importance of the conductor's role, but it prevails on him to function as much as possible behind the scenes in the background.

The absence of affirmation sometimes verges on the negative side, so that the technique may seem, to Americans at least, eccentrically unforthcoming. There is a defaulting tendency on the part of British group therapists that can mislead not only their colleagues but also their patients.

CONCLUSIONS

For a scientific purpose, a system of group psychotherapy should demonstrate certain characteristics: It should be impartable to students by the ordinary routines of training, including training therapy, and impartable to colleagues who do not wish to join an esoteric cult to complete their understanding; it should provide a therapeutic model that helps to explain the process of therapy and the process of change; it should carry out periodic research evaluations on the efficacy of its treatment; it should be flexible enough to develop and alter under the impetus of further knowledge and practice; its proponents should remain eternally vigilant with respect to the tightening grip of dogma and fully aware of the limitations as well as the assets of their particular treatment model; and, finally, the system should provide an economic, elegant, and powerfully explanatory theoretical framework linking together group psychology and group psychotherapy in an indivisible whole. There should be special regard paid not only to the individual patient's status and behavior in the current group but also to him as a member of many human groups from infancy on. Group psychology must become developmental if group psychotherapy is to develop further.

These unseasonable reflections may not be altogether in keeping with the contemporary mood, and the bias is often unashamedly blatant. But they do try, in Nietzsche's terms, to bring the past into a living contact with the present for the ultimate good of both. The past looks much better viewed in the context of the present, and the present gains enormously in the logic of its position when it is placed in the perspective of time. From such beginnings, each practitioner must improvise a serviceable history for himself.

REFERENCES

Abercrombie, M. L. J. Group Analysis International Panel and Correspondence, *2:* 145, 1970.

Ackerman, N. W. Some general principles in the use of group psychotherapy. In *Current Therapies in Personality Disorders*, p. 279, B. Glueck, editor. Grune & Stratton, New York, 1946.

Anthony, E. J. Reflections on twenty-five years of group psychotherapy. Int. J. Group Psychother., *18:* 277, 1968.

Bierer, J. *Therapeutic Social Clubs.* H. K. Lewis, London, 1948.

Bion, W. R. *Experiences in Groups.* Tavistock Publications, London, 1961.

Burrow, T. *The Social Basis of Consciousness.* Harcourt, Brace & World, New York, 1927.

Ezriel, H. A psycho-analytic approach to group treatment. Brit. J. Med. Psychol., *23:* 59, 1950.

Foulkes, S. H. *Introduction to Group-Analytic Psychotherapy.* William Heinemann, London, 1948.

Foulkes, S. H. *Therapeutic Group Analysis.* International Universities Press, New York, 1965.

Foulkes, S. H., and Anthony, E. J. *Group Psychotherapy, the Psychoanalytic Approach.* Penguin Books, London, 1957.

Freud, S. *Group Psychology and the Analysis of the Ego.* Hogarth Press, London, 1953.

Klapman, J. W. *Group Psychotherapy: Theory and Practice.* Grune & Stratton, New York, 1946.

Lazell, E. W. The group treatment of dementia praecox. Psychoanal. Rev., *8:* 168, 1921.

Le Bon. *The Crowd.* E. Benn, London, 1952.

Lewin, K. *Field Theory in Social Science.* Harper & Brothers, New York, 1951.

Main, T. F. GAIPAC Meeting, London, August 1969. Group Analysis International Panel and Correspondence, *2:* 133, 1970.

Moreno, J. L. *Who Shall Survive?* Beacon House, New York, 1953.

Mullan, H., and Rosenbaum, M. *Group Psychotherapy.* Free Press of Glencoe, New York, 1962.

Powdermaker, F., and Frank, J. D. *Group Psychotherapy.* Harvard University Press, Cambridge, 1953.

Pratt, J. H. The principles of class treatment and their application to various chronic diseases. Hosp. Soc. Serv., *6:* 401, 1922.

Schilder, P. The analysis of ideologies as a psychotherapeutic method, especially in group treatment. Amer. J. Psychiat., *93:* 601, 1936.

Slavson, S. R. *Analytic Group Psychotherapy.* Columbia University Press, New York, 1950.

Slavson, S. R. *A Textbook in Analytic Group Psychotherapy.* International Universities Press, New York, 1964.

Wender, L. Group psychotherapy: a study of its application. Psychiat. Quart., *14:* 708, 1940.

Whitaker, D. S., and Lieberman, M. A. *Psychotherapy through the Group Process.* Atherton Press, New York, 1964.

Wolf, A., and Schwartz, E. K. *Psychoanalysis in Groups.* Grune & Stratton, New York, 1962.

2

Basic Concepts in Group Psychotherapy

Edrita Fried, Ph.D.

INTRODUCTION

History

Although the practice of group psychotherapy greatly increased only after World War II, the origins of this treatment method go back to about the beginning of the twentieth century. Those who have followed its history usually place its beginnings in the work that Joseph Hersey Pratt, a physician from Boston, did with tubercular patients. He reported in 1907 that he had formed what we would today call homogeneous groups—all patients had in common a basic condition, namely their physical ailment. Pratt discussed with them their illness and its biological and psychological effects. One of the prime therapeutic factors on which Pratt leaned was what we call universality. His patients were strengthened by facing and sharing the effects of their common disease and its subsequent problems. Such joint sharing has always been considered one of the therapeutic agents in a group setting.

An important breakthrough in the development of group psychotherapy was made by the Viennese psychiatrist Alfred Adler. Contrary to Freud, Adler believed that society and its ills play a dominant role in creating mental disorders. To alleviate emotional illness, he used certain social situations as a remedy. For instance, he invited his patients to his own home so as to give them a better family climate than they were used to, thus creating an early impetus for the therapeutic community concept. (For

this and other information, the author is indebted to Alexandra Adler, M.D.) What is even more important in this context, he assembled the patients in groups, expecting a salutary effect from such meetings. Adler did not believe that the privacy of the patient and doctor was of primary importance, and indeed he went so far as to act on the idea that the sharing of problems was therapeutic because of peer identification. From 1918 to 1934 Adler founded many child guidance clinics where child therapy was done in the presence of parents, teachers, and doctors. In a way he is a pioneer not only in group therapy but also in family therapy.

Another advance in the development of group psychotherapy was made by Trigant L. Burrow. A student of Freud and Jung, Burrow found himself focusing on concepts of both of them and also on social forces that shape human behavior. With a number of patients, students, and colleagues, he spent summers in the Adirondack Mountains, exhorting both patients and therapists to analyze the behavior exhibited during the camp life. In this sense he helped to shape the here-and-now (contemporaneity) concept. Burrow's conviction was that people react to one another and to groups in terms of the particular social image expected of the individual. He believed that living up to a social image confines the individual and alienates people from one another, and his endeavor was to dissolve such social images. The idea of social image is related to the concept of role-playing, which social psychologists have observed

27

and described as inherent to groups and group processes.

Paul Schilder, who first started to conduct group psychotherapy in Bellevue Hospital in New York in the 1930's, and S. R. Slavson, who developed group therapy for children and teenagers, are also important pioneers in the field. Schilder, who, like Adler before him, saw little benefit in undifferentiated confidentiality between patient and doctor, talked in front of his patients with his interns about the patients' disorders. Later he developed group meetings, which often lasted two or three hours, where he emphasized certain psychoanalytic phenomena. He was keenly aware of the patients' transferences to the leader, namely the tendency to overevaluate and idealize him. He stressed that such focusing on the leader was the result of transference, namely the carry-over of feelings from childhood that made the patient's parents or other authority figures appear larger than life-size. He was aware of the various forms of resistance that patients put up, namely their temporary reluctance or inability to accept the insights that their doctors offer in the effort to help.

Slavson designed the model for activity group therapy with children. In his work he relied very carefully on screening and on composition to correct the children's behavior problems. For example, he put together children's groups in such a way that withdrawn children would be assured encounters with outgoing and aggressive children, and vice versa. This composition was for the sake of corrective experience. Slavson's work was studied systematically by Lawson Lowrey in 1943 and was found to be effective. Slavson, with a great capacity for organization, eventually established the practice of activity group psychotherapy at many clinics. His scientific curiosity and pioneering spirit led him into a number of further investigations concerning analytic group psychotherapy for adults. Many of his concepts combined with the ideas and clinical experiences of others to form the mainstream of group psychotherapy.

At the end of World War II group psychotherapy had spread into many settings and had been fertilized by many approaches.

Jacob L. Moreno, who is credited with having invented and publicized the expression "group psychotherapy," developed psychodrama and trained medical and lay practitioners in this approach. Alexander Wolf (1950) undertook and described the psychoanalysis of groups. Kurt Lewin (1945), a social and child psychologist, developed field theory, a system describing the perpetual interaction between individual and environment. In his way he contributed to the concept of contemporaneity, and he investigated experimentally various leadership styles. George Bach, a disciple of Lewin's, outlined his own method of group therapy and was the first to experiment with marathon groups. Their main characteristic is that they last more than 20 hours; in that time they break down defenses and the ego boundaries that normally separate people. From England came descriptions of techniques and research reports undertaken by S. H. Foulkes (1948) and W. R. Bion, who both emphasize the importance of interpretations to the group as a whole. The list of original thinkers and practitioners who formulated concepts in group psychotherapy is long indeed.

Types of Group Psychotherapy

The basic concepts presented in this chapter are the product of many theorists and clinicians and spring from a conflux of divergent ideas and schools. Today group psychotherapy, used in almost every outpatient department, ward, and clinic, and in schools, industry, and the offices of private practitioners, is practiced according to a number of models that are sometimes combined. Among the prime models are the following.

Inspirational-Supportive. In groups such as those used by Alcoholics Anonymous, one of the prime therapeutic agents is the idea that the individual has potential goodness in him and that others just like him have achieved resolution of problems similar to his.

Psychoanalytically Oriented. Here the range is wide. At one pole are the therapists who call their approach psychoanalytically oriented group psychotherapy. They do not necessarily assume that the outcomes of their groups are identical with those of classical analysis, and with certain modifications they have described them in detail. For instance, many assume that contemporaneity, the focus on what happens right at the moment between the members within a particular group, is of prime importance. At the other pole are approaches like that of Wolf and Schwartz (1962), who believe that with very little modification a regular psychoanalysis can be carried on in groups. Still other approaches do away with some, if not with all, psychoanalytic concepts. The existential group therapists do not believe in slowly resolving resistance but disregard this phenomenon and confront patients quite directly, and without particular timing, with their problems and incidentally with the therapist's own countertransferences. Therapists who use the transactional approach believe in and use reinforcement techniques (strokes) whenever the patient exhibits behavioral changes considered healthy.

Confrontation. In the treatment of psychotics this model is often used. At what is considered an appropriate time, usually early in treatment, the therapist lets the patient know in direct and clear language what his primary problems are. The confrontation model used on closed wards and also at times in day hospitals or partial hospitalization programs is combined with the therapeutic community model.

Therapeutic Community. A therapeutic community is created by sensitizing all personnel with whom the patient is in touch—doctors, psychologists, social workers, nurses, and aides—to their own feelings about the patients and to the patients' needs.

Discussion. This model relies on topics that are of major importance to the group members and that are debated in the presence of a leader, primarily on a cognitive basis but with some emotions emerging. Schools, camps, and various training programs—for instance, those for police officers and scout leaders—use the discussion group model. So do some schools for nurses, some day-care (partial hospitalization) projects,

etc. Family and sex education is but one specific form of the discussion group model.

Medication. Here the dispensing of drugs is accompanied by some patient discussion and interaction.

Activity. This group therapy model is for adult patients. Here the members' joint selection of an activity, the gradual learning of the decision-making process, the practice of cooperation in carrying out a joint task, and the chance for inarticulate people to have discussion flow from action are prime therapeutic factors.

BEGINNING A GROUP

Screening of Patients

Each participant should be thoroughly screened; that is, the therapist should have a history of the patient's family background, childhood, adolescence, and later years. He should also be acquainted with the patient's medical history.

Investigation of the patient's early family history, physical illnesses, previous mental and emotional crises, and sexual history must be augmented by preliminary diagnoses—in terms not of fixed psychiatric categories but of the most pertinent cornerstones of the personality. It is important that the therapist have some idea of where on the continuum between so-called normality and psychosis the patient stands. Does the prospective group member have a reasonably strong and flexible ego? Are his thinking processes appropriate? Does the patient go back and forth between good functioning and disturbances, as many borderline cases do? Is he an ambulatory schizophrenic who tends under pressure to lose contact with reality and engage in idiosyncratic thinking processes and perceptions? Or is the patient acutely schizophrenic, primarily out of touch with reality?

Thorough screening of each individual patient through careful interviews is necessary for two reasons. First, every patient accepted into a group should be understood as much as possible by the therapist. It is most helpful for the therapist to understand man. The borderline patient, especially, improved slowly but notably.

The First Meeting

It is not necessary to have the full membership assembled for the first meeting. A therapist can begin with as few as four or five patients and add other members gradually.

The therapist informs the initial membership of the meeting place, the length of each meeting (usually an hour and a half), and the number of group meetings a week (usually one or two). He states his fee, which is very often figured on a monthly basis.

Many patients who enter a group want an explanation as to how group meetings proceed. Experience shows that explanations given by the therapist are usually not very helpful in alerting the patients to the actual treatment course. Therapists who do not rely on the psychoanalytic model, however, tend to believe that preliminary explanations reduce anxiety. The psychoanalytically oriented practitioners, primarily preoccupied with intrapsychic processes (the emotional and mental currents going on inside the patient without particular reference to others) expect little anxiety reduction from explanations.

Once the first group meeting is under way, the therapist begins to deal with the patient's already-emerging feelings and thoughts. Since patients tend to act toward one another and the therapist as though they were members of their original family group, essential emotions come forth in the initial stage.

It is always important for the therapist to be aware that in the beginning phase of group therapy the patient's prime conflicts, concerns, and transference feelings—emotions carried over from the past, often unconsciously—deal with the problem of inclusion. What each member wants to know is whether he will be accepted by the leader, where he stands with regard to popularity with the leader, and to what degree others will show either tolerance or aggression.

Attendance

Punctual and regular attendance is a simple measure to evaluate the therapeutic progress of a group. As a rule, the stronger cohesiveness becomes, the more is accomplished and understood (the deeper the insight); and the more is understood, the more regular is the attendance of each member.

If therapy is psychoanalytically oriented and the majority of members are neurotic, ambulant schizophrenic, or borderline, they usually attend their group meetings regularly. It is, then, well to wonder what meaning occasional absences have. Even groups consisting primarily of outpatient schizophrenics will eventually attain rather regular attendance.

In many groups no member is absent for stretches of six or more months. Fairly frequent absences and latenesses suggest dissatisfaction, anxiety, and a wish to stop therapeutic alliance and development. It is always necessary and fruitful to discuss a disturbed attendance pattern with the group. At times segments of the group or the entire group is in a flight state, signifying that all or many members are primarily concerned with escape from the group and most likely from external commitment.

Conclusion

Difficulties in the initial stage of group psychotherapy frequently manifest themselves between the third and ninth sessions. Patients show extreme resistance and dissatisfaction by coming late, by missing sessions, by being very withdrawn or very agitated.

If the therapist is aware of his countertransference feelings and focuses on the here-and-now of interactions between the patients and between patients and himself, many difficulties can be overcome, and the prognosis is good. After initial resistances and difficulties are overcome, the group becomes a very important event in the life of the patients. The cancellation of a group session for any reason is felt as a grave loss.

THERAPIST AND GROUP

Most carefully conducted therapy groups have a leader. Leaderless groups are becoming more frequent, but for the sake of therapeutic safety the participants should be only those individuals who have already had a good deal of psychotherapy and who understand the workings of their emotions and mind. In fact, the members of leaderless groups are often psychotherapists themselves.

In the beginning of group therapy the leader is usually the focal point and frequently the recipient not only of attention but also of such narcissistic transferences as excessive admiration and overevaluation. Also, members identify with the leader, partly because they are convinced that he and not group interaction will provide a cure. As the group moves, this situation changes. Although the presence of the leader remains desirable, he becomes ever more realistically regarded. Most therapists attempt gradually to turn leadership over to the group.

Leadership Styles

Focus on the therapist's personality and the way he uses it has been growing. Well-trained therapists are attuned to a number of variables: (1) interactions between patients, (2) group dynamics, and (3) the therapist's countertransferences. Well-trained therapists are expected to use their personality on behalf of patient development. Lewin, Lippitt, and White have experimentally investigated the distinctions between autocratic, democratic, and laissez-faire leadership and the effects of these styles on group climate.

In the early phases of groups many therapists are more active than later on. Therapists who conduct groups psychoanalytically restrict themselves to interpretations of the underlying motivations for patient interactions. Existential and transactional therapists enter into vivid and deliberate interchanges with group members, often articulating their own feelings, whatever their cause. In general, group therapists reveal more of their own characterological structure than do those who practice individual therapy exclusively. But there are variations.

Countertransference

The existential school of psychotherapy has emphasized that not only do patients have transference feelings toward the leader —that is, feelings that are a carry-over from childhood and were originally aimed at family figures—but therapists, too, have feelings toward patients. Their countertransferences—sexual and aggressive impulses, narcissism, personal defenses, and guilt feelings—are a reflection of their own preoccupation, anxieties, and conflicts and are stimulated by their own past relationships, not by the patients.

Different group therapists advise different ways to use countertransference feelings. Psychoanalytically oriented group therapists expect merely to be as conscious as possible of their countertransferences. The existentialists counsel strongly that the therapist articulate his own countertransference reactions. In the latter case there is the assumption that patients sense the therapist's nonverbalized feelings anyway and therefore become freer and less confused (less affected by the double bind) if articulation takes place.

Interpretation-Intervention

Most analytically oriented group therapists interpret the patients' defenses before they uncover underlying deep problems. But group members who are amateur interpreters and who are often instinctively on the right track, jump quickly to the core of painful problems. In such instances, which are frequent, the leader must intervene. Such necessary interventions call for great skill. Above all, the leader must be free from countertransferences. If the leader rejoices over the fact that group members try to pin down a resistive patient who, to them, seems arbitrarily recalcitrant, the anxiety of the member who is the target of these amateur interpretations easily becomes intolerable. Usually it is the early phase of group therapy that calls for dynamic understanding, for interpretations concerning the vehemence of certain group members, and for skill and tact by the leader.

the defense structure by which the patient protects himself, especially the extent to which denial and projection (attributing his own emotions to others) are used. Ego strength, ego flexibility, and the condition of such primary ego functions as thinking, reality-testing, and frustration tolerance should be reasonably evaluated. The same is true of the patient's focal problems—for instance, how great his dependency needs are and what types of defenses he erects against them. In many instances—in many clinical settings, for example—such screening is completed within one meeting. Yet, whenever possible, it is well worthwhile to spend several meetings on an evaluation of the patient's problems, needs, and potential.

Second, screening is necessary as a basis for deciding whether a patient will benefit from group treatment and what kind of group model should be advocated. If it is decided to place a patient in a psychoanalytically oriented group, an appropriate group must be chosen. An active, articulate, and fairly autonomous patient will get very restless if he is placed in a group that consists primarily of dependent, passive, and silent members.

Hal, a somewhat hyperactive patient who possessed much insight and a good deal of independence, was invited to a group consisting primarily of dependent, withdrawn, and leader-focused patients. The passive majority welcomed Hal, who acted as a strong catalyst. But Hal was very dissatisfied and restless to find himself the most advanced group member, and he threatened several times to leave. The situation was saved when the therapist succeeded in eliciting from the withdrawn members more direct expressions of their anger and their sense of abandonment and an understanding of the excessive use of withdrawal, repression, and denial. This incident shows that, at times, a placement that is not ideal can work out to everybody's therapeutic gain.

Although such experiences occur more often than has been described in the literature, one cannot generalize from them. Therapists vary a great deal in the criteria they apply for a patient's selection. Slavson

(1955), for instance, suggests that patients with intense sexual disturbances, regressive and infantile characters, and pronounced narcissism be excluded. Other group therapists (Fried, 1970) are convinced that many infantile personalities and highly narcissistic patients benefit particularly from group therapy. Indeed, therapists with broad experience (Freedman and Sweet, 1954) believe that not all but many of their sickest patients benefit particularly from group therapy.

Size of Group

Most experienced group therapists recommend that any group consist of seven to nine members. This size allows for a membership of divergent racial, social, and educational background. It also suffices to reflect the range of psychodynamics that a patient will encounter and have to cope within real life. And it allows for sufficiently variegated transferences to offer a rich therapeutic (learning) experience. Yet it permits the group leader and members enough time to study in each meeting at least some microcosms of behavior in detail; it allows the ego of each member to experiment with a new range of defenses, emotions, and healthier adaptations; and it permits thorough working through, that is, the repeated examination and absorption of detailed material.

Discussion groups, supportive groups, activity groups, and social groups permit a much larger membership. But psychoanalytically oriented groups that exceed the optimal number of seven to nine members offer too little occasion to go into depth, although the socialization experience has a supportive effect.

Some therapists, especially those who structure group experiences according to a preconceived scheme, such as going around from one patient to the next, have found that 10 to 12 members is an optimal group size (Sadock and Kaplan, 1969). They figure that this size allows for one or two withdrawn schizoid members and one or two absent members. There will, then, be about six to eight participating members at each meeting.

Heterogeneous Groups

All groups are heterogeneous with regard to the psychodynamics (personality traits and symptoms) of the individual members. Thus, even in the extreme case where one assembles a group composed exclusively of overtly homosexual males, the personality structures would vary considerably. In the sense, then, of relationship problems and defense structures, all groups share a goodly amount of heterogeneity, even where overt problems are alike.

An important decision in composing a group concerns the degree of pathology of the members. Heterogeneous groups may include one or two schizophrenics, patients with compensated psychosis, as well as members who, from time to time, exhibit borderline behavior.

But it is primarily certain external aspects —for example, age, educational level, and race—that are kept intentionally at variance in groups meant to be heterogeneous. As Kadis et al. say, it is contraindicated to place very young and sexually inexperienced adults in the same group with older adults. Nor is it indicated to place in heterogeneous groups patients who—because of . serious physical handicaps, stuttering, acute alcoholism, or extreme age—will arouse so much anxiety that the group either denies their affliction or focuses too often and too long on them.

A 38-year-old man with conspicuous facial disfigurement was included in a heterogeneous group. The other members avoided any articulation of their reactions to the patient's affliction and to his human problems. The ensuing isolation that he, with the help of the therapist, tried to break but could not was deemed by the therapist to affect the group adversely. The therapist suggested to the patient that he be treated individually. His removal from the group was traumatic for everyone and may serve as a warning not to include such cases. Yet it should be stressed that a good degree of heterogeneity is not only tolerable in most groups but does much to stimulate varied, deep, and thus valuable interactions.

Homogeneous Groups

Generally, it proves salutary to consider criteria such as the following in setting up homogeneous groups.

Adolescents. They are best placed in groups with their peers, although the attendance record of adolescents tends to be poor. They act out and tend to use absence as a means to express anger, anxiety, and confusion.

Older People. Those who are so isolated as to be unable to partake in the agenda of the young and middle-aged, who have neglected their appearance to a point that creates great anxiety in the beholders, or who have developed thought disturbances have to be placed in groups with others whom age has affected similarly.

Acute Psychotics. Those whose ego disintegration is very serious and of long standing fare best and, indeed, often extremely well in homogeneous groups.

Alcoholics. They also seem to fare best in homogenous groups, although some of them develop when, in addition or subsequent to participation in an alcoholic group of the Alcoholics Anonymous kind, they are included in a heterogeneous group.

The Seriously Handicapped. They should be placed in homogeneous groups unless they have overcome masochistic complaints about their affliction and have developed a strong and enterprising ego.

In screening patients for groups and in deciding on composition, one should consider not only criteria such as the ones mentioned but also the ego strength and initiative of the patient. If these qualities are well developed, he may be helped most if included in a heterogeneous group, and the group as a whole may well benefit from his courage.

A severely crippled 42-year-old man who had overcome many handicaps through tenacity and sense of humor was placed in a group of physically intact patients. Six of the other group members were neurotic, and one, a woman, was a borderline case. Gradually, everyone became stronger and much less masochistic and narcissistic, partly through contact with the handicapped

Contemporaneity (Here-and-Now)

Many therapists have found that focusing on the immediate interactions in the here-and-now situation of the therapy session is of high therapeutic benefit. When therapist and patients concentrate on the immediate transference reactions (reaction patterns in the treatment situation that are not provoked primarily by present-day behavior of others but are carried over automatically from the past), important discoveries are made, and changes emerge.

The concept of contemporaneity was conceived by Lewin (1936), who perceived all life situations as determined mutually by the individual and the field in which he operates. Lewin maintained that behavior at any one point is decided by the factors that converge in the field. The experiences in the past that have preceded the occurrences in the immediate given field cannot account solely or even primarily for operant, current motivations.

The focus on the transference reactions in the here-and-now should not be exclusive, however. At times, accounts of past experiences are most illuminating. They highlight the reasons and stresses that made it necessary for the patient in his formative years to adopt the particular character traits and defensive reactions that he exhibits in the present and specifically in the group. The very transference reactions that become apparent in the here-and-now are highlighted and comprehended through such occasional flashbacks. Everybody in the group then understands why a particular member suffers, creates his own obstacles, and behaves destructively, for it becomes clear how present neurotic patterns had to develop long ago because of the particular pressures that existed in the original pathogenic family situation.

Yet, on the whole, group therapy does not lend itself ideally to the full exploration of the origins of maladaptive behavior that has become rigid. Although group therapy is most effective in bringing about the understanding, working through, and modification of pathological ways, the totality of historical origins is rarely explored. The pace of therapy groups and the maze of data that emerge through the immediate interaction make the search for historic origins of present-day behavior slow and at times all too cumbersome.

Some group therapists who emphasize that direct parallels exist between psychoanalysis and group therapy oppose the stress on contemporaneity.

Co-Therapy

Many therapists prefer to work in a co-therapy setting, that is, with another therapist. This setup has the following advantages: (1) If one of the two therapists is male and the other is female, variegated transferences are more readily elicited. (2) Two people often understand the meaning of a particular group interaction differently. Many patients find it reassuring to hear the co-therapists exchange differences of opinion openly, provided that there is no hostility attached. (3) Less experienced therapists are reassured by the presence of another therapist. (4) The discussion between the co-therapists after a group meeting often helps to focus on countertransference reactions. (5) Some borderline and schizophrenic patients work well with co-therapists. They tend to focus their dependency needs on one leader and their aggressive feelings on the other, a situation that allows them to express, inspect, and work out their aggression more quickly and fully than might otherwise be the case.

Leaderless Meetings

Leaderless meetings before a regular group session, after a group session, or regularly alternating with group sessions led by a therapist are often used.

Alternate Meetings. These meetings are regularly scheduled, take place without the presence of the therapist, and are held on a day the leader-led group does not meet. The purpose of the alternative meeting, first conceived by Wolf (1949), is to give the patients additional freedom to challenge the authority figure of the therapist. Usually, alternate meetings last as long as the formal meetings.

A number of therapists oppose the alternate meeting because they believe that the patient works through his authority problems more deeply when the therapist is present. In terms of group dynamics this working through occurs primarily in the power phase.

After-Sessions. These get-togethers, sometimes called postmeetings, are dynamically related to the alternate sessions. When the leader-led session is over, some or all group members stay together, sometimes for extended periods of time, such as two to four hours. Acting out of sexual impulses and aggression is not unusual.

Experience shows that neither alternate sessions nor after-sessions are attended regularly by the full membership. One possible outcome is the formation of cliques and destructive pairings.

Premeeting Sessions. These take place immediately before the leader joins the group. They have been called by Kadis (1963) "a warming-up process."

Conclusion

It is essential that group therapists evolve their own style. They should not copy the style of their supervisors. A personal genuineness as well as an awareness of countertransferences usually guarantees success.

GROUP PROCESSES

Group therapists owe new knowledge, on the one hand, to social psychologists who have studied group behavior and, on the other hand, to practitioners who have focused on special dynamic currents that occur in group settings. Only the group therapist who is aware of group dynamics can maintain group cohesion, that is, a reasonable and continued regularity of attendance and progressive changes in interactions. Only a practitioner who knows of group dynamics can evaluate whether his group proceeds at a reasonable rate from one group phase to another, from inclusion

(Am I accepted?) to power (Dare I challenge the leader and other members?) to intimacy (I like to give, not only take).

Since all group members meet other human beings, not only in their therapy groups but in outside life, interpretations of group dynamics—for example, of envy toward a new member, of escapism from therapeutic work, of wishes for alliance formation—are usually helpful. They reduce social or interpersonal conflicts (conflicts between two or more persons).

Cohesion

Therapy groups, like other functioning groups, are unified by a certain amount of cohesion (connectedness, mutual bond) between members. It has been stated in many contexts (Slavson, 1943, and Scheidlinger, 1955) that such cohesion derives from identifications with and commonly shared feelings toward the leader. Stock and Thelen have studied and described another basis for group cohesion: the group's concentration on and wish to solve a nuclear conflict that arises in each group session. And Hare, Borgatta, and Bales have assumed that the need of any assemblage of human beings to build a social structure resembling the one from which they were split constitutes impetus for group cohesion.

At the same time, invariant group cohesion is an obstruction to group movement and to the development of individual members, as Slavson (1943) pointed out. What matters is that a pronounced although not static degree of cohesion prevails. The cohesion undergoes development in the sense that members feel committed to attend meetings yet become less dependent on the leader's attention or on each other's support. This kind of cohesion is a prerequisite for a working group.

In dynamically oriented therapy groups, cohesion stems from the members' wish to get well, develop individuation, and at the same time achieve a modus vivendi with others. Cohesion that is therapeutically useful and valid is usually not the result of homogeneity between members in terms of sex, education, or problems. Groups based on a homogeneous cohesion of this kind are assembled relatively rarely and only under specific circumstances.

Developmental Phases

Numerous systematic observations and some experiments have been conducted regarding phases or cycle regularities in group development. Essentially, the definition of group phases is the work of social psychologists and group dynamicists. However, many group therapists who do not specialize primarily in group dynamics find the differentiation of group phases or stages helpful.

Group phases are seen as corresponding to the developmental phases in individual life as they have been specified by psychoanalysts. In the life of the individual the psychoanalytic ego psychologists distinguish (1) narcissism and symbiosis, (2) individuation, and (3) object constancy and mutuality.

In parallel fashion, group phases run the gamut of the following stages: (1) inclusion (primary is the question of whether the patient is loved and accepted and belongs), (2) power (primary are questions as to whether the patient can gain autonomy from the leader and whether the patient dare challenge the leader's power, formerly considered exclusive), and (3) affection (primary are concerns with equality and giving as distinguished from taking only). Those group developmental phases have been described by Schutz and by Kaplan and Roman. Other group-dynamics-oriented observers, such as Semrad and Arsenian, differentiate more phases in the sequential development of a therapy group.

Group Dynamics

When several human beings meet collectively, processes are mobilized, properties emerge within each person and within the collective, and laws of behavior are formed that are subsumed under the term group dynamics. For example, a person is likely to respond to a frustration differently when he is alone and when he is a member of a group. The discrepancy between the individual reaction and the group reaction varies from case to case. But the fact that a discrepancy exists is not a variable.

Therapy groups experience special processes. The combinations of these processes make for a constant state of flux. The chief emotional currents noted in the beginning phases of a therapy group differ from those that stand out during later phases of the group's existence. What the group therapist faces is an almost perpetual change of dynamic interactions, differently motivated and differently integrated.

Connections between Group Dynamics and Group Therapy. To maintain group cohesion and group development from the narcissistic phase to inclusion to power to intimacy, the leader needs to be attuned to group dynamics. If the interaction patterns and mobilized group dynamic patterns are overlooked or misunderstood, groups fall apart or come to an impasse.

In a group of nine members, six patients were struggling for autonomy, power, and independence from the therapist. They leveled very harsh attacks at the leader. Two patients were still very dependent and in the second group phase, where the prime questions concern whether or not the individual is part of the whole; they experienced increasing anxiety as they saw the leader attacked. One very advanced woman, who had benefited from a good deal of treatment, was in the final phase of development, that is, she was capable of peer feelings with and friendly affection for the therapist.

To reduce the high tension level of this group, in which many members were concerned at the same time with power and autonomy, the therapist used two measures that proved effective. (1) She repeatedly interpreted the attacks as a rightful defense of equality, which reduced aggressiveness and made the power struggle less fierce. (2) She mentioned a number of times that the autonomy-demanding group members were really quite close to the level of development the mature woman patient had reached. Subsequently, the patient became not a target of envy but a healthy ideal whom the others tried to emulate.

For therapeutic purposes, an understanding of group dynamics and individual dynamics is necessary. The two outlooks have come to a rapprochement, as Durkin has described. Any group, in any given time period, is concerned with such problems as status, alliance formations or alliance avoidances, and relations to the leader (group dynamics) *and* with individual idiosyncratic emotional conflicts and their solution.

Research and History. Among the first and foremost observers of group dynamics were Lewin (1935), his collaborators, Lippitt and White, and his disciple Bach. The special place and use of psychoanalytic propositions were examined by Thelen et al. and by Whitman, Lieberman, and Stock, who tested out experimentally to what degree and in what dynamic ways a group, during a specific meeting, partakes emotionally in a focal conflict and uses its ego forces to find a solution. The concepts of the last-mentioned authors, although they are not generally accepted and are considered too inclusive by some group therapists, do allow for the perception of an important merger. Each member's contribution is understood both on the merits of his own personality structure and as a contribution to the solution of a common group problem.

Group Process

The term group process is sometimes used in a specific way, and at other times it is used to mean the same thing as group dynamics. Used specifically, group process, as the term was coined by Foulkes (1957), denotes the patterns of interaction that groups develop during different periods. Group process conveys the members' specific feeling and fear patterns, either manifest or latent.

After a summer vacation, all eight members in a psychoanalytically oriented group were concerned with the value of the meetings. It turned out that their questions really concerned the inclusion of a new member, a covertly aggressive woman. Adam, who had considered the group meetings the most essential events in the week, deliberated whether or not to leave. Roger spoke with more anxiety of his problems. Edith ignored the arrival of the newcomer and attacked the leader more aggressively. Hillel doubted his own worth and attractiveness and questioned whether therapy helped him. What was evident was that such crosscurrents of reactions clustered around the hot issue of introducing a newcomer

who threatened the group, not so much by her arrival as by her hostile and complex patterns. Such a convergence of diverse reactions on one basic issue is called group process by Foulkes.

Conflict

Intense intragroup conflicts may signify pathology or health. As Bernstein says:

Conflict does not necessarily need to engender hostility, but it may be useful to hate each other when in conflict.

In group psychotherapy, intrapsychic conflicts usually manifest themselves in interpsychic conflicts between the members or between members and the leader.

Edda joined a group because she often blanked out when she drank liquor, even in tolerable quantities. Also, she had serious identity difficulties. She adopted one type of behavior in the morning, shifted to another one at noon, and was a third kind of person in the early evening. These shifts from one type of personality to the other bewildered her relatives, her friends, and the patient herself.

It was quite clear that one of the reasons for the patient's problems was her multiple and instant repressions. For instance, after one of the male members of the group had called this unusually beautiful woman a middle-aged lady, she returned the next time quite cheerfully. As she tried to say something to the man who had insulted her, she was unable to remember his name. The tendency toward repression revealed itself in the relationship between these two people and in many other interpersonal ways.

Focal Group Conflict. The concept of focal group conflict was borrowed by Whitman, Lieberman, and Stock. Focal group conflicts are produced by shared wishes, tensions, or fears in which all or most members partake. The usually unconscious attempts to solve the focal conflict produce forces that hold the group together. Focal group conflicts and their solutions can center on the arrival of a newcomer, with the charter members gradually attempting to integrate their variegated responses to the inclusion of the new arrival. Sharp divisions in the group's attitude toward the therapist, divided feelings about a secret held by one or several members with the permission of the therapist or unbeknown to him—these are a few examples of focal group conflicts. Not everyone shares the conviction that focal conflicts are a unifying force in therapy groups, since solutions are frequently not achieved jointly.

The Group as a Whole and Individual Patients

In terms of psychotherapeutic aims, the connections between processes that affect a group as a whole and those that affect each patient in the group have not yet been adequately clarified. At best, the following generalizations can be supported by practitioners.

Various, although not all, observations and interpretations of group-as-a-whole phenomena (group dynamics) serve therapeutic purposes. Such interpretations are necessary to sustain the group, that is, the desired therapeutic setting. For example, a majority of the group may linger a long time in the first group phase, that of problems concerned with belonging and dependence on the leader (inclusion). A small minority—already preoccupied with problems of individuation, autonomy, and independence from the leader (power)—may be experienced by the majority as so aggressive as to arouse intolerable anxiety in the large dependent subgroup. If the leader then explains (interprets) the minority aggressiveness as a sign of forward movement, group cohesion will be strengthened. Also, it is likely that this group dynamic interpretation will further the therapeutic cause. There are many instances where the understanding and interpretation of group dynamics is necessary to keep groups together and at the same time serve progress.

Unless group dynamics are understood and interpreted by the leader, patients may be damaged rather than helped by group participation. The group leader, therefore, must understand and offer interpretations whenever a group attacks one participant. The singled-out member may evoke great anxiety; he may be a therapist substitute; or he may demand so much attention that everyone else is deprived and, therefore, attacks.

Bion (1961) and Stock and Thelen are among those who are convinced that the therapist's understanding and interpretation of group-as-a-whole phenomena (group dynamics or group process) further the development of all individual patients. The emergence, understanding, and interpretation of the various transferences that occur in every group are indubitably of great therapeutic value to each participant. Quite frequently, such transferences clearly illuminate intrapsychic processes.

New Members

New members are often welcomed by a group if they possess and show such assets as openness, compassion, and tact, not unusual in patients who have improved through previous individual treatment. Leopold's assumption that every newcomer encounters reactions that are derivatives of sibling rivalry cannot be borne out.

New members arrive only in open-ended groups, where places become free because someone has completed treatment or has dropped out. Closed groups are deprived of the experience of integrating a new member, an experience that usually stimulates new reactions in the old members.

Pairing

The term pairing was first used in a significant and clearly defined manner by Bion. He interpreted pairing as an expression of emotional, instinctual, and defensive needs as contrasted with cooperative behavior. According to the complex conceptualization of Bion, pairing supports or reinforces patients' existing problems. Two or more group members may pair, for example, to give each other mutual support because they have not yet comprehended the essence of cooperative behavior in a group. Nor have they developed the skills to interact with all members of the group, through differentiating between the various members.

Currently, the word pairing is used loosely and primarily in a positive way. Many members of the staff of day hospitals or hospital wards look upon pairing between two patients as an expression of first attempts to make contact and break narcissistic isolation.

Basic Assumptions

Groups have been conceived of as pre-occupied with one chief theme at any given time. Three major topics overshadow all others, according to Bion (1951)—dependency, fight-flight, and pairing. These three themes can be related to the three major phases of group development that are evisioned by many concerned with group dynamics—inclusion (dependency), power (fight-flight), and intimacy (pairing). Such schemes help the group therapist to perceive the multiple events in any one therapy group according to an orderly summary of progressions.

To many therapists, Bion's basic assumptions and those development schemes appear too scant and rigid to reflect the multitude of events that occur. However, Bion's theory of basic assumptions has been widely quoted in the literature and has received much attention.

Group Mobility

When the interactions of the group members and the rhythm of progress follow no predetermined pattern, Slavson (1956) calls the process group mobility. It makes for a high degree of spontaneity and generally induces more participation, but it also produces more anxiety than does highly structured and predictable group interaction.

Conclusion

The therapist needs to be aware of group dynamics so as to keep the group coherent and to sustain group movement. Furthermore, interpretations of group dynamics help patients in their social lives and occasionally with their intrapersonal problems. Every therapist who understands group dynamics and applies it is bound to be successful, provided that he is also keenly aware of personal dynamics.

PSYCHOANALYTIC PHENOMENA

A large number of therapists utilize psychoanalytic concepts, although modifications occur when these concepts are applied to a group setting. Psychoanalytic concepts are applied in very specific ways within groups consisting exclusively of psychotics. But groups composed of patients with symptom neuroses, character neuroses, and borderline and ambulatory schizophrenic conditions are usually conducted in considerable accordance with psychoanalytic theory, albeit with adaptations to the group milieu and the group dynamics unfolding within it.

With the large number of character disorders that come to the attention of the private practitioner, it has to be assumed that to effect lasting changes in the personality, group treatment has to take at least two years. This does not mean that interminable group treatments are recommended.

Transference

Transferences occur in groups when feelings and defenses (largely unconscious) and other behavior patterns (character traits) or isolated acts (acting-out behavior), formerly directed at and associated with primary figures of childhood, are repeated toward the therapist and group members without being related to on-going stimuli.

It remains an unsolved question whether analytic group psychotherapy can or should further the development of a full-blown transference neurosis. The transference neurosis occurs in classical analytic treatment partially because the analyst makes a point of remaining neutral and, indeed, becoming a silent screen for the patient's responses. The point can then be strongly made that intense and prolonged feelings of love, hostility, etc., are clearly the result of distortions on the part of the patient who has entered the transference neurosis. The purpose of the silent-screen method is to convince the patient how little his established reactions have to do with on-going stimuli.

In groups, where the therapist's expressive movements are seen, where his behavior—of necessity more active—is observed to reflect some of his predilections and opinions, where his personality in general is more bound to show, it is naturally more difficult to evoke and sustain the classical transference neurosis. Yet despite the therapist's more realistic involvement in treatment and the reduced chances for transference neurosis, group therapy for various reasons does make it possible for patients to observe transference distortions.

Although group therapy rarely produces full-blown transference neuroses that sharply reflect the discrepancy between the patients' feelings and the objects and situations that arouse them, other aspects of the group setting help to clarify the transferential nature of emotions and defenses. What many a patient comes to see—that eventually he comes to produce the same feelings or defenses toward many, although rarely all, group members—helps to illuminate the fact that feelings and defenses are a carry-over from the past and not a response to the actual characteristics of other people and situations. Transference feelings become interrupted or fragmented due to interruptions of others, who react with their own concerns and feelings, but the frequency with which identical feelings return, regardless of present-day reality, does convince many members that they are stuck in a rut that was imprinted in the soil of the personality long ago and from which an exit must be sought. As Durkin says, the understanding of transference in a group is, on the one hand, "more devious," but "the working through process is reinforced by . . . all members working together."

In the beginning periods of treatment, group members' transference feelings focus on the desire for acceptance and nurture. Defenses against these feelings in the form of timidity, submission, or placation are frequently seen. Later, feelings of competition with other group members and of challenge toward the leader emerge. Again, these feelings are often covered up by defenses. Eventually, tenderness and affection emerge, frequently hidden behind the facade of teasing or hostility.

When very intense transferred feelings—primarily of hostility, love, or suspicion—are for long periods of time, for half a year or longer, directed at persons who do not send out stimuli to justify such feelings, the therapist must question whether borderline, schizophrenic, or psychotic processes are at work and rendering the patient unsuitable for group therapy.

The 40-year-old Gilda participated in two different groups. In both groups she addressed intense and unmitigated hostility toward the therapist and one or two female group members. Her rage was interpreted as stemming in large measure from unsatisfiable demands for protection and nurture and from the envy engendered toward anybody who had the therapist's attention. But no interpretation alleviated her rage. Eventually Gilda and the therapist together came to an agreement that she needed individual treatment exclusively. Very gradually, after many years of individual treatment, this woman's rage subsided.

Dilution of Transference. Some group therapists believe with Slavson (1956) that transferences toward the leader are watered down because of the greater number of recipients for the transference phenomena. This opinion is not shared by other group therapists, who observe that for long initial periods the members of a group focus on the leader. The members check out with him whatever reactions are expressed or merely felt, since they see the leader as the primary person in the group.

Multiplicity of Transferences. One of the often-quoted advantages of the group setting is that it provides the patient with a broader range of targets toward whom to beam transferential feelings. For instance, if a therapist is patently reliable, even, and void of anxiety, it becomes difficult to unload on him retaliatory wishes to punish by abandonment. A patient with such a need, stemming from the very early years of life, may find a more suitable target in a group member.

Hillel, whose father died when the patient was three and whose mother stayed away from home a great deal, felt as an adult a hang-over need to punish others by threatening abandonment. When Tina entered the group in which Hillel had been a member for two years, he lit up because he saw her as a suitable human target for his abandonment threats. As soon as Hillel and Tina drew close, he would in one way or another bring up the fact that he played with the thought of moving to another city and hence having to leave the group. Such insinuations invariably created intense anxiety in Tina, an orphan whose prime concern focused on the possibility of abandonment, which aroused overwhelming anxiety in her. Two people with transference feelings that dovetailed had found one another.

In this, as in most similar cases, the intensification of the transference, because of the addition of a target that was especially suitable for special transferences, greatly helped to throw the transferential nature of the feelings and fears into sharp focus. Transference dissolution was gradual but greatly facilitated by target multiplicity.

When group patients are ready to struggle for autonomy and independence (in the power phase, according to the Schutz scheme), they are likely to deflect hostility from the leader figure toward group member targets. Many group therapists believe that such displacements of hostility need to be pointed out repeatedly so as to facilitate ventilation of anger toward the central authority figure.

Resistance

The mere belonging to a group often temporarily reduces an individual's reluctance or inability to get rid of symptoms and undergo character changes, as Freud (1940) observed. However, as spelled out by Slavson (1964), permanent symptom relief and personality changes can only be achieved within a group if resistances and transferences are interpreted and understood and if changes occur on a deep level. These changes, as a rule, set off anxiety, which in turn intensifies resistances and multiplies their manifestations.

One of the major patient fears, that pressure will be put on a group member to speak on issues for which he does not feel ready, is alleviated by therapists who use the group to gradually dissolve the patient's resistance to disclose. Some therapists, such as Sadock and Kaplan, believe that pressure is therapeutically valid. In various medical schools this method has proved effective during certain phases of therapy.

In the conduct of group psychotherapy one can distinguish between the resistances of individual patients in the group and group resistances that arise either in a majority of members or in the entire group. Resistances by individual members take many forms: (1)

protracted and repetitive transference reactions either to the group leader or to one or several members, (2) long-standing infatuations or hostilities, (3) extensive biographical accounts of childhood history, (4) frequent or uninterrupted silences, and (5) taking the part of assistant to the therapist. The last two forms of resistance are aided by the group situation. There are many other resistance manifestations.

Edith used her considerable intelligence and poise to explain to other group members and especially to Tina, a member whose hostility she feared, how they functioned. Her observations were so astute that the other members were eager to learn from Edith and to gain benefits from her interpretations, especially since her own rather substantial hostility was so repressed that it showed neither verbally nor nonverbally. After repeated interventions by the therapist, Edith and the other group members could no longer ignore the fact that Edith was not getting anything for herself out of the group. When Edith felt compelled to drop her particular resistance, she became so anxious that she missed a few sessions, got mixed up about the dates of the meetings, and could speak only with a quavering voice.

Resistances by the entire group or a majority of group members take on forms related to the above-mentioned ones: (1) silences shared by many group members, (2) prolonged dependency on and overevaluation of the therapist, and (3) hostile and snide attacks on the therapist. There are also other forms of resistance by the group as a whole or the majority of the members.

One group, because of basic flaws of group composition, had two fairly inarticulate and dependent members and six participants who were highly articulate and concerned with issues related to the group's power vis-á-vis the therapist. Moreover, among the majority members there were two women whose hostility to the leader was so intense that any remark by the therapist was misinterpreted in paranoid fashion or taken as proof that the two hostile members were unwanted. Since both women were also extremely dependent on the therapist and the group, it was nearly impossible to interpret successfully either to the two women or to the rest of the group that the hostility stemmed largely from guilt, feelings of dependency, etc. Because of very early abandonment traumata it was not advisable to transfer one or both of the hostility leaders to other groups. The deadlock seemed insurmountable. The situation changed after the summer vacation when, according to a long-standing practice of this therapist, some changes in group composition were made.

Some group leaders, such as Wolf and Schwartz (1962) and Aronson (1967), maintain that the interpretation and dissolution of group resistance does not further the development of the patients in the group, since the interpretation and dissolution detracts from the therapist's preoccupation with the individual patient's resistance. Many group therapists would not concur with this view, since they feel that the observation and explanation of group dynamics is an essential aspect of group treatment, one that sustains the desirable degree of group cohesion and facilitates the development of healthy adaptive patterns in patients.

Existential group therapists like Mullan (1955) bypass the phenomenon of resistance. In practice these therapists rupture and undercut resistances, going directly to what they sense or know to be central conflicts, without examining the patient's ways of hiding behind the bulwark of resistance because of anxiety.

Frequently, hostility is expressed in groups in order to resist the exposure of tenderness or love. This is true in some measure of all patients but especially of borderline cases and psychotics.

Aggression

According to psychoanalytic ego psychology, the child can glean the beginnings of mutual (give-and-take) love only after two previous stages have been completed. He has first to go through a symbiotic phase, where he feels one with the mother, and then he must struggle for individuation-separation from the parents, which usually has to be accompanied by certain negativistic and aggressive behavior. Once the child has attained some degree of separateness and individuation, he is able to move further and glean what mutuality is like.

Groups are sometimes said to induce a diffusion of aggression, meaning that aggression is neither distinctly felt nor clearly discharged toward a specific target. Yet many clinical observations show that, especially in the middle phase of group therapy (the individuation or power stage), strong aggressive forces are released. It becomes necessary, for the sake of group cohesion and movement, to use complex therapeutic skills to maintain a manageable degree of the aggressive forces, the aim of which is to win the power struggle with the therapist leader, member leaders, or factions of the group experienced as representing authority.

The point has been made by some group therapists, such as Hobbs, that, since a high degree of emotional support by the group as a whole or by a substantial number of group members represents a major therapeutic factor, hostile or aggressive individuals should be excluded from group treatment. Therapists who approach groups psychoanalytically do not go along with this view and will consider exclusion of an aggressive group member only if the aggression is unyielding to any intervention and its level does not change over a five- or six-month period.

Universality

In the group setting many superego pressures are ameliorated. The members come to see that others share their guilt, their real or supposed offenses, and their conflicts. Universality, as this shared awareness that "you are like everyone else" is called (Slavson, 1956), reduces the severity of the superego and alleviates guilt feelings.

Biographical Material

It is important that the therapist be familiar with crucial data that shaped the past of each group member. Especially important is the anamnestic history of repeated processes precipitated by the early environment that traumatized the patient by their frequent occurrence and halted the developmental trend, thus making excessive defenses and maladaptations a necessity.

The patient's insistence on narration of past events instead of immediate reactions to the present is often a resistance in group therapy, where the here-and-now of interactions is the focal source of data and the prime therapeutic agent. Biographical material is readily marked as resistance, as Wolf (1963) has pointed out. Irrelevant and evasive excursions into biography occur frequently in groups, but the members' boredom readily identifies the resistive character of these excursions.

Acting Out-Acting In

Acting Out. When, during a course of group psychotherapy, a patient expresses conscious or unconscious desires, conflicts, or fantasies—usually they exercise a particular pressure—in outside action rather than in articulate statements within the group, he acts out. Acting-out tendencies increase when internal or environmental stimulation is particularly charged and chaotic. Moreover, certain characters gravitate toward acting out. Patients whose motility is hyperactive, whose transferences are intense and divided against many group members, who have psychopathic character structures as distinguished from psychoneurotic or neurotic character symptomatology—these are the most likely candidates for acting out.

Groups intensify acting-out behavior because they offer a great deal of stimulation and an opportunity for multiple and divided transferences. Only when the group leader and the group members achieve a reasonable amount of organization does acting out gradually subside. The setting of group psychotherapy enhances the proclivity toward both activity and acting out, two phenomena that should be distinguished. In general, those who initially are psychopathic and gravitate toward acting out are among the few patients who should be only cautiously introduced into groups.

Acting-out behavior can be measured on a destructive-constructive continuum. Therapeutically speaking, not all acting out can be condemned as destructive. A measure of it can be constructive by furthering individuation and the rebellion that antecedes and accompanies movement toward autonomy and individuation.

Group leaders limit destructive acting out whenever a group majority or individual patients incline in that direction. Groups in and by themselves do not limit acting-out behavior, despite the claim of Wolf and Schwartz (1962):

> Every therapeutic group . . . sets limits on the acting out of its members. The therapist can encourage limits on acting out as follows: (1) by asking that all extramural group activity be reported to all members and the therapist; (2) that its therapeutic value be clarified in different instances.

Acting In. Acting in signifies the patient's nonverbalized and hence behavioral re-enactment of his conflicts, desires, and life history. Acting in is a phenomenon that occurs frequently in group psychotherapy and one that may often escape those who behold it. As Ormont says, persistent and unchecked acting in may disrupt and demoralize a whole group and may sometimes bring it to a disastrous halt. Acting in is a form of nonverbal communication, albeit of a destructive kind, and group members have to be alerted to its disorganizing effect. In any psychotherapy that has validity, the point has to come when the patient verbalizes rather than acts his problem if he is to understand its full meaning and function. Since acting in has an ego-syntonic quality, the struggle between the therapeutic forces and the undermining ones is quite pronounced.

Working Through

In order to resolve old conflicts clustering around infantile desires, long-standing transference reactions, and ego defects, group members have to go over basic experiences again and again. In psychoanalysis proper, it is assumed that a turning backward toward the emotions originally surrounding the conflictive experiences (regression) helps the process of working through.

The heightened reality elements in groups make regressions less likely or curtail them to a considerable degree. Nevertheless, certain aspects that are inherent in the group setting aid the working-through process. For instance, the fact that a member distorts not one but several people in the same manner helps him to comprehend that transference (carried-over) feelings are at work. The other group members' encouragement to discontinue the repetition of transferences (carry-over feelings) and to see novel stimuli in a fresh light is helpful. Pressures stemming from the superego (conscience) and prompting the patient to uphold his pathological behavior are reduced partially because other members encourage him not to keep up with self-harrassment and partly because confessions of guilt before peers lead to less self-blame than confessions made exclusively to an authority figure.

Brian had undergone two years of private individual therapy with a male analyst whom he alternately admired and appeased. Two months after he entered a group conducted by a female leader, he was able without oppressing guilt to express homosexual feelings toward a strong man in the group. He declared that he wanted alternatively to imbibe the other man's strengths and to appease him. It became quite clear in the ensuing discussion that the declaration of homosexual desires was aided by two factors: (1) Brian's guilt feelings were ameliorated by the rather casual tone that prevailed among the group members. (2) Brian expected that his peers would censor him less heavily than the leader would.

Group Psychoanalysis

Psychoanalysis within the group setting appears quite feasible, provided that the therapist is attuned to and interprets transference and resistance phenomena, which Freud and his desciples declare as the all-important cornerstones. As Durkin says:

Neither Freud nor Fenichel insisted on a fixed mode of implementing the essential process.

Narcissistic transferences, pre-oedipal fears of abandonment, attempts at individuation, oedipal transferences, archaic superego pressures, various libidinal demands—all those are manifested in groups. They can be interpreted, and incisive changes can be brought about, provided that the therapist is psychoanalytically skilled.

Probably the least accessible conflicts are those centering around very early oral deprivation. With a therapist who divides his attention among six or more members and with limited opportunities for prolonged regression, the conflicts stemming from oral deprivation, which are most basic, can often not be put to rest. For example, patients who have a history of considerable autistic experience in infancy, many of them with an obsessive-compulsive superstructure, tend either to withdraw too much or to insist on too much attention, thus provoking either neglect or hostility. However, some patients with problems stemming from extreme oral deprivation experience their group as a substitute mother and family.

Many psychoanalysts, such as Kubie and Stein, have formulated the reasons why they do not believe that psychoanalysis in groups is feasible. Almost as many group therapists, such as Wolf and Glatzer, have described how it can be done. Probably the most farranging and deep therapeutic effects can be accomplished by combining individual and group psychotherapy. One way to enable a patient to work through residual problems of early deprivation is to start with individual analytic therapy and continue with analytic group psychotherapy.

Combined Therapy

When a patient's treatment consists of regularly scheduled individual and group meetings, this arrangement is called combined therapy. Many therapists—such as Fried (1954) and Kaplan and Sadock (1971) —consider the advantages of combined therapy considerable.

In individual meetings the patient has ample opportunity to develop the trusting, individualized, and dependent relationship with the therapist that represents one aspect of a positive transference and that in large measure initially, and in lesser measure in the middle and later phases of treatment, helps him to muster the frustration tolerance and ego strength often needed to get through intense group therapy stresses. Rarely does group therapy provide patients who have pronounced depressive leanings due to inadequate mothering with that make-up experience that the one-to-one relationship of individual treatment offers. This is true even if a first narcissistic phase and the struggle for inclusion in the group are skillfully handled.

Group therapy has the advantage of offering the patient multiple transference objects and hence a rich variety of transference reactions.

On the other hand, the multiplicity of stimuli in the group can create fragmentations that some patients can tolerate only through the integrative work in parallel individual therapy.

Often the group therapist, flooded by impressions, is aided by combined treatment to make significant connections between various and divergent transferences exhibited by one and the same patient in the two situations. When he cannot relate the meanings of the transference tangle either to past events or to the object relation phases that the patient tends to misapply in the present, such connections can be made in the quiet setting of the one-to-one relation.

The individual sessions that are part of combined treatment allow a thorough working through of the rich, group-induced frustrations.

Dubin related to the therapist in a rather polite manner in individual treatment. This transference, which became resistance, seemed impossible to analyze and to change. In the group the patient showed positive feelings for few of the female members, but, once again, he was quite courteous toward them, obviously so fearful of his enormous rage that he never let go. When a new member, Sheila, was added to the group, Dubin reported in his private sessions that he felt intense resentment toward her. He started to express his resentment cautiously in the group session during a holiday session, when the group was small because three members were away on Southern vacations. Steadily and clearly it turned out that Dubin's anger toward Sheila focused primarily on very slight undercurrents of self-pity and concomitant accusations that were expressed more in her tone of voice than in her words. Genetically, here was a transference with a constantly complaining and accusing mother. Functionally, in the here-and-now situation, the male patient was actually terrified to express himself not only because he was certain that he would attack too strongly and possibly physically but also because he feared that Sheila's clever twists would shut him up quickly.

Only a minority of patients reserve certain material for individual sessions, for example, homosexual drives and actions, psychopathic behavior, or murderous feelings toward a group member. In all such instances it is important to examine the material in detail and gradually diminish resistances that stand in the way of equally free disclosures in the two combined-treatment modalities.

Conclusion

The group setting is an excellent medium for conducting a thorough-going character analysis. Many shy and withdrawn patients become open and enterprising. Many manic patients find nuclei of their own selves and calm down. Rectification of specific symptoms, however, is usually not accomplished as promptly in a group as in a series of individual meetings. Many group psychotherapists disagree with the above statements.

SUPPORTIVE-INSPIRATIONAL GROUPS

Supportive-inspirational groups are used in specific settings, such as in Alcoholics Anonymous meetings, in outpatient clinics, in day hospitals, and in the offices of some private practitioners. The underlying idea is that the self-esteem of the patient is affirmed not by characterological changes and by independent ego strengths but by the direct encouragement of the therapist, who is seen in an exalted position. In other words, a transference cure takes place. The patient does not change within himself but feels changed because the supposedly powerful therapist acts benevolently. Moreover, in supportive-inspirational groups, a member who has accomplished some feat tells his confreres about it and lifts their spirits because they identify with him.

Peer Identification

In supportive-inspirational groups, members whose self-esteem is shaky are exposed to members whose self-esteem is high because they have reached some special goal.

The self-doubting members are uplifted through feeling at one with the members who have scored an achievement. This process is called peer identification.

Peer identification also occurs in psychoanalytically oriented groups. However, in this therapeutic setting, the identification is not left untouched but is subjected to investigation and interpretation, with the result that peer identification may be a starting point for self-development and not the prime vehicle for increased self-esteem.

Mutual Support

In supportive-inspirational groups, the leader gives clues that members are expected to encourage one another. Each person is a cheer leader, so to speak, who signals to the others that they either do well or have done well. Motivations for wanting to do well, for doing well, or for doubting whether one does well are not explored.

This kind of mutual support is different from the kind that occurs in psychoanalytically oriented groups. In such groups, members are frequently helpful to one another, but the prime aim is to examine the motivations of behavior and to alter behavior. Therefore, encouragement can evoke anxiety in these groups.

Idealization

Both leaders and members are idealized. This is by no means very different from the manner in which psychoanalytically oriented groups start out. But in supportive-inspirational groups the idealization is allowed to remain untouched. In psychoanalytically oriented groups, by contrast, the idealization is gradually understood, through interpretations, to constitute an overevaluation of either the leader or the powerful members.

Colette, who belonged to an Alcoholics Anonymous group, returned from many meetings in an elated state. She had listened to the accomplishments of other members and was filled with hope and ambition to emulate them. Such idealization helped her over a long period of time. It has to be added, however, that depression eventually set in. As Colette observed that idealized members faltered, she lost faith. As she gradually noticed

that she could emulate them only rarely and not invariably to the degree that they reportedly attained, her self-doubts increased.

Conclusion

If the group members have strong identification with the leader, the cause, or the spokesman in their group, the supportive-inspirational treatment works well. But the success of this treatment is precariously balanced on the members' trust in what they consider an extraordinary leader and extraordinary experiences. When the spiritual nature of the group wears off, members tend to be discouraged. In such instances, the membership gradually declines.

PSYCHOTIC PATIENTS

Clearly, psychotic patients can benefit from group psychotherapy, as can be observed in day hospitals and outpatient clinics.

In dealing with psychotic patients, one must understand that the patient's isolation from the other members and his seemingly inappropriate comments and looseness of language are frequently determined by a thread that runs through his group behavior. Although he appears to be isolated from others who are present in his group and his utterances reflect a discontinuity, a connectedness that is not readily apparent does exist and can be deduced by the therapist. The socialization offered to psychotic patients through group psychotherapy is most salutary.

As a result of group therapy, many patients become more cooperative with the hospital staff and their fellow inmates. More frequently than is often assumed, psychotic patients can be rehabilitated gradually after successful treatment.

Importance of Nonverbal Behavior

Psychotic patients on wards, in day hospitals (partial hospitalization), in outpatient departments, and in the offices of private practitioners respond to the therapist, to the group, and to other group members on a nonverbal level. To help them, the therapist has to be attuned to the fine antennae of the psychotic. Every psychotic patient senses immediately whether the therapist, some other member of the staff or office team, or another patient is angry without admitting it, lacks understanding and interest, or is not open and direct. When psychotic patients are on to duplicity, double messages, disinterest, etc., they refuse to open up and to make attachments. Distrusting the clinicians and many members of the clinical team more than their own peers, they are likely to communicate with another patient when they would not speak up to authority figures.

A near-catatonic patient, whose most recent depression occurred after his girl friend left him, refused to speak to any member of a day hospital staff. Finally, the decision was made to send him to a state hospital. The day before his admission to the state hospital, a young woman patient in the day hospital sat next to this distraught and silent man. Attuned to most of his needs, she would get up from time to time to close a window, to fetch a glass of water, or to perform some other minor service. After two hours of this companionship, the man started to talk to his newly found friend. When he spoke a few words during the next morning to one of the female aides, the decision was made to extend his stay at the day hospital.

Articulating the Unconscious Links

When the majority of the group members are psychotic, they often speak in what appears to be a collective monologue. Everybody seems to be an entity unto himself. Much of the speech is incoherent. At times a group member gets up and does something in the room that seems unconnected with what is going on. Many, although not all, unrelated behavior patterns are actually linked together in ways that a trained therapist can understand. When the therapist articulates the connections that have remained unconscious to patients, hope, trust, and communication gradually develop.

A paranoid, middle-aged woman in a day hospital group got up, left the room, and returned with a pitcher of water whenever any physiological function, particularly sex, was mentioned. The patient then walked over to the plants in the room and watered them. This much-repeated action expressed her feeling that the body, specifically the sex organs, was dirty and that a cleansing ritual was necessary. Eventually, the therapist addressed this patient as though she had spelled out her feelings in explicit words. She was visibly pleased to have been understood.

Setting Limits

In treating psychotic patients, the therapist must set limits to aggressive behavior, most forms of sexual exhibition, and overt sexual approaches among patients. Violence can never be tolerated in a group setting or, for that matter, in the therapeutic community in which many psychotics live. Provided that the therapist distinguishes between firmness, which is necessary, and an autocratic, overbearing attitude, which is contraindicated, the psychotic patient appreciates the injunctions that are appropriate. Until his own ego controls are better developed, he leans on the ego strengths of the therapist, whom he senses to act on his behalf.

Setting up too many injunctions at the same time confuses psychotic patients. It is better to set up just a few injunctions, repeat them at intervals, and express satisfaction when they are observed.

Epithetic Withdrawal

Invariably among the emotions that motivate epithetic withdrawal are anger and punitive intent. Group therapy has the advantage that other members may help to articulate the withdrawn patient's anger. They do this by simply assuming that it exists and inviting the silent member to join in the discussion. Or else another patient's show of anger can set a precedent. Some therapists who are basically good-humored and not hostile can pierce the withdrawn facade by humor and challenge.

Confrontation Techniques

In recent years on some wards, psychotic patients have been confronted directly, although with few words, with their prime problems. If this is done with authority but not autocratically, if the timing is right, and if the therapist proceeds without angry countertransferences, the method can be highly effective. After such confrontations it is wise to discuss with the patients how their problems—for instance, a fear of their own violence—can be handled through conscious, direct control rather than through psychotic symptomatology.

Therapeutic Community

Among the reasons why many psychotic patients do well in a hospital or clinic setting is the existence of the therapeutic community. A few of the many features that characterize the therapeutic community are these: (1) Staff and patients live together. (2) The staff is sensitized to the patients' need for directness, to their nonverbal behavior, and to the need for empathy yet firmness. (3) Communications that are contradictory, double-bind messages, are avoided. (4) All staff members approach the patients according to a jointly shared understanding of what is needed to provide corrective experiences.

Conclusion

Psychotic patients tend to be immensely helped by groups. In fact, it is hardly possible to make headway with them without utilizing the therapeutic community and certain group settings. The progress of psychotic patients is usually very slow, but sometimes it is startlingly quick. Group psychotherapy is strongly recommended for this category of patients.

TERMINATION

The distinction between premature drop-out and termination has to be clear in the therapist's mind. Premature drop-out occurs because the patient cannot master his anxiety, because the group has reduced his self-esteem, and because he is a minority in a group. By contrast, termination occurs when the patient has resolved his major conflicts, has acquired self-esteem, and feels decisively that he and the group engage in a mutual give-and-take.

Indicators for Termination

As a rule, group members begin to weigh the value of terminating treatment after the following accomplishments: Anxiety has decreased both in the group and outside, and so has hyperactivity. The expression of impulses has become freer, and control is primarily conscious. Narcissism, both in the form of being isolated and of leaning on the powerful, is markedly reduced. The range of deliberately chosen defenses is wider. The patient displays his changes clearly and over a period of time toward the group, the members, and the leader. These changes coincide with improvement in his life outside the group.

Mutual Discussions of Termination

All patients who contemplate reasonable termination, rather than dropping out, discuss and weigh their notions with the group. Invariably, the members of the group express some feelings of sadness when the departure of a member is considered to be appropriate.

If a patient leaves because he has made gains, rather than because of resentment and anxiety, he should give two or three months' advance notice to the group.

Bud, after three years of group psychotherapy, discussed with some hesitation his feelings of ambivalence about leaving the group. On the one hand, he was convinced that he had resolved many basic conflicts. No longer was he looking for the overprotection of a solicitous mother; no longer was his leading mood one of depression; no longer did he feel worthless either in his job or in regard to women. Yet Bud still felt some dependence on the group and the therapist and was unsure whether he could replace the authentic relationships he had established with group members by turning to friends on the outside. For roughly two and a half months this back-and-forth of emotions was debated until Bud decided, and the group agreed, that he would gather more adult strength by leaving. It turned out that this thoroughly considered termination was appropriate. For five years after termination, Bud behaved without tension and with much adult strength. Only once did he ask for a private consultation with the therapist.

Conclusion

If the mentioned criteria for termination are heeded, the patient will, after termination, conduct his private and working life successfully. Frequently, he returns off and on for a few individual sessions with the therapist. After a genuine termination he may feel a wish to return to the group—but he does not act on it.

REFERENCES

Ackerman, N. W. Psychoanalysis and group psychotherapy. In *Group Psychotherapy and Group Function*, pp. 250–260, M. Berger and M. Rosenbaum, editors. Basic Books, New York, 1963.

Aronson, M. L. Resistance in individual and group psychotherapy. Amer. J. Psychother., *21:* 86, 1967.

Bach, G. *Intensive Group Psychotherapy*. Ronald Press, New York, 1954.

Bernstein, S. *Conflict in Group Work, Explorations in Group Work*. Boston University School of Social Work, Boston, 1965.

Bion, W. R. *Experiences in Groups*. Basic Books, New York, 1961.

Durkin, H. E. *The Group in Depth*. International Universities Press, New York, 1964.

Fidler, J. W. Group psychotherapy of psychotics. Amer. J. Orthopsychiat., *38:* 688, 1965.

Foulkes, S. H. *Introduction to Group-Analytic Psychotherapy*. William Heinemann, London, 1948.

Foulkes, S. H., and Anthony, E. J. *Group Psychotherapy*. Penguin Books, London, 1957.

Freedman, M. B., and Sweet, B. S. Some specific features of group psychotherapy and their implications for selection of patients. Int. J. Group Psychother., *4:* 355, 1954.

Freud, S. *Group Mass Psychology and the Analysis of the Ego*. Boni and Liveright, New York, 1940.

Freud, S. Beyond the pleasure principle. In *Standard Edition of the Complete Psychological Works of Sigmund Freud*, vol. 18, pp. vi–97. Hogarth Press, London, 1955.

Fried, E. The effect of combined therapy on the productivity of patients. Int. J. Group Psychother., *4:* 42, 1954.

Fried, E. Combined group and individual therapy with passive-narcissistic patients. Int. J. Group Psychother., *5:* 194, 1955.

Fried, E. Some aspects of group dynamics and the analysis of transference and defenses. Int. J. Group Psychother., *15:* 44, 1965.

Fried, E. Narcissism: how it curbs and can be curbed. Presented at the Annual Conference of the American Group Psychotherapy Association, New Orleans, January 1970.

Glatzer, H. T. Working through in group psychotherapy. Int. J. Group Psychother., *19:* 292, 1969.

Hare, A. P., Borgatta, E. F., and Bales, R. F. *Small Groups, Studies in Social Interaction*. Alfred A. Knopf, New York, 1965.

Hobbs, N. Group-centered psychotherapy. In *Client-Centered Psychotherapy*, pp. 278–319, L. R. Rogers, editor. Houghton Mifflin, Boston, 1951.

Jones, M. *The Therapeutic Community*. Basic Books, New York, 1953.

Kadis, A. Coordinated meetings in group psychotherapy. In *Group Psychotherapy and Group Function*, pp. 437–448, M. Berger and M. Rosenbaum, editors. Basic Books, New York, 1963.

Kadis, A., Krasner, J., Winick, C., and Foulkes, S. H. *A Practicum of Group Psychotherapy*. Harper and Row, New York, 1963.

Kaplan, H. I., and Sadock, B. J. Structured interactional group psychotherapy: a technique paper. Amer. J. Psychother., in press.

Kaplan, S. R., and Roman, M. Phases of development in an adult therapy group. Int. J. Group Psychother., *13:* 10, 1963.

Kubie, L. S. Some theoretical concepts underlying the relation between individual and group psychotherapies. Int. J. Group Psychother., *8:* 3, 1958.

Leopold, H. S. The new member in the group: some specific aspects of the literature. Int. J. Group Psychother., *11:* 367, 1961.

Lewin, K. *A Dynamic Theory of Personality*. McGraw-Hill, New York, 1935.

Lewin, K. *Principles of Topological Psychology*. McGraw-Hill, New York, 1936.

Lewin, K. The research center for group dynamics at Massachusetts Institute of Technology. Sociometry, *8:* 126, 1945.

Lewin, K., Lippitt, R., and White, R. K. Patterns of aggression in behavior in experimentally created climates. J. Soc. Psychol., *10:* 271, 1939.

Lowrey, L. (chairman), Slavson, S. R., Spiker, D., Peck, H. B., Glauber, H., and Ackerman, N. W. Group therapy special section meeting, 1943. Amer. J. Orthopsychiat., *13:* 648, 1943.

Moreno, J. L. Psychodrama and group therapy. Sociometry, *9:* 249, 1946.

Mullan, H. The group analyst's creative function. Amer. J. Psychother., *9:* 320, 1955.

Mullan, H., and Rosenbaum, M. *Group Psychotherapy*. Free Press of Glencoe, Glencoe, Ill., 1962.

Ormont, L. R. Acting in and the therapeutic contract in group psychoanalysis. Int. J. Group Psychother., *19:* 420, 1969.

Pratt, J. H. The class method of treating consumption in the homes of the poor. J. A. M. A., *49:* 755, 1907.

Sadock, B. J., and Kaplan, H. I. Group psychotherapy with psychiatric residents. Int. J.

Group Psychother., *19:* 475, 1969.

Scheidlinger, S. The concept of identification in group psychotherapy. Amer. J. Psychother., *9:* 661, 1955.

Schilder, P. Results and problems of group psychotherapy in severe neurosis. Ment. Hyg. *23:* 87, 1939.

Schutz, W. C. *Firo: A Three-Dimensional Theory of Interpersonal Behavior.* Rinehart, New York, 1958.

Semrad, E. V., and Arsenian, J. The use of group processes in teaching group dynamics. Amer. J. Psychiat., *108:* 358, 1951.

Slavson, S. R. *An Introduction to Group Therapy.* The Commonwealth Fund, New York, 1943.

Slavson, S. R. *An Introduction to Group Therapy.* International Universities Press, New York, 1954.

Slavson, S. R. Criteria for selection and rejection of patients for various types of group psychotherapy. Int. J. Group Psychother., *5:* 3, 1955.

Slavson, S. R. *The Fields of Group Psychotherapy.* International Universities Press, New York, 1956.

Slavson, S. R. *A Textbook in Analytic Group Psychotherapy.* International Universities Press, New York, 1964.

Standish, C. T., and Semrad, E. V. Group psychotherapy with psychotics. In *Group Psychotherapy and Group Function*, pp. 477–486, M. Berger and M. Rosenbaum, editors. Basic Books, New York, 1963.

Stein, A. The nature and significance of interaction in group psychotherapy. Presented at the Annual Conference of the American Group Psychotherapy Association, New Orleans, January 1970.

Stock, D., and Thelen, H. H. *Emotional Dynamics and Group Culture.* National Training Publication, Washington, 1958.

Thelen, H. H., et al. *Methods of Studying Group Operation.* Human Dynamics Laboratory, Chicago, 1954.

Whitman, R. M., Lieberman, M. A., and Stock, D. The relation between individual and group conflicts in psychotherapy. Int. J. Group Psychother., *10:* 259, 1960.

Wolf, A. The psychoanalysis of groups. Amer. J. Psychother., *3:* 524, 1949.

Wolf, A. The psychoanalysis of groups. Amer. J. Psychother., *4:* 16, 1950.

Wolf, A., and Schwartz, E. K. *Psychoanalysis in Groups.* Grune & Stratton, New York, 1962.

3
Comparison of Different Types of Group Psychotherapy

Hyman Spotnitz, M.D., Med.Sc.D.

INTRODUCTION

The practice of group psychotherapy is based on the finding that mental illness and mental dysfunctioning can be ameliorated through the psychological effects of several persons upon one another. The fact that improvement in mental functioning tends to alleviate and may eventually cure mental illness has inspired countless efforts to exploit the healing force of the group to meet the therapeutic needs of a widening range of patients—people with highly diverse problems seeking treatment at all phases of the life cycle. Concurrently, the commitment of virtually all schools of psychotherapy to group practice and its elaboration in their respective conceptual frameworks have encouraged the parallel development of a wide array of group psychotherapeutic approaches. These approaches have developed so rapidly and have been described so idiosyncratically by some of their proponents that the literature gives the impression that there are as many different ways of treating groups as there are group psychotherapists.

That impression is also generated by the therapist's use of himself as a professional instrument. In psychological treatment, personal influence cannot be discounted. Each practitioner is a unique personality. His style of conducting a group cannot be duplicated by another therapist, however similar their professional qualifications, treatment philosophies, and clinical skills may be.

Nevertheless, group psychotherapy as a scientific discipline owes its development to the systematic application of validated discoveries about the therapeutic needs of people with psychological problems and to carefully formulated specifics about the planning and conducting of their treatment, the selection and grouping of patients, and related considerations. These specifics are indices to the built-in limitations and potential values of group psychotherapy and thus offer a means of comparing its different forms.

This chapter serves two purposes: (1) It helps the student penetrate barriers of theory and language that separate the different systems of group psychotherapy and distinguish their actual differences from their common factors. (2) It suggests general guidelines for determining the specific effectiveness of one or another approach for a given patient. No attempt is made to discuss or even mention all the group methods that have been reported, but this comparison does encompass those methods that dominate contemporary practice.

DEFINITION OF GROUP PSYCHOTHERAPY

The presence of three or more persons in the same place at the same time is essential to qualify a procedure as group psychotherapy. The triadic formations covered by the term include one patient working with two therapists as well as a pair of patients, often a married couple, working with one therapist. Another essential factor in group psychotherapy is that they meet for the express purpose of influencing one another, directly or indirectly, by psychological means. Still another requirement is that this reciprocal influence be therapeutic to the participants—in no wise harmful to any of them—and help them improve their functioning as human beings.

Defined loosely in terms of those core requirements, group psychotherapy is a procedure in which three or more persons assemble at an appointed time and place for a definite period to beneficially influence their mental health and functioning by psychological means.

The main value of that broad designation is that it serves the purpose of this chapter, specifying only the factors that distinguish all forms of group psychotherapy and accommodating the innumerable diverse factors associated with its practice—factors related to the participants and their joint activities. Among the major differences are the subjects of the treatment, the composition of the group, the therapist's general orientation and specific strategies, the goals of the treatment, and the nature of the results achieved. Experimentation with these variables, which has recently increased, accounts for the kaleidoscopic character of contemporary group psychotherapy.

Descriptive terms frequently used in the literature convey some of the most obvious differences. Groups are dichotomized as large and small, inpatient and outpatient, long-term and short-term, continuous and time-limited, open and closed. Groups based on specific criteria for membership are referred to as structured; those whose composition follows no plan are blanket groups. The dichotomy of heterogeneous and homogeneous also relates to composition.

The labeling of the established procedures is haphazard. The name may be derived from any one of the group's properties or dimensions, such as its size, membership, field of application, duration, or operational principles. The theroretical framework in which the group is conducted may or may not be indicated. For example, "family therapy" is a label attached to groups whose only shared characteristic is that they are composed of members of the same family. More adequately identified are groups whose names derive from two or more variables, such as "psychodramatic family therapy" and "activity group therapy for latency-age boys." In striking contrast are the catchy names attached to tangential variants referred to as personal growth groups, the human potential movement, etc. A strong element of salesmanship pervades such christenings as "nude marathons," "basic encounters," and "group grope."

VARIATIONS IN PRACTICE
Size

The number of participants ranges from one patient with two or more therapists, as already indicated, to one hundred or more group members. There is no fixed boundary between large and small groups, but those referred to as small or face-to-face usually contain no fewer than four patients and no more than ten. Some practitioners regard six, seven, or eight patients as the ideal number. Small groups prevail today. Even though depth of treatment is primarily a function of the therapist's technique, it is not possible to work effectively for characterological change in groups that are too large for member-to-member interaction.

Groups larger than 12 and with an upper limit of 20 or 30 patients are sometimes designated as intermediate groups. They provide a suitable format for lectures and the discussion of common problems. In larger formations, therapy necessarily merges into educational, morale-building, or social activity. Large therapy groups, usually conducted in institutional or community settings, are more or less limited to the repressive-inspirational approach. Such groups are often organized to work on a specific problem—for example, alcoholism or obesity. Some are known as self-help groups because they operate without a professional leader. In many cities, Recovery, a self-directed group of psychiatric patients discharged from institutions, conducts a supportive program known as will training.

Composition

Although groups composed of patients of the same age or sex are sometimes referred to as homogeneous, that term is more strictly applied to those in the same diagnostic category or presenting the same problem. Persons suffering from different forms of psychoneurosis or from the same psychoneurotic condition, such as hysteria or phobia, may constitute a group. Similarly, the group identified as homogeneous may be made up of homosexuals, drug addicts, or patients with the same psychosomatic condition. In medical group therapy, those with a particular organic illness, such as cardiac disease, are treated together.

The majority of groups treated in private practice are heterogeneous, selection being based on the principle of mixing rather than matching personality types. This practice, begun as a matter of expediency, has been reinforced by the finding that the balancing of persons with diversely structured personalities facilitates the development of therapeutic interchanges, provided their socioeconomic backgrounds are reasonably compatible. Thus, different diagnostic categories are represented in heterogeneous groups, among them psychoneuroses, personality disorders, the milder psychosomatic complaints, borderline conditions, and some prepsychotic and postpsychotic states.

Therapists who conduct heterogeneous groups try to exclude persons who would not benefit from the shared treatment experience or who might be a disruptive influence on others, but there are no generally accepted criteria for exclusion on the basis of psychiatric classification. Whereas some authorities, notably Slavson, exercise extreme care in selection and advocate the exclusion of patients in specific diagnostic categories from group treatment, others pay scant attention to diagnosis. For example, Berne stated that almost any patient, if properly prepared, can be assigned to a group. He advocated the policy of picking candidates at random or in order of application, on the assumption that such selection favors heterogeneity.

Some practitioners, the author among them, rather than ignoring the diagnostic factor, regard it as an inadequate source of information on how patients will behave in the group setting. Therefore, these therapists try to ascertain the types of defenses that each candidate activates in interpersonal situations. The assessment of current impulses and defenses is one aspect of achieving a balancing of personality types, which facilitates the functioning of the group as a unit. The blending of placid and excitable persons with some who tend to arouse excitement and others who check it is sought by therapists who conduct group treatment as a primarily emotional experience.

Some differences in individual modes of conducting groups are dictated by the personal characteristics of their members. Their age, sex, and one or another particular about their life status are often reflected in the labels attached to their groups.

Age. Therapy groups are conducted for people in all age categories. Groups for adults often include the middle-aged as well as young adults, but the age span is narrower in those groups conducted for children, adolescents, and elderly people. Children treated together are generally at the same developmental level.

Sex. Private practitioners customarily treat men and women together. However, participation in some groups is limited to members of the same sex.

Kinship. Some therapy groups are composed of strangers, others of persons in real-life relationships. Outstanding among the natural groups are those consisting of members of one family. Some practitioners of family therapy treat several families together; the creation of an artificial group through the fusion of natural groups has also been reported in the treatment of married couples. Relatives of patients with similar conditions—for example, parents of severely disturbed children or the spouses of alcoholics—participate in groups organized to deal with the management of these patients. Friends and neighbors as well as family members are assembled in social network therapy, a brief series of meetings organized to deal with a crisis situation in the life of a schizophrenic person; the tribal support of his natural group is solicited as a possible alternative to his hospitalization.

Socioeconomic Affiliations. People who work together may be assembled for a specific therapeutic purpose, such as sensitivity training. Although these groups are usually characterized as group work for normals, some are so conducted as to be relatively indistinguishable from conventional therapy groups. Sensitivity training is also carried on under the auspices of social organizations and churches.

Professional Status. A prime example of groups constituted on the basis of professional identity are those conducted under the aegis of training in psychotherapy. To an increasing extent, group training in the behavioral sciences is oriented to therapeutic goals.

General Orientation and Approach

Most group therapists adhere to a theoretically grounded approach, the labeling of which reflects, implicitly or explicitly, their *modus operandi* and treatment philosophy. To identify a practitioner as an analytic group therapist, as a psychodramatist, or as a behavior therapist, for example, is to give important clues to how he views and addresses himself to his patients' problems. However, some therapists rather consistently apply the procedures consonant with their own school of therapy while others operate more empirically—a difference conveyed by the terms "strict methodology" and "fluid methodology."

The majority of therapists who conduct outpatient groups practice analytic group psychotherapy. The therapist who operates according to psychoanalytic principles, as adapted for the shared treatment experience, and applies the working concepts of transference and resistance remains a relatively unobtrusive figure in the group, intervening primarily to interpret behavior. Within that frame, three somewhat different approaches have developed: Some therapists

treat the individual *in* the group; others treat him *through* or *by* the group; and still others take an intermediate position, treating the individual as much as possible through the group as an entity and focusing on him separately to the extent necessary to resolve specific problems. Parloff has referred to these positions, overlapping in some respects, as intrapersonalist, integralist, and transactionalist or interpersonalist. The intrapersonalists place the least emphasis, and the integralists the most emphasis, on the role of group processes. The interpersonalists or transactionalists try to extract maximal therapeutic leverage from group processes in order to facilitate concurrent characterological change.

The theoretical divergences are reflected in the labeling of the analytic approaches. Therapists referred to as intrapersonalists have established such designations as "group psychoanalysis" and "psychoanalysis in groups" for their procedures; "psychoanalysis" has been abjured by other therapists. For example, Whitaker and Lieberman identify their system as "psychotherapy through the group process," and Foulkes introduced the terms "group-analytic psychotherapy" and "therapeutic group analysis."

Specific Strategies

Among therapists operating in the same general frame of reference as well as among those of different persuasions, much variability in therapeutic strategies and personal functioning in the treatment sessions is reported.

Probably the most obvious difference is the way therapists relate to patient-members of the group. Personal styles of conducting treatment range from authoritarian through didactic, blank screen (where the predominant attitude is passivity), and permissive to leaderless. The term "leaderless" may denote the therapist's physical absence from some or all treatment sessions or his attitude of scientific detachment, an attitude maintained by some research-oriented practitioners. But in the present context, "leaderless" refers to the disclaimer of more responsibility for the operation of the group than that assumed by the patients—an attitude characterized by Mullan in 1955 as status denial. Leaderlessness in that sense usually implies a high degree of personal involvement, the communication of information about the therapist's real-life identity, values, and immediate emotional reactions— all expressed in behavior as well as in words in some of the new approaches.

Diversity in professional backgrounds among practitioners of group psychotherapy helps to account for the wide spectrum of strategies and attitudes reported. Rather than adhering to the traditional view of their role as one of healing sick people, some therapists implement other assumptions about the problems of their group members. Practitioners, physicians among them, who depart from the medical model to an appreciable extent find it more congenial to view the therapy group as a social system and relate to its members in terms of sociological, philosophical, or theological systems of thought. The specific problems presented by patients are often regarded as social tensions, dynamic pressures, and the like. Surveying this variegated picture, Lieberman, Lakin, and Whitaker stated:

Therapeutic strategies range from those in which the therapist possesses a total encompassing charisma and, much like a guru, acts as the interpreter of reality and the center of emotional cathexis, to those in which the therapist acts as conductor or a social engineer.

Little is known about the therapeutic implications of these departures from the more or less established role of parent surrogate.

Sessions without the Therapist. The majority of practitioners maintain the policy of conducting all sessions of a group. Others incorporate meetings without the therapist in the treatment process. This practice was introduced by Wolf and Schwartz, who refer to these regularly scheduled gatherings as alternate sessions.

Use of Co-Therapists. Most groups are conducted by a single therapist, but current reports suggest an appreciable increase in the number treated by two or more. The practice of dual therapy was probably introduced for training purposes, with the second therapist serving primarily as a recorder and observer while his more experienced colleague actually conducted the group. However, many co-therapy teams today are composed of a male and a female therapist who share this responsibility.

Co-therapy is a controversial practice. Authors who question its value argue that it compounds countertransference phenomena, that it tends to contaminate the transference reactions of patients, and that their treatment is also interfered with because competitive strivings and even serious differences between the team members develop more or less inevitably. Exponents of co-therapy claim that the family constellation is replicated with the presence of mother and father transference objects, thus facilitating the progress of specific categories of patients. Exponents also point out practical considerations, such as the fact that one therapist can conduct the group in the absence of the other.

Since 1957, when Spitz and Kopp investigated the wide range of methods employed in co-therapy, including the treatment of one patient by as many as ten therapists, many additional variations have been reported.

Group Stimulus Situations

In any type of group psychotherapy, the stimulus situation is fundamentally different from that in the one-to-one treatment relationship. In individual analytic therapy, for example, the patient is stimulated mostly through verbal communication and auditory feedback, from his own words and the interventions of the analyst. The group setting adds to these the important factor of visual stimulation and visual feedback.

In the verbal group therapies, the therapist may limit himself to intellectual communication, which is generally effective in dealing with emotional problems that originated in the oedipal stage of development. Patients whose problems are associated with pre-oedipal (preverbal) stages are usually more responsive to emotional and symbolic communications.

Group therapists have traditionally limited themselves to auditory and visual modes of influence. The major exceptions are found in psychodrama and in the play and activity group therapies for children, in which feedback from action is a significant source of stimulation. The plethora of group methods recently introduced, some under the aegis of therapy and others characterized as growth experiences, relegate auditory and visual stimulation to a less important role. These new methods operate primarily through bodily sensations, including tactile and kinesthetic. Participants are encouraged to touch one another and to engage in other forms of physical contact—sexual or aggressive or both. Even taste and smell sensations may be stimulated.

Much experimentation is going on at the present time to determine whether such stimulation is necessary or desirable in psychotherapy. In the author's experience, physical contact and tactile stimulation do not contribute to significant personality change. In some instances, they preclude successful treatment.

HISTORY OF CLASSIFICATION

Various sorting racks have been devised to accommodate the multitude of practices designated as group psychotherapy and to elucidate their significant similarities and differences. But few schemata in this field have escaped the fate of rapid obsolescence. No generally accepted classification exists today.

Early attempts to classify the group methods reflected the initial need to know the different ways psychotherapy can be conducted in the group setting. Descriptive classifications are characteristic in an early developmental period, but, after one knows how to do it, answers are needed to the questions "For whom?" and "What does it accomplish?" Successive classifications have moved somewhat closer to supplying answers to those questions, although these classifications are still hampered by the clinical-impressionistic nature of the reports on treatment and the consequent difficulties of conducting evaluative research. The classifications discussed below in chronological sequence were made over a period of 25 years, and they illustrate how different investigators have attempted to rise above the level of descriptiveness in an immature field of practice.

1943

Giles Thomas, following Merrill Moore's simple differentiation of the individual psychotherapies, discerned two major categories of group psychotherapy—the repressive-inspirational and the analytic—"with various degrees of combination of the two." Accordingly, he arrayed the methods reported by the early 1940's along an axis, with Schilder at one end and Alcoholics Anonymous at the other end (see Figure 1). In the accompanying review, Thomas stated

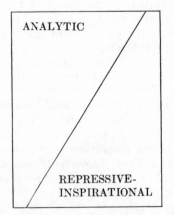

Schilder

Wender
Lazell

Chappell
Marsh

Pratt, Rhoades, Buck, Harris, Hadden, Snowden
Schroeder
Altshuler

Alcoholics Anonymous

Figure 1. The first and best-known descriptive classification of the methods of group psychotherapy, by Giles W. Thomas. (From *Psychosomatic Medicine*.)

that good results had been claimed in a "large proportion of the patients treated (more than half)" but that it was not possible to compare them.

Thomas's survey, published in the journal *Psychosomatic Medicine*, was introduced by the following editorial note:

This is a new field, and the review covers extremely heterogeneous material: therapeutic procedures based completely on rough empiricisms like Alcoholics Anonymous, together with therapeutic efforts like Schilder's carefully analyzed and planned experiments and the experimentation of psychodrama based on definition of psychodynamic observations and concepts.

The critical reader may receive the impression that this field is not yet ripe for this type of descriptive reviewing and needs above all a critical evaluation of the methods employed and the results reported. However, the Editors feel that this review gives, if not a complete, a rather broad descriptive view of the various attempts of group therapy and might stimulate interest in the obvious possibilities of this type of treatment.

That statement, expressive of the customary reaction of practitioners trained in the principles of scientific reporting on treatment, is of more than historical interest. The classification that provoked this reservation has attracted much attention over the years; Thomas's schema is still used and is regarded as one of the most helpful descriptions of the group approaches. Moreover, the above-quoted comment, published in 1943, has not, regrettably, lost its pertinence. Similar views have been expressed, particularly by those engaged in evaluative research in the field. For example, Goldstein, Heller, and Sechrest observed in 1966 that

group psychotherapy literature as a whole has remained at the earliest and most primitive level of observation and inquiry. . . . The plateau of descriptiveness which the current group psychotherapy literature represents must be built on, developed, and elaborated.

1945

J. L. Moreno formulated a table of eight polar categories and three points of reference to accommodate all the group approaches. He suggested that the methods be categorized as follows:

Subject of Therapy

(1) Constitution of the group (amorphous or structured on the basis of diagnosis); (2) Locus of treatment (natural life setting or special clinical situation); (3) Aim of treatment (causal or symptomatic);

Agent of Therapy

(4) Source or transfer of influence (therapist-centered or group-centered); (5) Form of influence (spontaneous and freely experienced or rehearsed and prepared);

Medium of Therapy

(6) Mode of influence (lecture or verbal, dramatic, or other actional mode); (7) Type of medium (conserved, mechanical, unspontaneous, or creative); (8) Origin of medium (face-to-face or presented from a distance, as from radio or television).

Actual distribution of the group methods under this comprehensive plan was not reported.

1957

Raymond J. Corsini, making a distinction between methods per se and the different ways each is applied, identified more than 25 methods by name. He distributed them under the headings of directive and nondirective to indicate the degree of control exercised by the therapist. The directive therapist was described as setting limits on the group members, the nondirective as setting limits on himself; the crucial factor was considered to be the

latitude permitted for decision making, especially in regard to interpretations.

Under his main headings, Corsini arranged the group methods under four subheadings: verbal-deep, verbal-superficial, actional-deep, and actional-superficial:

Directive

Verbal-Deep: (1) *Multiple therapy* (Dreikurs, Adlerian school)—one patient meeting with two therapists; (2) *Analytic therapy* (the circular-discussional approach common to the analytic schools, the main difference in its use being in the nature of the interpretations provided); (3) *Co-therapist methods: Behind-the-back technique;* (4) *Projective methods* (circular discussion of the spontaneously produced drawings of members);

Verbal-Superficial: (5) *Will training* (A. A. Low) in large and self-directed groups; (6) *Adlerian group counseling;* (7) *Lecture methods* (Pratt's class method, the repressive-inspirational procedures employing music or other attention-getting devices, repetition lectures, and procedures utilizing visual aids); (8) *Case histories* with discussion initiated by the therapist (Wender); (9) *Anonymous participation* (answering of questions written on unsigned slips of paper); (10) *Group bibliotherapy* (including J. W. Klapman's textbook-mediated therapy); (11) *Mechanical group therapy* (short recorded messages over a loudspeaker system);

Actional-Deep: (12) *Psychodrama* and related procedures introduced by Moreno;

Actional-Superficial: (13) *Dramatics* (theatrical productions by hospitalized patients); (14) *Puppets* (used for psychotherapeutic purposes in mental hospitals); (15) *Acting-out techniques* (as introduced by Ernst Simmel for release of repressed hostilities); (16) *ABC* (alphabet writing and other simple tasks performed cooperatively by patients using a blackboard);

Nondirective

Verbal-Deep: (17) *Client-centered method* (Carl Rogers); (18) *Leaderless therapy* (Bion-Rickman's research-oriented method, in which the therapist may engage himself verbally but assumes no special responsibility); (19) *Round-table psychotherapy* (introduced by McCann and Almada, in which the therapist is inactive while a small panel of patients sits around a table and many more constitute an audience);

Verbal-Superficial: (20) *Social-club therapy* (Joshua Bierer); (21) *Alcoholics Anonymous;*

Actional-Deep: (22) *Psychodramatic group therapy* (an adaptation of psychodrama with the group meeting in a circle);

Actional-Superficial: (23) *Activity group therapy* (Slavson); (24) *Music therapy;* and (25) *Auroratone* (abstract color films synchronized with music).

Corsini's classification, which affords a panoramic view of the practice of group therapy in the 1950's, illustrates the rapid rate of attrition in group methods. Many of the methods he listed have virtually disappeared from the current literature. The schema, moreover, does not distinguish between small and large groups. But the chief drawback of Corsini's classification lies in its failure to indicate the specific values and limitations of each method listed, the types of patients for which it is effective, and what it can accomplish.

1959

Although the classification proposed by J. W. Klapman in the second edition of his textbook on group psychotherapy has similarly outlived its usefulness, it represents the first attempt to categorize methods of group therapy on the basis of their suitability for patients. Decrying a preponderance of emphasis on any one approach as well as the waning status of approaches that he regarded as most appropriate for severely regressed patients, Klapman formulated a gradient classification presenting criteria and indices for

any given patient at any given time at any given level of aberrant psychic functioning.

He suggested that patients entering treatment in groups structured for the most disturbed patient population should be "upped" in due time to groups permitting a greater degree of autonomy. Consonant with those views, he described three degrees of disorganization observed in adult patients and matched these personality states with the optimally applicable group methods.

Patients in minimally disorganized states, encompassing most of the patients who qualify for treatment on an outpatient basis, were designated as patients of choice for analytic group therapy, psychodrama, and client-centered group therapy. Klapman listed about a dozen approaches as optimally applicable in moderately disturbed states. Among these approaches were a hierarchy of didactic procedures oriented to an improvement in intellectual functioning in groups small enough to permit two-way communication. For his third category—severely and relatively severely disorganized personality states—he recommended a score of methods oriented to different levels of ego functioning, from calisthenics and other physical activity to textbook-mediated therapy. The majority of the approaches described by

Klapman have fallen into disfavor, and his idea that the therapist is perforce limited to the lecture methods when treating psychotic patients has not been sustained. Nevertheless, the schema itself is notable in a period dominated by method-oriented classifications.

The classification by Frank and Powdermaker, also presented in 1959, has been more widely used. It suggests that the group treatment procedures, though marked by a considerable degree of overlap, fall into five general categories:

Didactic Groups, with guided discussions based on lectures by the therapist directed toward the promotion of intellectual insight and also allowing emotional interaction, used primarily with hospitalized psychotic patients;

Therapeutic Social Clubs, conducted especially for promoting skills in social participation among patients discharged from hospitals, and organized along parliamentary lines with the therapist intentionally maintaining an unobtrusive role;

Repressive-Inspirational Groups, designed chiefly to arouse positive group emotions and build morale through strong group identifications, in which the therapist gives inspirational talks and conducts relaxation exercises or group singing, and the patients may present testimonials or recitations;

Psychodrama;

Free-Interaction Groups, encompassing the various forms of group psychotherapy conducted by psychoanalytically oriented therapists and also group-centered psychotherapy, which promote an atmosphere conducive to the free verbalization of feelings and to the exposure and correction of immature attitudes.

1964

In a schema elucidating differences in depth of small-group approaches, S. R. Slavson distinguished group psychotherapy from group counseling and guidance, reserving the first term for procedures aiming at significant intrapsychic change in subjects with real pathology. By contrast, counseling and guidance, identified as different levels of psychonursing, are concerned with ego functioning and offer assistance with immediate and specific reality problems. Counseling is viewed as the most superficial and time-limited method, designed to clarify a course of action; guidance deals with emotional impediments to carrying through action by providing support and clarification without, however, tracing the blockages back to their source. Four major types of group therapy are discerned: activity group therapy for children, analytic for adults, para-analytic—a therapy of less depth for adolescents, the elderly, and specific diagnostic categories of adults, among them schizophrenic and borderline patients—and directive.

Slavson's classification illustrates one of the terminological confusions in the field, that generated by different conceptions of group counseling. Nonmedical therapists, in particular, tend to use the term group counseling interchangeably with group psychotherapy or regard it as a more intensive procedure than group guidance.

1965

Instead of compartmentalizing the systems of group treatment, some classifiers have represented them as constituting a continuum. Max Rosenbaum, for example, discerns a succession of interrelated methods, ranging from repressive-inspirational to regressive-reconstructive, which reflect the two extremes in the extent of personality change worked for. Between them he places the supportive and reparative therapies, the latter being oriented to the building up of weak defenses. A directive-didactic category, including behavior therapy in groups, is differentiated from nondirective methods, such as the group version of client-centered psychotherapy, psychodrama, therapeutic social clubs, and analytic group therapy.

1968

Howard A. Blatner's chart (see Figure 2) shows further progress toward specificity. It has a dual significance. Proposed as an aid in the selection of the type of group experience that will meet the patient's therapeutic

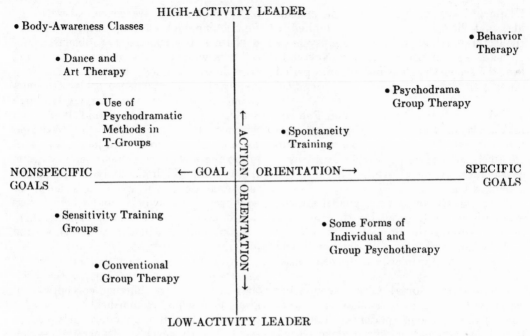

HIGH-ACTIVITY LEADER

• Body-Awareness Classes

• Behavior Therapy

• Dance and Art Therapy

• Psychodrama Group Therapy

• Use of Psychodramatic Methods in T-Groups

↑ ACTION

• Spontaneity Training

NONSPECIFIC GOALS   ← GOAL   ORIENTATION →   SPECIFIC GOALS

ORIENTATION

• Sensitivity Training Groups

• Some Forms of Individual and Group Psychotherapy

• Conventional Group Therapy

↓

LOW-ACTIVITY LEADER

Figure 2. Classification of group procedures in relation to goal orientation and action orientation, by Howard A. Blatner. (From *Voices.*)

needs most efficiently, this schema appears to be the first to focus on the group approaches that were introduced during the 1960's. Moreover, methods are differentiated in terms of factors that were not mentioned in earlier classifications—the amount of structured activity imposed on group members by the therapist and the degree of specificity of the goals on which they agree. Of interest in this context is Eric Berne's suggestion in 1966 that therapies in which the practitioner's goals are limited or diffuse be identified as "soft," while those geared to more far-reaching, clearly defined goals and to achieving these goals expeditiously be identified as "hard" therapies.

A comparison of Figures 1 and 2, reproduced from clinical reports that span a period of 25 years, highlights the on-going shift from method-oriented to goal-oriented classifications. The comparison also suggests that group psychotherapy has been developing from an assortment of more or less similar instruments for doing psychotherapy in a general sense into an armamentarium of different instruments fashioned to achieve highly specific objectives.

SIGNIFICANCE OF GOALS

In the absence of scientific findings on the comparative values and limitations of the different types of group therapy, recommendations for treatment are usually based on clinical judgment and experience. By and large, the personal predilection, theoretical allegiance, training, and expertise of the practitioner whom the patient happens to consult determine the type of group experience he undergoes. Happenstance in selection, understandable as it is in this still primitive stage of development of group psychotherapy, is undesirable. It may deprive the patient of the type of treatment experience that would be most efficacious for him; it may also expose him to a distinctly harmful treatment experience. Rapid expansion of the group psychotherapeutic armamentarium increases the responsibility of the practitioner for discriminative selection of the instrument to be applied in each case.

Specificity in treatment will eventually be facilitated by objective evaluations of the results achieved through the different approaches. Without such evidence, however, the most reliable guide to specificity is a comparison of the stated treatment goals and results reported by the proponents of each procedure. The theories applied are of some significance because they indicate how the therapist attempts to influence the group through his behavior. But primary consideration needs to be given to what is sought, anticipated, and achieved through the use of the procedure. In short, the preferred method for a patient can best be determined by investigating the respective goals and results achieved through the alternatives available.

With increasing effectiveness in the matching of methods to patients, such data will probably be included in classifications of the group treatment approaches. At the present time, the facts have to be extracted from the professional literature—a laborious and not very rewarding task, owing to the unscientific nature of much of the reporting. Differentiations are vague; the range of applicability of some methods may not be defined; follow-ups are exceptional, claims in some instances being based exclusively on behavioral change in the treatment sessions.

Like individual psychotherapy, group psychotherapy has only one *raison d'être*—to benefit the individual. Although that justification may seem too elementary to mention, the prolonged preoccupation with methodology has tended to obscure it. *How* the patient is treated in the group setting has received much more attention than the precise benefits the therapist was striving to accomplish through his procedure. Nevertheless, distinct differences in the goals reported are readily discernible.

Distinctions are made in psychotherapy between *attainable* goals and *ideal* goals. An attainable or practical goal is commonly viewed as one that helps the patient achieve the optimal level of functioning consonant with his financial resources and material circumstances, his motivations when he enters treatment, and his ego capacities. It is generally recognized that such goals represent a modification of what theoretically constitutes the ideal objective of psychotherapy—personality maturation. What this

notion implies offers a desirable criterion for a comparative evaluation of the goals reported.

Personality Maturation

Undoubtedly, the most ambitious goal that is pursued in psychotherapy is that of arresting an illness, repairing its ravages, and helping the patient outgrow his emotional immaturities so that he may realize his potential in life performance and happiness. Such an outcome, although more far-reaching than symptomatic relief or social recovery, does not necessarily mean that he has been relieved of all his problems or that he will not encounter new ones in the future. That outcome does signify, however, that he has the ability to feel, think, and behave appropriately in all normal situations and to meet the impact of extraordinarily traumatic experiences with considerable resiliency. Emotional versatility is an important measure of recovery because the seriously disturbed patient entering treatment tends to be bogged down in the essentially gross feelings of the young child. In the process of refining them and acquiring more discriminatory feelings, the patient eventually commands the hierarchy of feelings that characterize emotional evolution. The author therefore conceptualizes such curative change as the emergence of the emotionally mature personality.

Personality maturation is considered to be the natural outcome of biological and psychological growth in a succession of reasonably favorable internal and external environments. Highly specific reactions to disruptions of these growth processes at different developmental levels constitute the spectrum of functional disorders to which the psychotherapist addresses himself. The earlier the processes were thrown out of gear, the more damaging the impact on the organism. Disruptions of the maturational sequences that unfold during the first year of life are associated with psychosis. Other disruptions during the pre-oedipal period (the first two years) are associated with the impulse disorders, character disorders, severe obsessive-compulsive illness, and some psychosomatic disturbances. Vicissitudes encountered at later maturational levels are linked with psychoneurosis and the relatively minor disturbances experienced by the normal person in emotionally stressful circumstances.

In a person suffering from a deep-seated disorder, the psychotherapist usually recognizes two types of interferences with further personality growth: fixations and maladaptations. Both types are associated with the failure to meet maturational needs. Fixations result from exposure to situations of undue frustration or gratification or both. Maladaptations are perceived as the persistence of certain repetitive behaviors, patterned in these deficiency states, that drain off psychic energy into circuitous processes. These defensive maneuvers may interfere with the meeting of needs that are subsequently experienced. The psychological ingredients that would satisfy the later needs are usually available but cannot be assimilated because of the deviant patterns formed to compensate for the original deficiencies.

Patients succeed in liberating themselves from the compulsive operation of the maladaptive patterns when they are helped to engage in defense-freeing exercises and to re-experience the original fixations. They also require, concomitantly and subsequently, experiences that contribute to further growth.

Treatment oriented to the goal of personality maturation entails three essentially different dynamic operations. In this discussion, these dynamic operations are referred to as discrete steps and are focused on in the order in which each operation dominates the psychotherapeutic process, but they are overlapping concerns.

Step 1. In the treatment situation, reactivate and deal with the forces that prevent the patient from meeting his maturational needs. This step is what the psychoanalytically trained therapist refers to as controlling the development of transference. The interfering forces are aroused, analyzed, and influenced in terms of dealing with transference resistance.

Step 2. Help the patient meet his own maturational needs. This step is, in a sense, a tactical operation, engaged in to help the patient give up the maladaptive behavior. During the treatment, he experiences many psychological needs, such as a need for some immediate gratification, but in principle these needs are not met. The therapist extends aid only for meeting those needs that hamper emotional growth.

Step 3. Help the patient give up the maladaptive behavior without endangering the degree of personality maturation that he has achieved. In technical terms, this step is referred to as the working through of transference resistance.

Case History

John, 35 years old, was frequently referred to by the co-members of his group as "the great protector." He talked repeatedly in the sessions about disagreements with his wife concerning her disciplining of their 10-year-old son. John's tendency to rush to the little boy's defense whenever he was reproved for misbehaving and his refusal to associate himself with his wife's disciplinary measures gave rise to much friction in the family.

In the treatment sessions, John characteristically came to the defense of a young man whenever he was criticized by another member, a middle-aged woman. John made no effort to investigate the merits of the criticism. Objections to this behavior were voiced by several members of the group.

In the process of dealing with this maladaptation, the group came to recognize it as a component of John's infantile personality. His early years had been marked by emotional deprivation. After his parents' divorce, when John was two, he never saw his father. John eventually disclosed that he felt like a little boy. The pattern of "the great protector" appeared to represent an indirect attempt to call attention to his own need to be taken care of. The other group members responded to this understanding by helping him with his current problems with his wife. A progress report on his home life was often demanded of him in sessions when he did not volunteer such information.

As a group member, John functioned more and more appropriately as his need for help was satisfied. He tried to understand the communications of the other patients and to be helpful to all of them.

The resolution of the pattern of automatically jumping to the defense of the young man in the group was followed by a gradual but observable change in John's behavior with his family. He began cooperating with his wife in the upbringing of their son. John informed the group that he felt like a husband as well as a father.

In this case, the group therapist worked primarily on Steps 1 and 3. He conducted the treatment in such a way as to maintain a transference climate, addressed himself to the obstacles to cooperative functioning in the treatment sessions—illustrated by John's little-boy feelings—and helped the patient work through these interfering forces in the context of innumerable treatment situations. Step 2, on the other hand, was performed mostly by the group members themselves. His feelings of being understood and cared for by his co-patients, for example, helped him significantly in outgrowing the "great protector" pattern.

Emotional Feeding

As a matter of principle, the majority of analytic therapists who conduct individual treatment to produce significant personality change do not help the patient meet his maturational needs. They assume that the understanding they provide through their interpretations will suffice to free him to meet them himself through the emotional nourishment inherent in ordinary social situations. In the shared treatment experience, on the other hand, patients spontaneously "feed" one another, session after session, with feelings that satisfy different kinds of psychological needs.

Much of this emotional feeding is of little or no significance for personality growth; it provides momentary gratification without influencing the obstacles to change. But in addition to nutriments that create spells of excitement and dilute feelings of depression and alienation without helping to induce corrective change and the more conventional verbal communications of support or reassurance—all viewed by the author as meeting gratification needs—patients also pick up from one another specific feelings that stimulate growth processes. One of the special values of group psychotherapy lies in the contribution of patient interaction to the reciprocal meeting of maturational needs.

TYPES OF GROUP THERAPY

A classification of the various group procedures in terms of the type of problems they deal with and their relative effectiveness in clearing up these problems is not yet possible for reasons that have already been mentioned, notably the lack of specificity in the practice of group psychotherapy and discrepancies in the standards of reporting in the field. At the present juncture, however, these procedures can be differentiated roughly on the basis of the operational principles applied. The extent to which the practitioners employing each procedure deliberately address themselves to the three operations entailed in resolving the forces that have blocked personality maturation serves as the principal criterion in the assessment of each type of group therapy discussed.

Taking a phenomenological stance, the author has attempted to picture the field of contemporary practice and has, therefore, included in his sampling, along with the major established approaches, some that are innovative and unvalidated and whose status as psychotherapy is moot. Clinical concepts and techniques are delineated when deemed necessary to clarify their relation to the manifest goals of the treatment or the composition of the group or to facilitate the evaluation of the claims made.

Goals, it should be borne in mind, do not necessarily convey the therapeutic power residing in a method. In the course of the method's development, the results achieved most consistently come to be identified as its objectives. Goals are thus an expression of therapeutic outcome most efficaciously secured through past applications rather than a final pronouncement on therapeutic action. Hitherto untapped values may emerge in the future with somewhat different applications. As already mentioned, however, the goals currently enunciated and information on the extent to which these goals are attained provide the most reliable evidence available on the suitability of a procedure for a given patient and the predictable outcome of the case, assuming that the therapist is reasonably proficient.

The procedures surveyed below cover the spectrum of contemporary practice. The sequence in which they are discussed does not accurately reflect the order in which they were introduced; psychodrama, for example, antedates the cluster of analytic approaches that are reviewed first. Procedures with relatively similar goals are viewed in succession. The progression is from long-term to short-term, with approaches of the most recent vintage completing the series.

The author's impressions are based primarily on information provided by practitioners adhering to the procedure under review. Their assumptions, clinical practices, observations, and claims have been gathered from the literature. Personal communications from patients were another source of information. The claims advanced for each procedure were assessed on the basis of the data available.

Analytic Group Psychotherapy (Freudian)

It was pointed out earlier that therapists whose procedures are derived from individual psychoanalytic therapy differ substantially in the extent to which they integrate group processes into their conceptual framework as well as in their modifications of the parent techniques. In general, however, they conduct treatment on a long-term basis to produce significant characterological change in persons who are highly motivated to achieve such change. The treatment is conducted in a transference climate; transference and resistance phenomena are analyzed and, in some cases, worked through; the group equivalent of free association is employed; dreams are interpreted. Great reliance is placed on the acquisition of insight. Rapid change is not looked for, and the therapist does not necessarily apply himself to help the patient improve his interpersonal functioning.

Careful attention is given to the selection and grouping of patients, but criteria for admission vary. Patients with psychoneurotic conditions, character disorders, and other disturbances of the oedipal type are widely regarded as the most likely candidates. Practitioners who conduct analytic groups on an ambulatory basis usually exclude patients with more severe disorders or limit the number of such patients in composing a group. For instance, Wolf reported in 1968 that for psychoanalysis in groups he accepts persons with borderline and mild psychotic conditions and specifically excludes paranoid and hypermanic patients, those who hallucinate, severe stutterers, the seriously psychopathic, alcoholics, mental retardates, and patients with some types of cardiac disorder.

Some analytic group therapists structure treatment to include regular sessions without the therapist. Wolf claims that these alternate sessions promote

more spontaneous interactivity as well as more inappropriate responses and impulsivity.

This practice is predicated on the assumption that the group members will not seriously misbehave in the therapist's absence. Other therapists, including the author, challenge the assumption and believe that alternate sessions are undesirable for groups with acting-out or potentially psychotic patients. But such meetings may conceivably be recommended for the promotion of spontaneity in rigid and overcontrolled patients.

The goals of this method are defined in terms of psychosexual maturation. The therapist addresses himself to resolving the emotional forces that thwart maturation and focuses on the working through of maladaptive behavior (Steps 1 and 3).

Cautious assessment of ego strength and tolerance for regression is important before exposing a person with a severe disturbance to this regressive-reconstructive approach. The more deep-seated his problems, the more retrograde movement he has to engage in, and the more difficult it becomes to influence him effectively by interpretive interventions. Problems rooted in the preverbal period are more responsive to emotional and symbolic communications. Moreover, it is difficult to work on these problems without stimulating regressive tendencies that threaten the degree of adjustment to reality that the patient has achieved.

Consistent and confirmed techniques for the individual treatment of pre-oedipal patients have been reported, but the development of such approaches for group treatment oriented to meaningful change has not been claimed. Analytic therapists who accept severely disturbed persons in their groups do so within the framework of combined treatment.

Analytic Group Psychotherapy (Neo-Freudian)

Therapists who adhere to the theoretical constructs of the cultural and interpersonal schools of psychoanalysis differ notably from those who implement Freudian principles in their interpretations and formulation of goals.

Adler School (Individual Psychology). Adlerian therapists, notes Dreikurs, view their group members as social beings whose behavior is purposive and directed to social survival and self-realization. Although the group members have not learned to live together as equals, their life styles are based on self-set goals, and they do only what they intend to do. Frequently, they are unaware of these goals and intentions. Another principle of Adlerian psychology is the unity of the personality, which is viewed as an intertwining of dynamic, somatic, psychological, and social processes. Interpreting the phenomena observed in the group sessions, particularly the social aspects of the patients' problems, the therapist strives to bring them into awareness.

Psychotherapy is conducted primarily as an educational process in which emotional experience reinforces intellectual learning. Insight is not viewed as a prerequisite for change. Patients are encouraged to improve, recognize, and correct value systems that militate against desirable social functioning. An atmosphere of social equality and mutual helpfulness is created to counteract fears, anxieties, and emotional isolation. Intrapsychic dynamics are explored, and understanding is communicated, but more emphasis is placed on social reorientation and the counteracting of fears.

Changes in attitudes toward life are reported to express themselves in the alleviation of symptoms, improved functioning, and a sense of general well-being. Changes in the patient's early recollections are characteristic.

The goals are to increase the patient's self-respect and self-confidence—to remove feelings of inferiority—and to enhance his faith in his own worth and ability to grow.

Character traits and ego functioning of the mature personality are described, but precisely how these improvements are brought about is not clear from the data available. The therapist concentrates on correcting maladaptive behavior (Step 3). The goals as conceptualized do not encompass the identification and meeting of the maturational needs that preserve the illness. Unless feelings of inferiority are permitted full expression in the process of removing them, the risk of producing fresh repressions is courted. In that case, improvement may be temporary, and psychosomatic problems may ensue.

Horneyan School. The therapist, notes Rose, assumes that a unifying process goes on in the group that can be turned in a healthy direction and used to work through neurotic blocks to growth. Sensitive to group atmosphere, the therapist distinguishes between cohesiveness that serves merely to relieve basic anxiety (feelings of weakness and isolation from the real self and the feeling that others are hostile) and cohesiveness that develops when the patients get to feel that belonging to the group is a healthful experience. Conflict and the emergence of anxiety are encouraged, but the anxiety is not permitted to become so intense that patients withdraw from the group.

The democratic values of the group help to liberate strivings toward cooperative mutuality, but, when corrective processes fail to operate, the therapist may intervene on any one of three levels, focusing on the group atmosphere, on interpersonal behavior, or on intrapsychic mechanisms. Through their interpersonal reactions, the group members repeatedly demonstrate the multidimensional and self-perpetuating nature of their individual neurotic patterns. The therapist permits these patterns and their consequences to be experienced for the purpose of encouraging new modes of behavior (Step 1).

Emphasis is placed on the here-and-now. Childhood memories are used as a vehicle for the expression of immediate feelings, and neurotic reactions are seen in terms of present character structure. The idiosyncratic defensive patterns of the patient are identified not in terms of repetition-compulsion or transference reactions but in terms of abnormal character structure, originating in childhood disturbances that led to a distorted concept of the self and the world (Step 3). Interpretations elucidate discrepancies between the idealized image of the self (the ideal self) and the real self.

The goal of the treatment, in Horney's term, is self-realization. The therapist works for significant and enduring character change, a restructuring of the personality. Self-realization is correlated with the capacity to feel free and independent and possession of a unified personality, a sense of inner-directedness, and a recognition of one's responsibilities and limitations.

The group therapeutic process is aimed at producing the mature personality. The therapist arouses and deals with transference resistance (identified as patient-patient and patient-therapist relationships) and works to remove maladaptations. The meeting of maturational needs is not described.

Sullivanian School (Interpersonal Psychiatry). The therapist who operates in the framework of Harry Stack Sullivan's interpersonal theory, notes Goldman, conducts himself in the group as a representative of constructive culture. He engages in interpersonal transactions with the patients to correct their distorted perceptions and socially ineffectual behavior, and he communicates attitudes of acceptance and respect. He focuses on feelings, particularly anxiety and loneliness, rather than on unconscious memories. Maladaptive behavior, the motivation for which is explained in terms of avoidance of anxiety and the search for security, is explored in historical perspective. Much attention is given to nonverbal behavior. Transference phenomena are regarded as one among various types of personalized childhood fantasies that are carried over into the immediate situation (parataxes); these fantasies are elucidated as an aid in correcting misperceptions and modifying present behavior. Acceptance of the therapist's interpretation

of a patient's defense maneuver is facilitated by identical reactions of other group members (consensual validation), which helps each member to become aware of his behavior and to analyze it.

The therapist, as an expert in human relations, attends primarily to problems raised by the patients. In the final phase of treatment, he summarizes what has gone on in the therapy and suggests ways of improving future functioning.

The goal of treatment is to help the patient become a well-integrated and socially effective person who tends to see things as others in his culture see them and who behaves in ways they approve of.

This operational approach focuses strongly on the elimination of maladaptations (Step 3). The development of transference is not controlled because the therapist presents himself as a real person. The degree of personality maturation achieved through understanding of the patient's history and interpersonal relations and through correction of his misperceptions is not made clear.

Since the full expression of feelings and the meeting of maturational needs do not appear to figure in the therapeutic process, the improvement achieved may be superficial in nature. Later somatic illness is a possibility.

Psychotherapy through the Group Process

The model of treatment developed by Whitaker and Lieberman is illustrative of systems of group therapy that supplement concepts of individual therapy with the findings of group dynamicists. The therapist views the movements of the group as successive attempts at the resolution of unconscious conflict. The immediate behavior of the members represents a compromise between conflicting motives—disturbing and reactive—and the quality of the group climate is determined by whether the solutions worked out are restrictive or enabling.

The group members are described as homogeneous in terms of vulnerability of defensive structure and heterogeneous in their areas of conflict and ways of dealing with conflict. Candidates evaluated as highly vulnerable, including the acutely psychotic and some neurotics, are not accepted. The consistently silent patient is thought to obtain only limited benefit from the therapeutic process. The group is regarded as the major vehicle of treatment, and patients are not seen routinely on an individual basis.

As the successive group conflicts elicit habitual maladaptive behavior and attitudes originating in the patient's interpersonal relationships, the therapist focuses on modifying those maladaptations and facilitating new learning. Individual patterns that are irrelevant to the focal conflict are not investigated. The contribution to changes in behavior made by reality-testing in a climate of safety is emphasized.

The therapeutic experience itself is regarded as the core factor. Insight and catharsis may occur, but they are not regarded as significant mechanisms. The promotion of permanent change is not claimed; it is pointed out that behavioral change in the group sessions does not automatically carry over into life.

The goal of the therapist is to promote the growth of the patient. He tries to achieve growth by working on maladaptation patterns (Step 3).

Referring to the maladaptive behavior patterns that the patient brings into the group, Whitaker and Lieberman state that "some may yield, others may not." A corrective emotional experience is offered, but the therapist disclaims responsibility for resolving the patient's fundamental problems as they become manifest in the group conflict. The observation that changes in behavior may not carry over into the life situation suggests that the transference is not deep enough or that the maladaptations are not worked through sufficiently.

The inactivity of the therapist may largely be accounted for by the primacy of his interest in studying group dynamics. Whitaker and Lieberman, like Bion and others, have made important contributions to the study of group processes by withholding their influence and permitting the group to go where it wants to go. As research-oriented therapists shift their attention from group processes per se to the investigation of how these processes can be exploited to facilitate personality growth, they will probably function as more active therapeutic agents.

Existential-Experiential Approaches

These unstandardized and vaguely differentiated procedures, reported by psychoanalytically trained therapists, appear to represent a multifaceted protest against the traditional concern with childhood experience and ego psychology. Existentialists commit themselves to here-and-now interaction with their patients. Experientialists stress the primacy of experience and relatedness over understanding. Some practitioners identify themselves as both existentialists and experientialists.

Among those whose theoretical framework reflects the teachings of existential philosophy, Hora describes existential psychotherapy as a process of cognitive unfoldment and as one in which the practitioner "lives" psychotherapy instead of trying to "do" it. Rather than interpreting, evaluating, and judging, he opens himself up to existential encounter and clarifies what he understands.

The existential groups, designed for study as well as treatment, are composed of from eight to ten persons in diverse diagnostic categories. They are viewed as suffering from disturbed modes-of-being-in-the-world. Their emotional and somatic problems are attributed to preoccupations with the need to confirm one's being. Since their capacity to communicate meaningfully is restricted, they experience frequently recurring conflicts and a sense of isolation.

Revealing themselves at the start as inauthentic people who are concerned with releasing tensions, existential group members move through phases of self-discovery and growing understanding, of being burdened by their defensive strivings and of giving them up, of learning to accept their own anxiousness, and of ultimately discovering themselves as being authentically in the world. On the road to authenticity, they achieve truthfulness in expression, develop mutual regard and respect for the integrity and freedom of one another, and become more perceptive and creative in their thinking.

Group communications focus on the immediate experience. The past may be revealed through proper elucidation of the present, but this revelation is not regarded as significant. Unconscious motivation is not explored. Emphasis is placed on helping the patient achieve harmony with life.

Some existential group therapists apply the working concepts and techniques of analytic psychotherapy, despite their philosophic divergences. Others reject the operational concepts of transference, countertransference, and resistance.

Experimental therapists stress the feeling experiences of the patient. They view sickness as dynamic pressure rather than as disease, and they view health as continuous personal growth, which expands the capacity to choose. The therapist works actively to augment this capacity, using his total person and striving through his preconscious and unconscious responses to stimulate reparative forces working within the patient. The transference relationship, the function of which is to permit the development of responsiveness and counterresponsiveness, is eventually replaced by a nontransference or existential relationship. As Malone et al. state:

> The intrapersonal experiences of both therapist and patient function as reciprocals primarily through nonverbal communication.

Goals are formulated by existential therapists in terms of liberating cognitive and creative potentialities, self-discovery, and deepening understanding. They appear to be working for personality maturation and, in the results claimed, come close to describing it. Experientialists aim for characterological and other growth changes, the breaking up of repetition-compulsions, and the release of the patient from impassed living. Other goals of the experiential therapist are to promote congruence between the patient's intrapsychic realities and his manifest attitudes and behavior and to help him expand his feeling repertoire. Little attention is directed to alleviating symptoms or to improving the patient's social adjustment.

When diagnostic inquiry is bypassed and treatment is based on the therapist's advance assumptions of what his patients need, some patients may be exposed to a group experience that will not meet their specific therapeutic needs and that may, indeed, be harmful. This problem, though by no means limited to practitioners of existential psychotherapy, is well illustrated in their reports. The nature, origin, and history of each patient's disturbance are not investigated; instead, it is assumed that he will benefit from communing, interpreting, valuing, being spoken to truthfully, and the like. But, truthfulness in expression, for instance, is not likely to improve the interpersonal functioning of the person who is insensitive to the feelings of others. It is necessary at times to withhold information of a sensitive nature from group members who tend to be destructively truthful with one another. Suicidal reactions have been reported in patients who were informed by co-patients that they were latent schizophrenics or latent homosexuals. Full and conscious participation in the process of existence is not desirable for those persons in whom it arouses intolerable impulses and anxieties.

These are a few illustrations of the neglect or damage that a patient may sustain when his problem is viewed through the prism of the therapist's blanket assumptions rather than being studied. Such assumptions, whether or not they are derived from a philosophical system of thought, are not applicable to all patients and may interfere with the meeting of their particular therapeutic needs.

An exclusive focus on immediate experiencing (here-and-now) prevents the full mobilization of regressive states and makes it impossible to deal with the patient's primitive maturational needs. Controlled regression is essential for the resolution of patterns of maladaptation that originated in early-life situations.

Transactional Group Psychotherapy

Eric Berne, who introduced this approach, has referred to it as (1) a "happy remedy" for the unsuitability of psychoanalysis for conditions other than the transference neuroses, (2) an effective procedure in a transference neurosis when psychoanalysis, the treatment of choice, is not available, and (3) an appropriate forerunner of other procedures, being more general than any of them and overlapping with analytic and existential therapies at late stages.

Initially the transactional therapist focuses on loosening up resistances—the troublesome games the patient plays in the group sessions. After the patient becomes symptom-free, resistances may be analyzed, but the uncovering of the cause of his problems and of unconscious material is not stressed. It is hypothesized that the patient, by learning to control his free energy, becomes capable of shifting his authentic self from one ego state to another by an act of will. External stimuli are first relied on to accomplish such shifts, but, as treatment progresses, they are made more and more autonomously. Authenticity in social behavior is stressed.

The transactional group therapist accepts patients in many diagnostic categories. They are picked at random, with a view to forming as heterogeneous a group as possible. Rapid improvement and results as stable as those achieved through other approaches are claimed—especially in borderline cases, for which the treatment seems to be designed. Patients are reported to express confidence in the method. It is also claimed that the transactional approach is easily learned.

The goal of the treatment is to cure the patient—for example, as Berne states, to "transform schizophrenics into nonschizophrenics"—and all techniques at the therapist's disposal are used to effect a cure as expeditiously as possible.

The transactional group therapist appears to work for personality maturation, primarily by addressing himself to Step 3. The significance of Steps 1 and 2 is impossible to determine, but the use of techniques for facilitating deep transference is not described. The gratification needs of the patient are identified but not distinguished from maturational needs.

The playful character of the presentations reported may obscure the development of serious relationships. The crucial question is whether, in the course of the clever games they engage in, the patients and the therapist come to develop real feelings for one another. These feelings are indispensable for the maturation of the pre-oedipal personality.

Adaptational Approach

Broadly representative of much group treatment conducted on a supportive level in outpatient as well as institutional settings is the practical approach detailed by Johnson. Patients are helped to overcome uncomfortable and distressing manifestations of emotional illness through understanding of the anxieties they develop in group situations as a defense and protection against the dangers of close relationships. They are also helped to "practice new methods of adaptation," initially in the group sessions and later in their regular social relationships. The therapist does not attempt to remove deep-seated conflicts or to change the basic personality.

Neurotic and psychotic adults are treated in separate groups; a major criterion in the selection of the members of a group is the patient's ability to tolerate anxiety. Children, adolescents, juvenile delinquents, and geriatric patients are among the other subjects with whom this group-oriented model is employed.

The group therapist is an authority figure. He maintains control in the sessions, by active measures when necessary. He refrains from doing individual therapy in the group. He stimulates mutual analysis of the maladaptive behavior observed and encourages the ventilation and recognition of hostility. In the process of clearing away hostility, he serves as the group's scapegoat but does not attempt to work through the hostility completely. The precipitation of psychotic behavior in the group sessions is carefully avoided.

Goals, concretely formulated in advance, vary with the type of patients treated but are in all cases moderate: to improve reality-testing, promote socialization, foster awareness of how feelings are related to anxiety and behavior, and motivate patients for additional psychotherapy on a group or individual basis. The therapist strives to provide a learning-relearning experience that enables the group members to perceive the similarities between their maladaptive behavior in the treatment sessions and their habitual behavior with their life associates.

These general goals are applied in a restrictive manner in groups of psychotic patients. In long-term therapy, psychotics are permitted to become more dependent on one another and on the therapist. Specific goals for a group of psychotically ill patients are the strengthening of defenses, provision of support and dependency, and increase in repression.

This supportive approach is illustrative of the traditional group therapy programs at many mental hospitals, although the practitioners do not invariably lead their groups in an authoritarian and directive manner. Reports indicate that many of these groups are too large to permit much patient-to-patient interplay.

Undeniably, such groups perform a practical function, enabling the patient to achieve more comfortable control of his feelings and behavior. His adjustment to his present environment is improved, and his symptoms may be temporarily alleviated.

An attempt may be made to control transference and deal with common transference resistances. Maladaptive defenses are recognized, and some maturational needs are inadvertently met. Common bonds of interest develop, and feelings of isolation are reduced by the socializing effects of the group sessions.

But the results achieved are not usually self-sustaining. There is no assurance that the postpsychotic patient will not fall apart again after the group experience ends. Since the working through—emotional *unlearning* —of his deep-seated patterns of maladaptation is not attempted, he is likely to revert to them in stressful circumstances. By and large, therefore, the changes effected cannot be equated with personality growth to maturation.

Psychodrama

This multifaceted procedure, introduced in 1925, has been employed in a variety of settings with children, adolescents, and adults. The use of this approach in marital counseling is also reported.

As formulated by J. L. Moreno in the context of his theories of role behavior and group structure, psychodrama requires a large staff and an elaborate format for the directed acting out of problems, but modified versions are employed by practitioners applying other theories, including psychoanalytic concepts. Some elements or techniques of psychodrama, such as role-playing, enter into the contemporary crop of procedures, which also borrow from Moreno's terminology. Moreno and Kipper characterize psychodrama as an elaborate form of encounter, the scientific exploration of the truth by dramatic methods, and the depth therapy of the group.

The acting out of immediately pressing problems or past situations is based on the principles of therapeutic interaction, spontaneity, catharsis, and reality-testing. Five instruments are described: the group (as audience and participants), the patient-protagonist, the stage, auxiliary egos (other group or staff members playing assigned roles), and the director (the therapist). Numerous techniques are employed, some of them to stimulate spontaneity of body and in action.

Psychodrama is reported to benefit persons with psychological and social problems and related somatic disturbances. Among the problems specified are psychomotor disturbances, such as tics, stuttering, and bedwetting; marital maladjustments; and inhibitions in self-expression. Psychodrama is employed with hospitalized schizophrenic patients.

The goals of the psychodramatist are to help people express themselves with greater ease, to structure internal and external experiences, and to bring forth their thoughts and feelings in structured form. An unstated goal appears to be the stimulation of spontaneity and creativity.

Some reports on this procedure suggest that emotional growth does occur, but the goals to which it is addressed do not encompass the notion of producing the mature personality. No distinction is made between gratifying a patient and helping him to mature. Dramatic experience and encounter are therapeutic only in the sense of providing some needed gratification. The psychological needs of the patient in a regressed condition are not met.

In describing the structuring of a psychodrama, Moreno and Kipper point out that

by forcing the protagonists to stick to actualities, he [the director] warms them up to present the facts directly and to express their actual experiences.

The failure to permit random behavior in the treatment setting may serve to foreclose the full development and integration of the personality. The capacity to use one's own initiative freely is an important attribute of the emotionally mature individual. Procedures that force the patient to comply with specific instructions and that do not provide him with opportunities to express himself freely or to develop awareness of the pressure of self-demand are essentially driving rather than growth therapies.

Group-Centered Psychotherapy

This short-term procedure, introduced by followers of Carl Rogers, corresponds to the client-centered method of individual counseling and is widely applied in a variety of educational, social, and industrial settings. Initially, this nondirective and nonclinical approach was employed with maladjusted and neurotic children, adolescents, and adults, but its use with more disturbed patients, including chronic schizophrenics, has recently been reported.

Little attention is paid to diagnosis. It is hypothesized that the same psychotherapeutic principles apply to normal, neurotic, and psychotic persons. However, hostile or aggressive persons are excluded from these groups on the grounds that they might threaten the climate of safety and acceptance that the therapist strives to maintain.

The group members are not viewed as objects of treatment but as potentially adequate and responsible persons who became maladjusted by excluding significant experiences from awareness and by failing to value and integrate all aspects of the self. The therapist assumes that unconditional positive regard, communicated to the members

genuinely and sensitively, will enable them to deal constructively with their problems.

Reconstruction of the perceptual field of the group member or client is regarded as the therapeutic task. His mind is not directed into particular channels, nor is he provided with interpretations. Assuming the client's own frame of reference and paraphrasing the content of his communications, the therapist clarifies the feelings expressed and consistently conveys acceptance, empathic understanding, and respect (Step 2). Transference attitudes are not distinguished from other affect-laden expressions. No attempt is made to uncover or explain the conflicts that underlie problematic behavior.

The goals sought through this procedure are to help the group member achieve a more realistic perception of himself and to enhance his self-esteem, capacity for self-direction, openness to experience, and ability to cope with stressful situations. Significant changes in personality, in attitudes about the self and others, and in behavior are claimed.

Rogerian postulates on personality organization resemble those of the Sullivanian school of psychiatry, notes Glad. The practitioner of group-centered psychotherapy—in his nonjudgmental concern with the phenomenological world of the client, his commitment to direct person-to-person encounter, and his open reflection of the feelings and attitudes he is experiencing and may verbalize when they persist—functions in a manner similar to that of the existential therapist.

People who are exposed to this approach secure a great deal of emotional release. The climate maintained in the group is particularly appealing to persons who were subjected to discipline and domination early in life and who greatly resented it. It a so appeals to those who crave freedom from certain immediate personalities. The authoritarian personality is not likely to benefit from the experience, but it has been recommended for persons who have democratic attitudes and some ability to maintain understanding relationships with others.

Some degree of personality change can be achieved through this approach. The communication of understanding and acceptance serves to meet maturational and other psychological needs and leads to functional improvements. However, the treatment is directed to relatively limited goals. It does not provide the long-term psychological ingredients that are essential for emotional maturation of the individual with deep-seated problems.

Since patients are not diagnosed and are accepted on the assumption that their problems are psychological, there is some risk of mistreatment.

Behavioral Group Psychotherapy

Behavior therapy in groups encompasses a broad range of short-term procedures that are grounded in the premise that acts are more potent than thoughts and words for influencing human responses. The desensitization and assertive-training procedures focused on here were reported by Lazarus.

Group desensitization treatment, first applied to phobic patients, is now employed in a wide range of disorders, such as sexual impotence, frigidity, and, in a modified form, chronic anxiety. Psychotic patients are specifically excluded.

Various conditioning and anxiety-eliminating techniques based on modern learning theories are applied in homogeneous groups. These techniques are flexibly combined with didactic discussions and with techniques borrowed from other schools of psychotherapy, whose explanations are, however, rejected. Therapy is mainly in, not by, the group, primarily through patient-to-therapist communication. Results are evaluated in terms of the number of maladaptive habits that have been eliminated.

The therapist's attitudes in the desensitization group are didactic, sympathetic, and nonjudgmental. But in the assertive-training group he functions by and large as a participant-observer. Training in self-assertiveness implements the hypothesis that failure to assert oneself is in most cases a manifestation of anxiety. It is assumed that frankness in verbalization and the spontaneous expression of basic feelings will improve the patient's interpersonal functioning.

The group conducted for this purpose is small, carefully composed, and homogeneous, and the course of treatment usually covers from 15 to 20 sessions. The therapist opens the first meeting with an address on the art of relaxation, and preliminary training in relaxation follows. In later sessions, when productive interchanges are not going on among the group members, the therapist usually lectures. The techniques he employs may include open discussion, role-playing, modeling, behavior rehearsals, and psychodrama. A whole session is occasionally devoted to the needs of one member.

The goal of the desensitization procedure is primarily symptomatic improvement. By changing habits deemed to be undesirable, the therapist also endeavors to eliminate suffering and to increase the patient's capacity for productive work and pleasurable interpersonal relationships. It is claimed that the rate and extent of improvement achieved are superior to those produced through other procedures. Secondary benefits reported include changes in personality and self-concept, increased self-esteem, and the development of friendships among the group members.

The goals of assertive training are the acquisition of adaptive responses and the extinction of maladaptive responses. Quantitative measurement of the results achieved is more difficult in assertive training than in the desensitization procedure, but behavioral improvement in nearly all the participants is claimed. The majority of patients report that the improved modes of behavior are transferred to life situations and that they are able to develop more satisfying and enduring relationships with their associates.

The behavioral therapist exerts pressure on patients to change specific patterns of behavior. He secures improvements in functioning by extirpating maladaptations. The psychopathological forces in which these overt patterns are rooted are not investigated or dealt with.

Verbalization is permitted, but the therapist does not work for the expression of all impulses. The question thus arises: What is done with impulses that are not put into words? A person who is put under pressure to behave in ways not consistent with his impulses to action may find self-damaging ways of expressing those impulses. In patients who are not properly selected for these procedures, psychosomatic problems may develop, notably in those who have strong tendencies to repress and suppress their impulses. Patients with impulse disorders are more likely to respond favorably to this punitive approach, but they may later require treatment for a neurotic condition.

Some investigators report that personality *is* dealt with in behavior therapy. The crucial issue is whether the therapist does so sufficiently to prevent some part of the personality from becoming inhibited and repressed.

The value of this approach is that it is short-term and rapidly achieves demonstrable results. Reports do not delineate the possible long-term costs of the short-term improvement.

Gestalt Therapy

The experiential group approach developed from Gestalt psychology by Frederick Perls and his associates revolves around a flexible set of rules and games. These techniques are designed, according to Levitsky and Perls, to help the members of the group assimilate emotional and other psychological experiences with the active coping attitudes that characterize healthful feelings. They are influenced to stay with feelings they have a strong urge to dispel. Much attention is paid to physiological manifestations.

Rules are introduced as a way to unify thoughts with feelings, to heighten awareness, and to facilitate maturation. Communication in the present tense is encouraged; the past is not dealt with, other than to delineate present personality structure. The games, proposed by the therapist to meet individual or group needs, represent a commentary on social behavior and stress the polarity of vital functioning. For example, a need for withdrawal from contact is respected, but the patient may be asked to withdraw in fantasy to a place or situation where he feels secure, to describe it with feelings, and then to return to the group. The use of an awareness continuum is designed to guide the participants away from explanations and speculations to the bedrock of their experiences. Some games have a definite interpretive element, but their primary function is to move patients from the "why" to the "what" and "how" of experience.

The goals of the Gestalt therapist are to promote feelings, to prevent their avoidance, and to help the participants function in a more integrated way. It is claimed that group members become more self-confident and that the group experience increases their capacity for autonomous functioning.

The Gestalt procedure is focused exclusively on maladaptive behavior, and the therapist deals with it primarily by trying to knock out inappropriate patterns. No attempt is made to work them through or to meet the maturational needs that uphold them. The practitioner deliberately refrains from arousing old personality problems. Temporary improvements in feelings are effected by meeting present functional needs. Constructive modification of the current personality structure is sacrificed for short-term benefits.

This form of group therapy may benefit a patient who suffers from low drive. The stimulus of the situation will increase his drive intensity. But exposure of a high-drive patient to this procedure is contraindicated. The experience may traumatize him and provoke suicidal behavior.

Bio-Energetic Group Therapy

Alexander Lowen's procedure involves the body in the psychotherapeutic process and apparently does so more directly and more fully than other approaches that entail body activity and physical contact between participants. Lowen refers to the procedure as a double-barreled approach that provides insight more convincingly than the use of words alone. Personality change is not regarded as valid until it is paralleled by improvements in the form, motility, and functioning of the body.

The variety of techniques employed include simple breathing exercises to facilitate the expression of feelings, manual manipulation to soften chronically spastic areas of the body, embracing, and other types of physical contact expressive of acceptance, reassurance, and support. The participants are taught simple ways of easing tensions. Bodily expression is analyzed and interpreted as a reflection of mental functioning. Verbal interchange goes on primarily in the context of these activities. Therapeutic strategies include encouragement of the venting of negative feelings before expressions of affection.

It is reported that the participants develop a feeling of unity and a respect for the body and the uniqueness of others and are directed to new sources of health and pleasure. Hysterical episodes, precipitated by intense emotional experiences, have been brought under control through bodily contact and physical expressions of reassurance.

The goal of bio-energetic group therapy is to facilitate personality change and unification through activation of healing forces on the deepest and most powerful level.

This method is oriented to personality integration, which is certainly an aspect of emotional maturity. The therapist deals primarily with maladaptations. Maturational needs may be met indirectly.

The chief beneficiary would appear to be the person whose mental and physical functioning are not harmoniously coordinated. Another value is the rapidity of the improvements achieved, which is encouraging to patients. Discouragement may follow later if they have serious problems.

The procedure runs the risk of being a repressive form of treatment. The encouragement given to one form of activity may lead to the suppression or repression of other forms. The mobilization of more psychological energy than a patient can discharge appropriately, leading to impulse acting out or even psychotic behavior, is another possibility.

Marathon Group Therapy

George Bach, who was associated with Frederick Stoller in the development of this procedure during the 1960's, refers to it as a psychological pressure cooker in which genuine emotions emerge as phony steam boils away. He also calls it a

practicum in authentic communication, based on freedom from social fears conventionally associated with transparency.

Group pressure is exploited to generate psychological intimacy as quickly as possible. Stoller refers to the approach as accelerated interaction.

Concentrating therapy into a single experience of a day or two, often over a weekend, the marathon is an outstanding example of the continuous, time-extended format. Both clinical and nonclinical settings are used. Some practitioners conduct marathons in their homes and press their wives into service as co-therapists. Follow-up sessions may be held. Some psychotherapists report the use of the marathon as a supplementary rather than a basic procedure.

Patients are selected on the basis of interest in self-actualization and in undergoing an intensive experience. Usually strangers are assembled, but specialized marathons for marital couples and other natural groups are reported. The participants may or may not be undergoing conventional psychotherapy.

The therapist actively sets the tone and pace for intimate encounter by any means at his disposal, including rejection of professional status and assumption of the patient role to engage in the mutual exploration of feelings. The orientation is ahistorical; the participants are encouraged to own up to and share their immediate feelings and to try out new ways of being in the group.

The goals, as stated by Bach, are to produce a change in orientation and to find new and more creative ways of dealing with old problems. Rapid changes in behavior are reported. It is claimed that the participants become more interested and involved with others, more honest, and less defensive. Behavioral breakthroughs have occurred, but their permanence is admittedly unknown.

The marathon is structured to arouse emotions quickly, thus generating instant intimacy among the participants. The therapist addresses himself primarily to patterns of maladaptive behavior. The procedure is calculated to overpower such patterns by exposing the assemblage to a new experience that has an intense emotional impact. The assumption that the overpowering of defenses can be therapeutic in the long run has yet to be confirmed, notes Yalom. Pending such confirmation, the procedure should be identified as an experiment in group process rather than as a psychotherapeutic method.

Lengthy and fatiguing experiences of this nature are contraindicated for patients with psychosomatic conditions, for those who are in a prepsychotic or postpsychotic state, for people with a strong suicidal disposition, and for those whose marriages are unstable.

Disclosures made to the author by participants in weekend marathons reveal their variable effects. First, some of the values reported: Commitment to the treatment offers the hope of an immediately helpful experience, and some who have undergone it have referred to it as both enjoyable and educational—enjoyable because it dispelled feelings of loneliness and because they derived some gratification from the instant intimacy with strangers; educational because the experience helped them become aware very quickly of their own interpersonal problems. The stimulus of the situation and the exposure to a battery of emotions aroused intense emotions in them. One consequence was that innate tendencies that are usually held in check were uncovered in a matter of hours. The participants were thus able to discover what attracted or disgusted them and whether they had suicidal tendencies, harbored murderous wishes, were easily seducible, etc. One woman characterized the marathon as a dramatic introduction to individual and group psychology.

Other informants have supplemented published reports of social and psychological damage sustained in one-shot marathons or encounters. The uninhibited communications that the marathons encourage often lead to impulsive behavior. To be sexually seductive or to permit oneself to be seduced without regard for the consequences is all too often regarded as operating in the spirit of the occasion.

On returning home after a marathon, a man who had committed himself in treatment to preserving a shaky marriage told his wife that he had felt pressure from several female participants to engage in sexual intercourse during the weekend. He was puzzled to observe how enraged his wife became. Another crisis in their relationship had to be dealt with in his long-term psychotherapy.

A woman whose promiscuous behavior in the past had caused her much unhappiness participated in a marathon, where she met a married man who complained that he had never enjoyed sexual intercourse. She responded forthwith to the challenge. Because their intimacy during the weekend proved to be mutually gratifying, they ended up by having an affair. The man obtained a divorce but refused to marry his new sexual partner on the grounds that they were socially incompatible. Thus, her impulsive behavior, besides causing her fresh unhappiness, led to the dissolution of the marriage of two other persons. In other cases, guilt over the sexual stimulation of the situation has precipitated psychotic episodes.

Self-destructive tendencies of which a person has no awareness can be unleashed in an emotional experience that is highly concentrated in time and pervaded by a built-in sense of intimacy. A man, after discussing his business affairs during a marathon, was stimulated to act on the advice of other participants and commit himself to a foolhardy investment. A few days later, given the opportunity to explore his motives and weigh the risks involved, he changed his mind. In the process of marshaling the pros and cons of the new venture, he recognized that his mounting emotional involvement in the weekend events had significantly dulled his judgment. A state of manic excitement had propelled him into a decision that a person of his astuteness would not otherwise have made.

Sensitivity Training (T-Groups)

A product of the laboratory training movement associated with the National Training Laboratory at Bethel, Maine, programs for sensitivity training in groups have burgeoned in recent years, thrusting themselves into a variety of community, educational, and industrial settings for many different purposes. The members of these relatively unstructured groups participate as learners and use their on-going interpersonal transactions as data in the learning process. As the use of the group setting for experiential learning has expanded and as group leaders or trainers have tended increasingly to concentrate on affective blocks to learning, the boundaries between training and therapy have become more and more diffuse. Gottschalk and Pattison have delineated many overlapping areas. Moreover, sensitivity training itself is a far from standardized procedure. Garwood has pointed out that what occurs in the T-groups

varies with their composition and *most especially with the trainer* [her emphasis].

T-groups are generally short-term, time-limited experiences, concentrated into a week or two, with the participants meeting several hours a day in a special setting. Sometimes the group begins during a weekend in a special setting and then continues in a series of meetings conducted in the participants' own community. Originally the group format was used for the first-hand study of group processes, but the early focus has broadened to encompass the study of the participants' conscious and preconscious behavior and their interpersonal functioning. Some T-group leaders encourage the reporting of dreams and fantasies. The number of techniques employed has increased; some T-group leaders employ nonverbal techniques, including body-contact activities. Role-playing may be engaged in for the purpose of increasing self-awareness.

By and large, the leaders of T-groups state that they are not conducting psychotherapy but are trying to promote personal growth or provide positive and creative emotional experiences for the participants in order to make them more effective in their work and other life activities.

The goals of sensitivity training programs, as formulated by Gottschalk and Pattison, are the heightening of interpersonal coping skills, the sharpening of interpersonal perceptions, and the imbuing of life experience with authenticity and greater self-awareness.

Sensitivity training in groups is of value for developing leadership skills and helping people become more perceptive of their own feelings and the feelings of others, provided they are well-defended and not unduly suggestible personalities. But such training is not universally beneficial, and a substantial number of cases of serious psychological damage caused by these experiences have been described in the literature. Reports call attention to two limitations in these programs: (1) No criteria for evaluating per-

sonality strengths are applied in the selection of the trainees. (2) Sensitivity training is mandatory in many organizations.

Kuehn and Crinella recommend the systematic exclusion of four types of persons: psychotics, characterological neurotics, persons with hysterical personality traits, and those who are in a crisis situation. These authors suggest that the usefulness of the procedure depends on the maturity, experience, and expertise of the T-group leader, his knowledge of diagnosis and treatment, and the availability of professional consultation, particularly when psychiatric first aid is required.

Encounter Groups

Thirteen years after J. L. Moreno referred to encounter as a meeting on the most intensive level of communication, his wife and associate, Zereka T. Moreno, remarked in 1969, "Everybody under many flags, is doing what we started." In the interim, a philosophical concept that had permeated relatively few systems of psychotherapy became an umbrella term sheltering a variety of innovative methods, which some mental health professionals refer to as the encounter movement. Firm differentiations among these methods, some of which have already been discussed, are not yet possible. Hence, some labels are used synonymously—for example, T-group and encounter group. As a rudimentary distinction, Yalom points out:

Generally encounter groups have no institutional backing, are far more unstructured, are more often led by untrained leaders, may rely more on physical contact and nonverbal exercises, and generally emphasize an experience, or getting "turned on," rather than change per se.

Encounter as a psychotherapeutic procedure encompasses the investigation of immediate emotions in a dramatically direct manner. In contrast to the long-established approach of establishing a relationship before beginning to work on a problem, encounter therapy relies on the efficacy of blunt honesty. Total reciprocity in the revelation of feelings is worked for through a variety of verbal and action techniques. Many diverse constructs are applied. Candidates for the experience are accepted without screening.

Development of the ability to be honest and open and to express warmth freely is among the values reported. It is also claimed that buried feelings are worked through. The limitations of the procedure are the lack of appropriate safeguards for people with serious disturbances and the stigma placed on emotional unresponsiveness.

The goals of encounter therapy are formulated in terms of personal growth—to promote physical and mental awareness of self and others and of social realities.

Various explanations have been advanced for the proliferation of encounter groups. It has been attributed to the overpopularization of group psychotherapy and to widespread cravings for self-discovery and intimacy among the psychologically sophisticated. Encounter groups also serve to counteract a pervasive sense of estrangement, alienation, and loss of personal identity, produced by the accelerating tempo of technological and sociological change.

In the phenomenal development of the encounter movement, the author also discerns evidence of public dissatisfaction with the practical dictates of the established psychotherapeutic approaches and their doubtful results in severe psychiatric conditions. The length and cost of traditional treatment have stimulated a search for short cuts and guaranteed results—preferably through a less rigorous treatment experience than that oriented to personality maturation.

More specifically, encounter groups may evince a reaction to the limitations of the classical psychoanalytic method. Modifications of the orthodox psychoanalytic situation reach their extreme in the encounter groups. Instead of the dyad, for example, the groups engage as many as 20 persons. There are many variations in the number of group leaders and participants and in their modes of functioning. However, the initially directive and nonrevealing posture of the analyst and the cooperative, self-revealing attitude of the analysand are definitely renounced for mutuality in interchange. The careful control of regression, to permit the arousal and gradual working through of emotional blockages, is abdicated for more

dramatic breakthroughs and occasional peak experiences through direct onslaughts on the defense system. Instead of being limited to verbal communication, the encounter groups sanction nonverbal communication, including physical contact. Diverse activities and modes of communication are studied for their possible therapeutic effects.

Whether such experiences are harmful or helpful depends on the immediate emotional state of the participant. He is exposed to a great deal of stimulation. If he needs it and can assimilate it, the encounter will have a positive impact. If he does not need such excitement or cannot tolerate it in the heady dosages offered, the encounter is, from a therapeutic standpoint, a waste of time and the participant runs the risk of incurring damaging effects.

In general, these experiences appear to be more gratifying than therapeutic or educational. In the participant who is undergoing conventional psychotherapy, they may increase his resistance to working consistently to resolve his problems. Desires to take the easy way out are stimulated.

CURRENT STRENGTHS AND WEAKNESSES

The scientific importance of a psychotherapeutic procedure is determined by the type of problem it is addressed to and its effectiveness in clearing up that problem. As already indicated, there is a pressing need for a serious evaluation of group procedures in these terms, but outcome research has not yielded this information and is not likely to do so for some time.

One of the major shortcomings highlighted by a study of the professional literature is the lack of distinction between the group approaches that are designed to provide the patient with the type of experience he needs to become healthy and mature and those group approaches that are addressed to needs that have an immediate gratification value. Every procedure needs to be evaluated from this standpoint: Does it primarily offer a gratifying experience or one that will help the patient mature?

When this elementary distinction is made,

it becomes evident that what is really new about the procedural innovations that have become the object of controversy are the forms of gratification they provide. Feeling better in the present is often equated with characterological growth. But the success or failure of these experiences depends on their ability to produce long-range results.

Reports on the majority of the procedures reviewed suggest that contemporary practice is more involved in shoring up the personality at the premorbid level of adjustment and in teaching adaptive patterns of behavior than in working for self-sustaining change at a higher level. The procedures that are addressed to significant gains require an undue expenditure of time and effort to clear up the more serious of the oedipal-type conditions, and they fail rather consistently to clear up pre-oedipal problems. In fact, some of the approaches addressed to ambitious goals are not generally applied to patients with severe forms of mental illness. No procedure has demonstrated superiority in cases of this nature.

A moot issue among analytic group therapists is whether to adhere to the operational principles of individual psychoanalytic therapy or to extract as much therapeutic leverage as possible from group process. Many of these practitioners express their personal preference for one theoretical approach or the other, but their clinical reports do not demonstrate that better results can be secured from the approach they prefer.

The large majority of group therapists address themselves primarily to maladaptive interpersonal behavior. In one way or another, they help the patient to recognize it and to master better patterns of behavior. The acquisition of new action patterns, however, does not liberate the patient from the compulsive grip of the old patterns. Unless these patterns are freed of their emotional charge—unless they are emotionally unlearned through the solution of the underlying problem—the patient will continue to revert to them.

Each group procedure is based on a different assumption of the patient's therapeutic needs. To cite a few examples: The analytic group psychotherapist assumes that the way to help the patient is to reawaken

the fundamental problem or conflict in the treatment situation and to focus on early as well as present growth needs. Practitioners who reject the historical approach assume that all the patient requires is to learn to express himself more honestly, or to coordinate his present psychic and physical functioning, to develop more awareness of his feelings, to learn to stay with what he feels, to relate authentically to others, or to have powerful and concentrated emotional experience that will unmask his defenses, etc. The behavioral therapist assumes that change entails desensitization of the patient. The T-group leader assumes that the members of his group need to increase their sensitivity to feelings.

The assumptions on which the present approaches are based often diverge to the point of contradiction, but what each strives to accomplish is a potential contribution to emotional maturity. When the treatment achieves its objective, the patient has acquired some attributes of the mature personality.

APPROACHES TO SPECIFICITY

Group psychotherapy has definitely emerged from the period when its acceptance as an effective mode of treatment was in doubt. The question, "Can it help a patient improve?" has been answered in the affirmative. However, the results obtained through its indiscriminate use have aroused much dissatisfaction. Clinical experience has amply demonstrated that the efficiency of the group psychotherapeutic process hinges on the degree of specificity achieved in relating the procedure applied to the patient's condition. Little is accomplished through haphazard use of the group setting; patients do not secure appreciable benefits simply because they are treated together. Desirable change is a function of helping each group member deal with his particular problems. Consequently, there has been a concerted effort in recent years to secure more specific results. In the process of transforming what was all too often regarded as a panacea into a precise instrument, clinicians discovered that it could be refined to produce different results.

Group psychotherapy thus appears to be thrusting toward the development of a larger number of dissimilar procedures that will influence patients in different ways. This trend is very desirable. If the group psychotherapist is committed to help people become effectively functioning individuals, whatever their problems and stage of life, many different procedures are required. But the crucial issue is not the number of approaches at his disposal, but which approach is the best to use in each situation and for each purpose.

Clinical Experimentation

The 1960's ushered in a period of great therapeutic creativity. Along with efforts to increase the effectiveness of the established approaches and to make them less interminable, there was much experimental activity, which is continuing into the present decade. The fact that some of this activity has been misrepresented to the public as psychotherapy has stimulated negative attitudes toward experimentation per se.

Psychotherapy by its very nature requires experimentation, which was vital to the development of psychological treatment and is the key to further progress. However, the practice of psychotherapy does not readily lend itself to objective evaluation. The treatment process entails confidential relationships, subjective and objective assessment by the same person, and freedom to experiment as and when necessary to achieve an immediate objective. This state of affairs makes it difficult to determine at times whether one is engaging in responsible psychotherapy or in irresponsible experimentation. Evidence of the latter occasionally comes to the fore, and efforts are being made to lay a foundation for responsible experimentation.

General Guidelines. Two basic principles of clinical experimentation that the author recommends relate to mutuality and the selection of appropriate subjects.

1. In responsible experimentation, the patient is diagnosed, and his specific problem is carefully studied. On the basis of the diagnosis and with the goals in mind, a plan is formulated for working with him. The patient is then informed what the therapist is striving to accomplish and what results can be expected. The patient is not exposed to an experimental procedure unless he consents to it; his wishes in the matter are respected. It is also made clear to the patient that, if the attempt to help him does not yield the desired results, the therapist will at least explain to him why the failure occurred. This principle is applicable in group as well as in individual treatment.

2. The patients with whom it is most appropriate to experiment are those who do not respond to the established approaches. These approaches are effective in dealing with most of the conditions associated with oedipal development and with run-of-the-mill problems for which people solicit professional help; hence, little is gained from experimenting in such cases. The subjects with whom experimentation is justifiable and most likely to be scientifically rewarding are those with more severe disturbances.

Experimentation with Schizophrenia. The main challenge in the field of psychotherapy lies in the development of more effective approaches to the pre-oedipal disorders, especially schizophrenia. Despite the fact that many cases of schizophrenia appear to have more than one cause, the disorder invariably testifies to basic defects in the maturation of the personality. The author regards this condition as psychologically reversible in principle. In his experience, the schizophrenic patient does not respond on a long-range basis to individual or group psychotherapeutic experiences that are primarily gratifying. Quite the contrary. Such experiences tend to produce psychotic episodes —which is one reason why many therapists conducting treatment on an outpatient basis are reluctant to treat the schizophrenic patient. If the procedure employed does not contribute to the reversal of the illness, it is likely to have more gratification than maturational value. The response of the schizophrenic patient is, in a sense, the ultimate test of the procedure's effectiveness in dealing with fundamental personality problems. Since relatively few group therapists work with schizophrenic patients on other than a supportive level, the scientific importance of experimentation of the nature just suggested is obvious.

Schizophrenic patients do not respond to a purely neutral approach. They need an emotionally responsive therapist, one who can tolerate the patient's emotions and feed them back to him in a controlled, goal-oriented manner.

The schizophrenic patient's individual treatment was once thought to call for two or more analysts. If the first analyst was a man, the patient was usually transferred at some stage of their relationship to a woman, and vice versa. But even with a change in analysts, emotionally responsive though they might be, they could not, in the dyad, meet the schizophrenic's special need to experience different feelings simultaneously. The multiple charge of member-to-member verbal interchanges in the group setting makes an important contribution to the meeting of this maturational need. More difficult to meet in the shared treatment experience is the schizophrenic's high-urgency need for the adequate release of aggressive energy; his co-patients are not happy to hear how much he hates them.

Combined Treatment

Present evidence suggests that what will be most effective in the treatment of pre-oedipal disorders is a highly specific combination of individual and group treatment based on psychoanalytic principles, understanding of personality development, and incorporation of meritorious techniques of various schools of practice. To resolve pre-oedipal conditions through the exclusive instrumentality of group psychotherapy would be exceedingly difficult; in the group setting the therapist does not have as exquisite control of all stimuli, including his own responses, as he has in the one-to-one relationship. The patient's group therapeutic experience usually follows a period of individual treatment, during which he works on his bipersonal problems; but in some instances, generally when there are special transference difficulties, the patient begins treatment in a group. Properly timed, the shared treatment experience is particularly valuable for the

severely disturbed person who is totally unable to benefit from group association, such as the postpsychotic college student who told the author:

I've never known how to tolerate, feel close to, feel comfortable with, find myself accepted by, feel non-self-conscious in groups and group activity with my peers.

Supplementary Treatment

Although the new short-term procedures are not corrective per se, their specific values can be exploited when they coincide with maturational needs that are uncovered in patients undergoing long-term psychotherapy. For instance, a person who suddenly experiences a great hunger for human companionship may benefit from an encounter-group experience. For one who is totally divorced from his feelings, the T-group or marathon may serve as a springboard for their arousal and expression.

The use of these supplementary measures is likely to increase, but the practitioner who recommends them to patients needs to recognize the possibly psychonoxious effects of the experience on a person who demonstrates a strong need to withdraw from people. The advance safeguard, of course, is study of the patient's current functioning and understanding of why he says he needs additional stimulation to feel more deeply or to make his life more interesting and exciting. The patient's reaction to his initial venture in instant intimacy also needs to be investigated. If the experience does not lead to emotional withdrawal, loss of identity, sense of alienation, or similar signs of severe regression, and if the patient wishes to repeat the venture in accelerated emotional education, it will probably stimulate further improvement.

CONCLUSION

The introduction of community psychiatry is greatly enhancing the reliance on group psychotherapy as the most available approach for producing the socially effective individual. To meet this additional responsibility, the present armamentarium of emotional-impact instruments needs to be substantially refined and scanned closely for their specific therapeutic and antitherapeutic effects. Dissatisfaction with all psychotherapeutic procedures will continue until they achieve significant results more rapidly. New ideas for group formation will probably emerge in this era of therapeutic creativity, and they need to be studied, not rejected out of hand. No one knows all the answers today. A demonstrably superior approach may emerge for dealing with the enormous range of psychologically reversible disease states and states of dis-ease to which human beings are prone throughout the life cycle. This superior method is conceivable, but it is not on the horizon today. At present, the key to fulfilling the promise that group psychotherapy has held out to the public is more precise wielding of the instruments it has forged.

REFERENCES

Bach, G. The marathon group: intensive practice of intimate interaction. In *Group Therapy Today*, p. 301, H. M. Ruitenbeek, editor. Atherton Press, New York, 1969.

Berne, E. *Principles of Group Treatment.* Oxford University Press, New York, 1966.

Blatner, H. A. Patient selection in group therapy. Voices, *4:* No. 3, 90, 1968.

Corsini, R. J. *Methods of Group Psychotherapy.* McGraw-Hill, New York, 1957.

Dreikurs, R. Group psychotherapy from the point of view of Adlerian psychology. In *Group Therapy Today*, p. 37, H. M. Ruitenbeek, editor, Atherton Press, New York, 1969.

Foulkes, S. H. *Therapeutic Group Analysis.* International Universities Press, New York, 1965.

Foulkes, S. H., and Anthony, E. J. *Group Psychotherapy: The Psychoanalytic Approach,* ed. 2. Penguin Books, Baltimore, 1965.

Frank, J. D., and Powdermaker, F. B. Group psychotherapy. In *American Handbook of Psychiatry,* vol. 2, p. 1362, S. Arieti, editor, Basic Books, New York, 1959.

Garwood, D. S. The significance and dynamics of sensitivity training programs. Int. J. Group Psychother., *17:* 457, 1967.

Glad, D. D. *Operational Values in Psychotherapy.* Oxford University Press, New York, 1959.

Goldman, G. D. Some applications of Harry Stack Sullivan's theories to group psychotherapy. In *Group Therapy Today.* p. 58, H. M. Ruitenbeek, editor. Atherton Press, New York, 1969.

Goldstein, A. P., Heller, K., and Sechrest, L. B. *Psychotherapy and the Psychology of Behavior Change.* John Wiley, New York, 1966.

Gottschalk, L. A., and Pattison, E. M. Psychiatric perspectives on T-groups and the laboratory movement: an overview. Amer. J. Psychiat., *126:* 823, 1969.

Hobbs, N. Group-centered psychotherapy. In *Client-Centered Therapy,* p. 278, C. R. Rogers, editor. Houghton-Mifflin, Boston, 1951.

Hora, T. Existential therapy and group psychotherapy. In *Basic Approaches to Group Psychotherapy and Group Counseling,* p. 109, G. M. Gazda, editor. Charles C Thomas, Springfield, Ill., 1968.

Johnson, J. A. *Group Therapy: A Practical Approach.* McGraw-Hill, New York, 1963.

Klapman, J. W. *Group Psychotherapy: Theory and Practice,* ed. 2. Grune & Stratton, New York, 1959.

Kuehn, J. L., and Crinella, F. M. Sensitivity training: interpersonal "overkill" and other problems. Amer. J. Psychiat., *126:* 840, 1969.

Lazarus, A. A. Behavior therapy in groups. In *Basic Approaches to Group Psychotherapy and Group Counseling,* p. 149, G. M. Gazda, editor. Charles C Thomas, Springfield, Ill., 1968.

Levitsky, A., and Perls, F. The rules and games of Gestalt therapy. In *Group Therapy Today,* p. 221, H. M. Ruitenbeek, editor. Atherton Press, New York, 1969.

Lieberman, M. A., Lakin, M., and Whitaker, D. S. Problems and potential of psychoanalytic and group-dynamic theories for group psychotherapy. Int. J. Group Psychother., *19:* 131, 1969.

Lowen, A. Bio-energetic group therapy. In *Group Therapy Today,* p. 279, H. M. Ruitenbeek, editor. Atherton Press, New York, 1969.

Malone, T. P., Whitaker, W. C., Warentkin, J., and Feder, R. Rational and nonrational psychotherapy. Amer. J. Psychother., *15:* 212, 1961.

Moreno, J. L. Scientific foundations of group psychotherapy. In *Group Psychotherapy and Group Function.* p. 242, M. Rosenbaum and M. Berger, editors. Basic Books, New York, 1963.

Moreno, J. L., and Kipper, D. A. Group psychodrama and community-centered counseling. In *Basic Approaches to Group Psychotherapy and Group Counseling,* p. 27, G. M. Gazda, editor. Charles C Thomas, Springfield, Ill., 1968.

Moreno, Z. T. Moreneans, the heretics of yesterday are the orthodoxy of today. Group Psychother., *22:* 1, 1969.

Mullan, H. Status denial in group psychoanalysis. In *Group Psychotherapy and Group Function,* p. 591, M. Rosenbaum and M. Berger, editors. Basic Books, New York, 1963.

Parloff, M. B. Analytic group psychotherapy. In *Modern Psychoanalysis,* p. 492, J. Marmor, editor. Basic Books, New York, 1968.

Rose, S. Horney concepts in group psychotherapy.

In *Group Therapy Today*, p. 49, H. M. Ruiten-beek, editor. Atherton Press, New York, 1969.

Rosenbaum, M. Group psychotherapy and psychodrama. In *Handbook of Clinical Psychology*, p. 1254, B. B. Wolman, editor. McGraw-Hill, New York, 1965.

Rueveni, U., and Speck, R. V. Using encounter group techniques in the treatment of the social network of the schizophrenic. Int. J. Group Psychother., *19:* 495, 1969.

Slavson, S. R. *A Textbook in Analytic Group Psychotherapy*. International Universities Press, New York, 1964.

Spitz, H. H., and Kopp, S. B. Multiple psychotherapy. In *Group Psychotherapy and Group Function*, p. 391, M. Rosenbaum and M. Berger, editors. Basic Books, New York, 1963.

Spotnitz, H. The borderline schizophrenic in group psychotherapy. Int. J. Group Psychother., *7:* 155, 1957.

Spotnitz, H. *The Couch and the Circle: A Story of Group Psychotherapy*. Alfred A. Knopf, New York, 1961.

Spotnitz, H. *Modern Psychoanalysis of the Schizophrenic Patient*. Grune & Stratton, New York, 1969.

Stoller, F. H. Accelerated interaction: a time-limited approach based on the brief, intensive group. Int. J. Group Psychother., *18:* 220, 1968.

Thomas, G. W. Group psychotherapy: review of the present literature. Psychosom. Med., *5:* 166, 1943.

Whitaker, D. S., and Lieberman, M. A. *Psychotherapy through the Group Process*. Atherton Press, New York, 1964.

Wolf, A. Psychoanalysis in groups. In *Basic Approaches to Group Psychotherapy and Group Counseling*, p. 80, G. M. Gazda, editor. Charles C Thomas, Springfield, Ill., 1968.

Yalom, I. *The Theory and Practice of Group Psychotherapy*. Basic Books, New York, 1970.

4

Comparison Between Individual and Group Psychotherapy

E. James Anthony, M.D.

INTRODUCTION

Growing up in a family of closely related disciplines under the eye of a somewhat arbitrary parent discipline can be as painful as anything experienced by the developing human child in analogous circumstances. The ambivalence on both sides of the generation gap ensures that separation, individuation, and the recognition or acceptance of maturity is always fraught with vexatious misunderstandings and recriminations. No new discipline, under the age of 30, can expect complete cooperation.

The reason for this lack of cooperation is now a psychodynamic commonplace in the sphere of human development. Conflict is inherent in the nature of the dual development that takes place in parallel as the parents grow up alongside their child, responding to each phase of his development in an expectable phase-specific way. Redl has suggested that this situation has been the case in a number of progeny stemming from psychoanalysis, and he cites, in particular, child analysis and group psychotherapy. The latter, however, lacks an illustrious daughter to plead its cause with the parent institution. In his opinion, psychoanalysis, as the parent body for the analytic types of group treatment, the majority at the present time, has behaved abominably but phase-typically. At each stage of a new therapy's emergence, psychoanalysis has responded with characteristic suspicion,

contempt, surprise, condescension, and, finally, recognition of a marginal few. This developmental struggle is undoubtedly rougher for orthodox psychoanalysis than for the newer cultural variants, many of whose members have undertaken the mysterious leap from the couch to the circle without being ostracized or banished into affiliate status. But even the orthodox associations have come a long way from entrenchment, and it is possible today to be concurrently a member of the American Group Psychotherapy Association and a training analyst, which can be interpreted as representing a pinnacle of professional trust. Redl sums up the situation in the following way:

> In fact, it has been gradually conceded that clinical work in groups, if done well and by appropriately trained therapists, could at least take over what the analyst wouldn't be too eager to deal with anway, and group therapy has come a little closer to the position psychotherapy is allowed to hold in relation to "analysis proper."

This summation speaks for the existing condescension very well, and, in the face of such obscurantism, one is free to wonder at the degree of masochism that precipitates psychoanalytically oriented group therapists under the wheels of the juggernaut. Berne, for one, is troubled by this anaclitic relationship that led to Procrustean efforts on the part of group therapists to cut themselves and their theories to pieces in order to fit in with orthodox psychoanalytic theory and practice instead of evolving their own consistent, indigenous system directly based on the phenomena observed in groups. Not all contemporary group psychotherapists share this attitude, but they all suffer from its effect. Those who are antagonistic, says Berne, are hampered in their creative thinking by invidiousness; those who are neutral, by too much circumspection; and those who are reconciliatory, by the problem of divided commitment. Moreover, he believes that the position of those who claim that group psychoanalysis (either psychoanalysis in groups or psychoanalysis of groups) can do practically as well as individual psychoanalysis is untenable because there is in the literature not

a single convincing case history which shows that this whole analytic process was brought to completion in any course of group therapy alone: the development of a transference neurosis, a systematic interpretation of resistances, and the resolution of the neurosis with structural changes, leading to optimum adaptation, through the consistent use of free association.

Berne further states that no serious person can really expect a group psychoanalyst to do what his name implies. If it takes one psychoanalyst four hours a week for three years to cure one patient, how long would it take the same psychoanalyst to cure a group of eight patients meeting two hours a week? Berne comes up with the answer of 48 years but acknowledges that an alternative response from some practitioners would indicate that the whole job could be done 16 times as fast as in individual work because there are eight transference relationships for each patient in the group and the therapist's analysis of each of his countertransferences would, in addition, make everything go twice as fast. This facetiousness has an element of sense about it. Group therapists, according to Berne, should derive strength from Freud's authority not by conforming to orthodoxy but by resorting to their own creative observations. It is only then that many sincere, well-trained, and intelligent individual therapists will be attracted into the field of group psychotherapy.

Instead, an anaclitic tendency has brought about a preoccupation with questions of conformity and nonconformity and with terminological exactitudes. The task is no longer one of individuating from the parent body but of internecine conflict over what Freud has aptly called "the narcissism of small differences" between fairly similar therapeutic approaches.

History has a tendency to repeat itself in the absence of historical insight. The developmental problems of separation between parent and child may be inevitable but not necessarily devastating to further individuation. Admission to the therapeutic club as full-fledged members should not be made too exclusive, or else patients will be the ultimate sufferers. Therapists must cooperate generously and graciously with one another, if only for the sake of patients. The new therapeutic approach must be given every chance to prove itself.

There is a well-known story of a child and an accompanying adult who entered a crowded railway compartment, provoking the inevitable response from those already there. The child remarked:

I can hardly wait until the next station; then it will be our turn to hate.

Group psychotherapists should bear this comment in mind when new therapeutic measures enter their sphere of interest and demand a place. It should not be their turn to hate.

GROUP THERAPY VS. INDIVIDUAL THERAPY

A certain amount of rivalry between the individual and the group approaches is only to be expected. These competitive feelings are harder to live with when they occur within a person rather than between persons. The group therapist, coming from individual therapy, experiences two opposing reactions: He may feel that he is losing something important in the therapeutic situation. At the same time, he may feel that he is gaining a great deal more from the group situation than he ever obtained from the one-to-one relationship. He is, therefore, often hard put to say which method is better, but with increasing experience in both fields, he may eventually be able to work out to his own satisfaction at least a dynamic accounting of strengths and weaknesses and gains and losses.

Depth

Slavson has stated the case for the two sides as well as anybody:

The depth and thoroughness of this treatment does not reach those of an individual psychoanalysis [and he includes himself among those who believe] that the basic conflicts of the full-blown psychoneurotic can be resolved only by psychoanalysis. [Transference toward the therapist] obviously cannot be as intense in groups as it is in individual treatment [because of the dilution brought about by other members and also because in groups] interpretation seldom reaches areas in the patient's personality as deep as in individual treatment.

Slavson is, however, quick to add that in many conditions this interpretation is sufficient to eliminate not the nuclear conflicts but the derivative personality difficulties. An analytic group psychotherapy, he insists, is well able to do this. Furthermore, not all patients need and even fewer can avail themselves of as thorough a form of treatment as psychoanalysis.

On the positive side, Slavson remarks that

the universal observation by all group therapists is that patients are incomparably more productive in groups than in individual treatment, and that the therapeutic process is greatly accelerated.

The reason he gives for this facilitation of therapy in groups is based on a number of dynamic mechanisms peculiar to the group situation, such as identification, mutual support, catalysis, dilution of transference, a multiplicity of targets for aggression, and the liberating recognition by patients that other people have problems similar to their own. Clearly, he is not talking here of second-class therapy for patients who cannot afford something better; but he is cautioning therapists to be aware of certain limitations with regard to depth and intensity—cautions that have been echoed by other therapists.

Arsenian and Semrad insist that

the treatment of a patient within a group setting is so far removed from the psychoanalytic arrangement that it is misleading to call it psychoanalysis; at best, it is psychotherapy with a psychoanalytic orientation.

They also feel that free association belongs to psychoanalysis proper and cannot be applied in a group and it is free association that gives depth to the individual situation.

They raise an important question to which there is no ready answer: If group therapy induces transference without the opportunity for working through it, lays bare the primary processes without the opportunity for analyzing their history and function, demonstrates resistance without the opportunity for studying its origin and evolution, causes structural change without the opportunity for studying its meaning, and triggers off bursts of free association without the opportunity to pursue its course without interruption, why would any therapist undertake to involve himself in such inevitable and pervasive technical frustrations? If he views group therapy as a means for dissolving the nuclear neurotic conflicts of the individual patient, the therapist is going to be disappointed; but if he sees it as an unrivaled clinical instrument for the study of group dynamics and for the analysis of disturbances in interpersonal relationships, his enthusiasm will wax with every new group experience. What the group approach loses with respect to the individual patient, it gains enormously with respect to the group. As long as the therapist maintains his orientation to the individual patient, his group treatment will remain a poor substitute for individual therapy; once he develops a genuine group perspective, the added new dimensions will more than counterbalance the loss of some of the advantages connected with the dyadic arrangement. The patient, on his side, can gain certain ineluctable experiences from the group to compensate him for the sacrifice demanded of his uniqueness.

In his approach to the group, Freud was much more concerned with the gains and losses sustained by submersion within the collective experience, and he speculated about the ways in which the deficiencies in psychic functioning induced by the group situation could be overcome. If there are compensations, are they enough to satisfy the needs of therapist and patient?

The loss of depth is a hard one for the therapist to sustain. It impinges directly on his personal narcissism and on his self-image as a profound therapist. The dichotomous alternative is to be shallow or superficial. Arsenian and Semrad offer him some cold comfort:

While group therapy may not deal as thoroughly with depth material, it may be a more immediately influential corrective emotional experience which changes behavior.

Transference

The same is true for another magic word in therapy, transference, which is commonly regarded as the major dynamic mechanism at work not only in all forms of therapy but also in life itself. Depending on the nature of the situation, transference varies considerably in quality and intensity, and different levels of transference can be described. It is acknowledged that the phenomena subsumed under this term are at their most explicit in psychoanalysis, where they frequently take the form of a transference neurosis. Although today therapists recognize that a transference neurosis can develop in the group, it does so only to a limited extent. (The same is true of children in analysis.) The group situation, by its very nature, impedes the regressive movement required for full reactivation of the early dyadic and triadic relationships. As a result, the transference manifestations are diluted, as Slavson says, or fragmentized and therefore need to be analyzed piecemeal, as Durkin says.

The two situations work in almost opposite directions. The psychoanalytic one favors the development of the regressive transference because of its deeply infantilizing nature. The group situation focuses on the existential, the experiential, and the progressive. This is not to say that regression does not occur in groups—even the early observers like Le Bon and McDougall were well aware of regression in groups—but it does not take place to the same degree. To quote Spanjaard:

Over and over again one gets the impression that in comparison with psychoanalysis the blocking of the group toward full infantile regression, though oscillating, sticks fast.

He feels that the limitation is imposed by the mutual rivalry for the therapist engendered by the group situation so that the regression reaches and remains at the post-oedipal level—that is, the level of the five- to seven-year-old or of the adolescent attempting to wean himself from parental dependency.

Spanjaard makes two important points that would have gained the approval of Freud, since they stem logically from his great pioneering presentation on group psychology. First, if one keeps the group small—not more than five patients—keeps it amorphous rather than cohesive and organized, concentrates on the latent content, remains detached, and allows an infantilizing situation to develop without active intervention, then a transference analysis becomes possible. The group analyst in this formulation is modeled on classical psychoanalysis and adopts a more passive stance than in the Wolf groups. Second, Spanjaard is of the opinion that the tentative transference neurosis that develops in these analytically operated groups is impeded because of the development of group formations, taking his stand on the antithesis between neurosis and group formation postulated by Freud.

What does the group offer to supplement the dilution of transference? According to Bach, the group can add a host of interpersonal processes, such as identification, social symbiosis, contagion, coalition, role-playing, and security operation.

The substitutes do not always sound as good as the original but the analytic group theorists do their best. For example, Arsenian and Semrad write that

spontaneous work toward communication and sharing experiences moves from the less to more articulate modes of expression and toward better understandings. Perhaps this is the group equivalent of making the unconscious conscious.

The same authors feel that, although free association cannot be applied in a group and although group association is fairly infrequent, the same end can be achieved by acting out in the present with the challenge to understand what is happening. Slavson lays the same stress on the importance of acting out, especially in children's groups, and one is reminded here of Klein's equating free association with play in child analysis.

The working through of the transference situation in individual analysis has also been given its analogue in the group— namely, the observation and interpretation of the reaction of different individual members toward one another, toward the group, and toward the leader. Whether such modeling can substitute for the hard and detailed working through process of psychoanalysis is, however, doubtful.

Object Anxiety

Although the group, in the course of its therapeutic life, ranges over a wide spectrum of anxiety problems, it is with object anxiety that it becomes especially preoccupied. This preoccupation takes precedence over inner problems, and the members get an opportunity to appreciate it in all its ramifications. The group is altogether a more realistic place than the psychoanalytic situation, and reality-testing is a more constant requirement.

If the substitutes appear to offer less, the total group phenomena clearly offer more than is available in individual therapy. The group provides a sympathetic audience for one's suffering, a reference group for one's learning, an intimacy group for sharing one's feelings, a supportive group to bolster one's deflation, a critical group to prick one's bubble, and an understanding group to enhance one's insights. In more experiential and existential terms, the group offers the authenticating force and consensual validation furnished by peers and is, therefore, more effective. Because of the collective situation, it also offers more learning experience from better patients about how to function appropriately in the service of therapy, together with affective relearning during corrective emotional experiences. The need to differentiate self from other members brings about an increased personal

awareness and a greater appreciation of how one is seen by others.

In the end, it comes down to the old sense of belongingness that helps one to deal not only with a bad infantile past that continues to haunt him but also with the existential anxieties of being separate, lonely, and alone and faced by the specter of nothingness. The bad past, the lonely present, and the dread future obtain more expression in the group than they ever do in individual therapy. The group gives to each member a consoling sense of being in the same predicament and of sharing the same worries together with the help of mutual understanding and sympathy.

One must recognize that the two situations, the individual and the group, are intrinsically different in a wide variety of ways. In the group situation, there are more people to learn from and more people to learn about, more people to adjust to and more people to witness one's exposure. Instead of one unchanging, reliable, and unjudging person, there are many unstable and self-concerned individuals whose basic concern is not with the other but with themselves. It is some time before the egocentric perspectives abate sufficiently to allow the group to function as a therapeutic instrument.

Other Differences

Being in group therapy is different from being in individual therapy both for the patient and for the therapist. Lieberman has categorized some of these differences. The affects feel different in a group. The sense of intimacy, of risk, and of support is more acute, more exhilarating, and at the same time more frightening. When a patient passes from an individual to a group situation, he may have to endure, with some dismay, a loss of his sense of uniqueness, for which only his solid peer relationship can compensate him.

The therapist, too, may suffer from no longer being the only source of reference. At times, he may even feel excluded from the group. His influence is undoubtedly less powerful, and he cannot, as in the individual situation, shape the course of therapy by his interventions. (The group analytic therapists would object to this; for them, the archetypal image of the therapist loses nothing of its power when the therapist is silent or inactive. The more passive he is, the more powerfully the projections seem to act.) Lieberman concludes that the beginning group therapist, coming from individual therapy, may experience many problems because he tries to simulate the same kind of relationship in the group, which is, says Lieberman, a psychological impossibility.

In Lieberman's writing, one is struck by the phenomenon common to many academic psychologists who enter the field of therapy, either individual or group. They schematize and categorize excessively and appear to be not very much in touch with the unconscious as a therapeutic area in which the fantasies make of reality what they wish. On the other hand, Lieberman is right in that the patient coming to group therapy for the first time has to learn the hard way that help can come from any corner of the group, not merely from the therapist. The therapist, in turn, has to recognize and acknowledge the diminution in his omnipotence and omniscience. He is also less able to link his particular interventions to therapeutic improvements, as he does in individual therapy, and he may feel, at times, some stir of resentment at the multiple therapists around him. The therapist's function is less safeguarded in the group than in the individual therapeutic situation. In the group, he can play his role actively or passively, frequently or infrequently, equally or unequally, fully involved or detached. He can be a psychoanalyst, a teacher, a social engineer, a conductor, or just another patient. What he makes of himself is often less important than what the group, in its unconscious functioning, makes of him. In the end, all is transference.

INDIVIDUAL THERAPY AND GROUP THERAPY

In both individual and group psychotherapy, the therapist attempts to bring the patient to the point where he can function as a therapist toward himself. The capacity for self-analysis is the hallmark of successful analysis. It is not sufficient to cure a patient; one must make him, for preventive reasons, self-curative. The patient, therefore, learns from his therapist through identification to become what Szasz has referred to as metatheoretical—that is, he begins to use metapsychology in the service of his own insight. In the group, this dimension is extended further by the presence of other patients. The patient can interpret to other patients, who can respond in kind, and he can model his own patient behavior on the good patients around him. Once again, it is possible to view the two therapies not as competitors but as supplementary, complementary treatments that are perhaps suitable for different conditions.

Selection of Patients

Individual and group therapy have undergone similar historical developments with regard to selection. In the early days of psychoanalysis, the analyst—after excluding the old and the young, the organically impaired and the defective, the dullard and the perverted, the psychopath and the psychotic—was left with a nice, articulate, intelligent, middle-class, psychoneurotic patient to treat. As time went on, the analyst became less selective and less exclusive and began dealing with almost the whole range of psychiatric disorders, barring the organic. The reason for his extended activity was partly that he was gradually becoming more technically competent and partly that he was obtaining unexpectedly successful results, even with narcissistic patients. He had also discovered that classical psychoneurotics were a rarity and that he could starve while waiting for them to turn up at his office.

Group psychotherapy also began by excluding almost every patient except the neurotic, and even severe psychoneurotics were at one time felt to be inaccessible by this method. Organic patients, regressed patients, psychotic patients, asthmatic patients, depressed patients, perverted patients, narcissistic patients, paranoid patients, and even obsessional patients—be-

Table 1. *The Three Main Approaches to Group Psychotherapy*

Individual-Oriented Approach (psychoanalytic and analytic group psychotherapy)	Integrative Approach (group analytic psychotherapy)	Transactional Approach (group dynamic psychotherapy)
Classical psychoanalytic orientation and techniques based on psychoanalytic principles; preservation of patient's uniqueness; analysis of individual patient in interaction with others (sibling transference) and of bilateral transference to the therapist, viewed as crucial; concern with making the unconscious conscious	Focus on both individual patient and group; transference recognized and interpreted but emphasis on configurations of interpersonal disturbance and their location within the group rather than on analysis of regressive transference to the therapist; concern with both latent and manifest content	Group as focus of therapy with emphasis on the group-as-a-whole, group reactions, group interactions, group roles, group themes, group relationships and communications; concern with manifest content

cause of their monopolizing tendency—were regarded as untreatable. Today the story is different, and the range of patients who are found treatable and who are treated compares favorably with individual psychotherapy. There may even be a tendency in the opposite direction—to treat everyone until proved he is untreatable by failure in actual treatment.

Ackerman suggested in the 1940's that group psychotherapy was more appropriate for patients suffering from externalized syndromes than for those suffering from internalized ones—that is, from struggles between the patient and his environment, not from intrapsychic conflicts. This suggestion would limit group treatment to use in the social neuroses. No practicing group psychotherapist at this time would agree with this artificial division between internal and external conflicts, since external conflicts are often secondary to internal conflicts. Slavson has offered some evidence based on the Rorschach test that group treatment brings about definite intrapsychic changes, even by the activity approaches.

The convergence of the two therapies toward one another was inevitable, and soon many therapists began to look on the two methods as flexibly adjunctive rather than as competitive or mutually excluding techniques. Some therapists have even made the combination of individual and group therapy their habitual mode of treatment. There may even be an argument, although not a very strong one, for matching individual and group therapies so that, where intrapsychic emphasis has been predominant, an extrapsychic approach would follow, and vice versa.

Approaches

There are three main approaches to group psychotherapy with a fourth offshoot into the existential approach. The focus on the existential and experiential could develop within any of the three main techniques. All, to some extent and at some time, can claim to be existential and experiential, although they are disinclined to make this the total venue of approach.

In Table 1, the middle approach seems to be a compromise between the two extremes, but in fact it has developed along this path from the very beginning and is not a reactive therapy. The same three models have emerged in family therapy, and Haley has put forward the view that, whereas a totally one-sided view would be both unrealistic and impossible in actual practice, the statement of extreme positions provides clarification for theoretical purposes. Family therapists also worry, but more in theory than in practice, over the problem of leaving out the individual patient and his genetic, psychodynamic background, or, just as myopically, neglecting the family as a group with its complicated system of reciprocal roles and transactional processes.

There are, of course, extreme representatives in all manner of groups who refuse to believe that the other side has anything at all to offer. Wolf, for example, writes that

while group dynamics is admittedly an interesting and important subject for study by the social psychologist, it has little to offer systems of therapy for the individual.

The group dynamic therapists, on the other hand, have retorted that it is, in their thinking, a lesser sin, if one at all, to integrate concepts of group dynamics into group psychotherapy than to slavishly apply the concepts of individual psychotherapy to group psychotherapy. The individually oriented therapists, not to be outclassed, have pointed out that the emphasis on the therapy group as a group has led to a startling neglect of the neurotic difficulties of the individual members.

The existentialists have criticized all three of the main approaches for ignoring the existential anxiety that is basically troubling the group. All three varieties of group therapists, they claim, are intellectual thinkers who are simply motivated by curiosity and are little better than observers in the group, busy taking things apart by analysis but seldom troubling to put them back together again. The existential therapist, by contrast, is an essential thinker who pursues truth as a participant in the group and is concerned with wholeness and a mode of relatedness described by Buber as "mutual spiritual inclusion."

Combined Therapy

The noncompetitive outlook sees benefits in both individual and group models of psychotherapy and is prepared to use whatever will provide maximal benefits to the patient. The individual method has its advantages in eliciting historical material in the context of the one-to-one relationship. Group therapy concentrates on current relationships, especially within the group, and leads to a fuller understanding of the individual patient through the medium of multiple transferences. The group situation, by lessening anxiety, lessens resistance, increases productivity, enhances ego consciousness, and therefore provides a complementary measure of help.

It was, therefore, inevitable that a number of therapists would make attempts to combine the two approaches, individual and group psychotherapy. In so doing, they have opened up the spectrum of choice with regard to what can be offered to patients evincing a wide array of psychopathological disturbances (see Table 2).

Experience has shown that certain patients respond only to individual therapy and do best in this setting. The classical neuroses, especially obsessional types, are best handled in a transference analysis, although some analysts now believe that patients profit from a group therapy experience even after a long individual analysis. The value of this experience lies not only in the new insights that are provoked but also in the fact that it permits the patient to work out positive identifications based on healthy rather than neurotic needs.

A large number of patients, however, are best treated by concurrent individual and group therapy. The resistances created by the group are no greater than resistances deriving from other persons in the patient's environment, and there are many resistances that actually diminish as a result of the group experience. Some individual therapists, in fact, on coming up against a tough and immovable resistance, resort to temporary or permanent placements within

Table 2. *The Spectrum of Choice*

Individual therapy only	Individual therapy plus terminal group therapy to deal with residual social anxiety	Combined individual and group therapy, concurrent or sequential; sequence can be: group follows individual or vice versa, group inserted into individual therapy or vice versa	Group therapy plus occasional individual interviews	Group therapy only

Table 3. *The Role of the Therapist in the Group*

Leaderless Group	Leaderless Sessions	Therapist as Background Figure	Therapist as Foreground Figure
Therapist functions as patient in the group, totally involved to same extent as the patients; he is, however, the most experienced patient	Alternate sessions conducted without the presence of a therapist	Therapist functions as much as possible behind the scenes; his attitudes and behavior are determinant, but his control is subtle and unobtrusive	Therapist as psychoanalyst of the group—directional, stimulative, extensional, interpretative

a therapy group, and the maneuver often works successfully, although tough resistances can also be handled by transferring the patient to another therapist for more individual therapy.

In concomitant treatment, the therapist, if the same in both therapies, can use material from either type of session to further the patient's individual analysis. Some patients react to combined therapy by playing one against the other, by developing resistances, by keeping secrets only for or from his therapist, and by reacting traumatically when the therapist is attacked by others in the group. The therapist can use the multiple transferences of the group selectively in his work in individual therapy.

Slavson is of the opinion that, because of the many transference difficulties involved, it is better for different therapists to conduct the individual and group therapies. It would depend to some extent on whether all the patients in the group are also in individual therapy with the group therapist or only one or a few. The privileged position of those having combined therapy may create disruptive sibling transferences that cannot be adequately analyzed in the group for those receiving only group therapy. On the other hand, it is hard on the group therapist when his group patients are in therapy with several other therapists and a large part of their therapeutic lives is excluded from him. The patients may sense his concern and exploit it to the full, so that he is often left feeling impotent and frustrated and even irritated by the bad management that he detects in the outside therapists.

The role of the therapist in the group may also play a part in the outcome of combined therapy. In Table 3, the range of his activity is schematized. The nondirective, behind-the-couch therapist in individual therapy may perplex his patients and interfere with their smooth transference development when he emerges as a foreground figure in the group. The reverse is also true. An active analyst in individual therapy may create anxiety, amounting almost to panic, when he is viewed as impotent, passive, or unhelpful in the group. All these factors must be borne in mind when individual and group therapies are brought together for the same patient.

Model Building

Model building has become an essential part of advancing sciences that are not too sure of their next steps but are prepared to speculate concretely about them. Freud, whose adventurous mind frequently outran his clinical experience, occasionally resorted to model building and, by so doing, reified such abstract concepts as ego, superego, and id for later generations. On the group dynamic side, Kurt Lewin built his topological system so concretely that his blackboard figures began to take on a life of their own. It was only a short step from there to the emergence of the group organism functioning as a whole.

A series of five models has been constructed to represent the extension of the psychoanalytic model into the analytic, psychoanalytic, and group analytic models (see Figure 1). In the first two models, the individual patient and his unconscious system of objects are both the focus of attention of the therapist. In the second model, a certain amount of notice, but not too

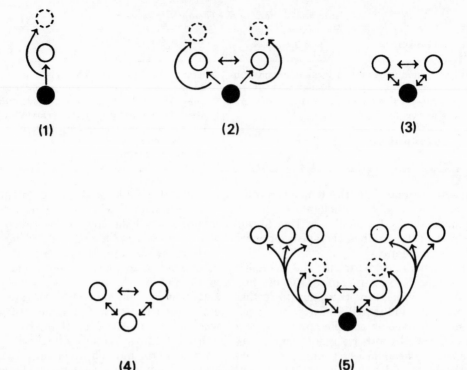

Figure 1. Model building—individual and group models. 1, Psychoanalysis. The analyst directs his attention to the "unconscious" family latent in the patient; 2, analytic and psychoanalytic group psychotherapy. The group therapist deals mainly, as in psychoanalysis, with the parental transference in each individual patient but also takes note of sibling transferences and interpersonal reactions; 3, group dynamic psychotherapy. The group leader gradually creates a milieu in which the therapeutic focus is exclusively on the interpersonal feeling responses in the here-and-now; 4, existential group psychotherapy. The therapist abdicates as completely as he can from his leadership role and becomes the best model of the "good" patient. Everyone in the group is in the same boat, dealing with the problems of life and death as openly and as authentically as he can; 5, group analytic psychotherapy. The emphasis is on the unconscious family of each patient as it gets transferred in the group, with the here-and-now interactions, and with the hidden impact of the existent family outside of the therapeutic process (the transpersonal network). This makes up the total T-situation.

much, is taken of the relationship between the two members. In the third model, the group analytic one, Foulkes has complicated the picture in several ways. The therapist is conscious not only of each member and his internal objects but also of the group matrix or interaction between two members. Behind each member is another system of external objects, the social network, that adds its influence to his reactions in the group. Anthony's addition to this model has been the group representation in the preconscious mind of each member. This internal group is constantly affected by the internal objects that operate unconsciously, and both inner systems attempt to manipulate the actual members of the group to fit transference expectations or the expectations raised by the preconscious group, signifying the manner in which the patient would like the actual group to feel and act. The fourth model is the group dynamic one, focusing on the here-and-now. The fifth model, the existential one, depicts the therapist as patient.

For clarification, these models could be better demonstrated three-dimensionally. It is also particularly difficult to include the factors of space and time in the same two-dimensional model. In Table 4, the ele-

Table 4. *Space, Time, and the Group*

Time Element	Space Element	Process	Reference Group
Now	Here	Existential analysis (interpersonal, experimental)	Group matrix
Then	There	Genetic reconstruction (remembering)	Family of orientation
Now	There	Displacement (transactions outside the group)	Social network
Then	Here	Transference analysis (parental, sibling)	Society of internalized objects

ments of space and time are shown in conjunction with each other. The *now* is the present time both inside and outside the group; the *then* is the infantile past of each individual patient in the group. The *here* is the group therapeutic space; and the *there* is the Lewin "life space" of each patient outside the group. The now-and-here is the existential situation, and the reference group is the actual therapy group; the then-and-there is the reminiscence that takes place in analytically oriented groups and refers to real or screen memories of early family life; the now-there refers to events taking place in the social network, which has its own repercussions on the group through the member concerned; the then-here is the shorthand for transference analysis, of either the parental or the sibling variety, and the reference group is the society of internalized objects.

Models can also be built delineating the course of treatment. Anthony has attempted to construct two such models, one for individual therapy and one for group therapy. Half of the model representing dyadic treatment depicts individual psychotherapy, and the total model outlines the course of psychoanalysis. A similar model was made for group therapy and group analytic therapy. Both models are divided into two phases.

Phase 1 of individual treatment is essentially an open system modeled on the early parent-child union, with its anaclitic-diatrophic form of relatedness. Communication is dominated by primitive ego functioning on the part of both therapist and patient, with heavy reliance on empathy, intuition, imitation, and identification. The patient's thinking is largely of the primary process variety and is apt to be colored by ideas of magic and omnipotence. The focal conflict has to do with dependency and the ambivalent feelings engendered by it. In keeping with this issue, the drives are predominantly pregenital in origin, with attacking and sadistic elements especially prominent. The symbiotic transference tends to be floating and sporadic, and the countertransference is parental in orientation, involving areas of care, contact, and control. The major therapeutic influences at work involve suggestion, persuasion, and catharsis; consequently, the therapist's personality plays a crucial role in directing the course of treatment. The therapeutic task for this first phase comprises the resolution of the ambivalent dependency, the crystallization of identifications into a more genuine object relationship, and a corresponding individuation of the patient as a whole.

Phase 1 in group therapy is leader-centered. The patients seem to relate individually and directly to the therapist and only tangentially to one another. The conductor is looked on as an archetypal figure of immense authority and power, possessing magical means of healing. The patients direct their more significant communications almost exclusively in his direction, seeming to regard the rest of the group as an interference with the one-to-one relationship that they seek constantly to establish with the therapist. Their principal reactions to fellow members are often ill-concealed envy and jealousy; they appear to expect nothing from one another and to give nothing. They do not listen closely to what other members are saying and frequently distort someone else's remark to suit their own train of thought. However, they do pay careful attention to what the therapist has to say. The other members are not recognized as an integral and indispensable part of the group. The system is essentially open, in that people can come and go without making much difference to the life of the group. A newcomer in the group merely reactivates sibling hostility, the main concern being how much the stranger will eat into each patient's share of the therapist. At this stage, the patients are more a collection of rugged individualists than a cohesive group. But at the close of this stage, identifications and counteridentifications begin to emerge, so that a process of mutual recognition prepares the group for the development of Phase 2.

The group therapist may respond to the individual pressures exerted on him by responding individually, so that the dyadic model of therapy is very much in evidence. His own proclivity may fixate the group at this level of interaction. Groups made up of patients with pregenital syndromes, character disorders, borderline disturbances, and early deprivation need not and often cannot go beyond this phase.

In individual psychoanalysis, Phase 2 is ushered in by the resolution of the separation-individuation problems of the first phase. During Phase 2, the therapeutic system is closed, and the working model is triadic, including both parent figures in an oedipal type of transference. Communication is characteristically verbal and explicit, and the thinking operations of both therapist and patient are of the secondary process type, with the observing ego demonstrating a capacity for carrying out some of the analytic work for itself. Libidinal rather than aggressive drives are prominent, and regression to Phase 1 responses becomes a feature of transference resistances. A transference neurosis gradually unfolds and is resolved with the systematic use of interpretation and defense analysis. The countertransference shows erotic and genital components.

Phase 2 in group therapy tends to take place spontaneously in groups organized on a neurotic basis. The imitations, identifications, and confrontations of Phase 1 slowly bring about greater mutual recognition within the group, and communications flow more smoothly and widely. It becomes evident that a group-centered group has developed, manifesting an array of group formations. The therapist functions both in relation to the individual patient and to the group, and the group becomes increasingly conscious of itself as an instrument of therapy. The therapist is altogether less active than in Phase 1. A multiplicity of group phenomena—mirroring, pairing, resonating, colluding, power-playing—make their appearance during the second phase. With the development of group formations, regressive tendencies subside, and transference in its more neurotic aspect becomes less manifest. There is some logic for equating group formations during group psychotherapy with the transference neurosis during individual psychoanalytic therapy, as the resolution of both leaves the individual patient more autonomous and healthily independent.

There is also some reason to believe that the model chosen by a particular therapist also has unconscious aims to gratify as many of his pre-oedipal or oedipal needs as can be examined in the course of therapy. There is nothing to be said against this—in moderation. Therapists need some measure of satisfaction to sustain them in their demanding work—love, status, cure, theory, money, and, most of all, comfortable and congenial working theories and techniques. But the unconscious should be made conscious, and the therapist should at least understand his choice of orientation and the reasons why he feels compelled to defend it with so much polemical fervor. The spectrum of choice is for him as much as for the patient.

CONCLUSION

Unfortunately, little work has been done on evaluation or follow-up of individual vs. group therapies, so therapists are not in a position to rate or rank them in terms of therapeutic efficacy. Like the man-in-the-street at the art exhibition, the therapist only knows what he likes. He feels it unscientifically in his bones, like his rheumatism. He practices what he pleases and what pleases him. He does not really know, deeply, what brings about changes in either his individual or his group therapies. At times, a change looks like a logical working out of rational theory; at other times, success descends like manna from heaven—unexpectedly, magically. A large part of the therapist's therapeutic systems, however much he is disinclined to admit it, still lie within the province of magic, and Slavson has reminded therapists that modern psychotherapy was preceded by incantation and that savage survivals persist in some present-day efforts.

There is a story told about a patient who was seen many years after a successful analysis. He was asked what he recalled most vividly as mutative in his treatment. He was able to remember no striking interpretation, no particular uncovering of infantile amnesia, no successful analysis of a crucial resistance, no dramatic clarification of a dream; in fact, he recalled nothing but a seemingly trivial incident. His analyst's waiting room was separated from his consulting room by a dark corridor that could be lit by a light operated by switches located at both ends of the corridor. On one occasion, the patient received his summons to the sanctum and entered the corridor, but, as he flipped the switch, the analyst, at his end, helpfully flipped his switch. The end result was that the patient was left in the dark. He did not, as he might have done, react to this event symbolically or berate his analyst for making a clumsy intervention or thank him profusely for being so attentive to his needs as to try to anticipate them. Instead, he was overcome with exhilaration at the thought that, in a perfectly magical way, he and his analyst had been, at one and the same time, connected together by the same thought and action, both wishing for the same thing and pursuing it in exactly the same way. The umbilical cord itself could not have functioned with more exquisite sensitivity.

As Hamlet said:

There are more things in heaven and earth, Horatio, Than art dreamt of in your philosophy

This is equally true for individual and group psychotherapy.

The author attempted in 1967 to express his own credo in this matter, and what he wrote then still sums up his point of view against the background of his particular bias:

In my manner of approaching this presentation, it seems as if I see myself primarily as a psychoanalyst and only secondarily as a group analyst. My tendency has been, therefore, to extrapolate from the dyadic to the group situation rather than the other way around. If I were to learn from Freud and from what he refers to as the older psychology, I would be tempted to reverse this procedure and find out to what extent the dyadic psychotherapist can learn from group psychology and group psychotherapy. Perhaps we should not be too competitive about who should learn from whom, provided we make sure that we learn from each other, and I think that both sides have a great deal to learn—still.

REFERENCES

Ackerman, N. W. Some general principles in the use of group psychotherapy. In *Current Therapies in Personality Disorders*, B. Glueck, editor. Grune & Stratton, New York, 1946.

Anthony, E. J. Dyadic and group psychotherapy. Int. J. Group Psychother., *17:* 57, 1967.

Arsenian, J., and Semrad, E. Individual and group manifestations. Int. J. Group Psychother., *17:* 82, 1967.

Bach, G. R. *Intensive Group Psychotherapy.* Ronald Press, New York, 1955.

Berne, E. "Psychoanalytic" versus "dynamic" group therapy. Int. J. Group Psychother., *10:* 98, 1960.

Durkin, H. E. *The Group in Depth.* International Universities Press, New York, 1964.

Foulkes, S. H., and Anthony, E. J. *Group Psychotherapy: The Psychoanalytic Approach.* Penguin Books, London, 1965.

Lieberman, M. A. The implications of total group phenomena analysis for patients and therapists. Int. J. Group Psychother., *17:* 71, 1967.

Redl, F. Psychoanalysis and group therapy: a developmental point of view. Amer. J. Orthopsychiat., *33:* 135, 1963.

Slavson, S. R. *Analytic Group Psychotherapy with Children, Adolescents and Adults.* Columbia University Press, New York, 1950.

Spanjaard, J. Transference neurosis and psychoanalytic group psychotherapy. Int. J. Group Psychother., *9:* 31, 1959.

Wolf, A. Group psychotherapy. In *Comprehensive Textbook of Psychiatry,* p. 1234, A. M. Freedman and H. I. Kaplan, editors. Williams & Wilkins, Baltimore, 1967.

5

Clinical Diagnosis in Group Psychotherapy

Harold I. Kaplan, M.D. and Benjamin J. Sadock, M.D.

INTRODUCTION

To be of help, the group therapist must have detailed knowledge of each individual patient's intrapsychic and interpersonal disturbances, and he must be aware of the patient's psychological strengths and assets. In addition, the therapist must understand how and why the patient's problems developed—which means that he must study the patient's developmental history. Finally, the therapist must try to identify the various causes of the patient's illness—the stresses, adverse social and cultural influences, and somatic factors. With all this information in hand, the therapist can then proceed with his formal diagnosis and begin treatment.

In one-to-one therapy, diagnostic evaluation and the first steps in treatment may sometimes be conducted at the same time. But not in group therapy. For one thing, the therapist is not able to concentrate on any one patient long enough to collect the extensive data he needs for accurate diagnosis. For another thing, the therapist may jeopardize the treatment of the group as a whole and the treatment of the individual if he is not aware of the patient's diagnostic classification beforehand. The presence of just one unsuitable patient in the group may reinforce the pathology of his co-patients and create intolerable tension.

Clearly, then, the therapist must see each prospective candidate for group psychotherapy individually before he is admitted to the group. One or more psychiatric interviews will give the therapist an opportunity to make his diagnostic evaluation. Of course, the therapist may later modify his initial assessment of the patient. Indeed, he must be alert to changes in intrapsychic and interpersonal functioning and in somatic structure and function. But he cannot start group treatment with any degree of confidence until he establishes the patient's diagnostic classification.

Diagnostic competence begins with an understanding of the psychodynamics of behavior—both how the patient acts and how his conscious and unconscious mind works.

PSYCHOANALYTIC THEORY OF BEHAVIOR

The Theory of the Instincts

The term instinct refers to the influence of body needs on mental activity and behavior. Mediated through the central nervous system, such influences are experienced. psychologically in the form of various sensations and various perceptions of the environment associated with the satisfaction or frustration of body needs. In the course of a person's development, psychological representations of these experiences become established in his mind and are referred to as drives or instinctual drives.

Certain behavior and psychic activity aim at contact, union, or closeness with objects in the environment. Other behavior and psychic activity aim at the destruction of objects. This difference suggests the presence

97

of two instincts—sexual instincts and aggressive instincts.

Libido. As defined by Freud, libido is that force by which the sexual instinct is represented in the mind. Sexual instinct undergoes a complex process of development and has many manifestations other than genital union. And sexuality is not limited to those sensations and activities typically considered sexual or to those parts of the body usually associated with erogenous zones.

Phases of Psychosexual Development. The earliest manifestations of sexuality involve bodily functions that are basically nonsexual. In the oral phase, which extends into the second year of life, erotic activity centers on the infant's mouth and lips and is manifested by sucking and biting. Between the ages of two and four, the child is increasingly preoccupied with bowel function and control, and his dominant erotic activity shifts from his mouth to his anal region. Usually by the fourth year, the child is increasingly aware of pleasurable feeling from his genitals. The penis and clitoris become the new erotic zones, and masturbatory activity is manifested.

Development of Object Relationships. In earliest infancy, the child depends on certain elements or objects in the environment and is driven to behave in ways that will assure the supply of these objects. Such behavior occurs without the infant's being aware of the external world or of the objects he seeks. In fact, he becomes aware of the objects partly because of some degree of frustration. Awareness of food evolves out of repetitive experiences of being hungry and then being fed. Awareness of his mother evolves out of separation and reunion with her.

At this point the mother starts to be recognized as the source of nourishment and as the source of the pleasure the infant derives from sucking. She becomes the first love object. Later sexual development and psychosocial development reflect the child's attachment to the crucial people in his environment and his feelings of love or hate or both toward them.

During the oral phase, the infant is essentially passive. His mother must gratify or frustrate his demands. But during the anal period his mother demands that he use the toilet, thereby giving up some of his freedom. And so the battle is joined as he attempts to continue enjoying the pleasurable sensation of excretion. Later on, he may derive even more pleasure by retaining the fecal mass, stimulating his anal mucosa. During this period, the child wields power over his mother by giving up or refusing to give up his feces. Expelling and retaining feces are endowed with erotic and aggressive meanings, symbolizing submission and defiance, love and hate, conflict and ambivalence.

During the oral and anal phases of development, the child makes some progress toward finding a love object, but most of his libidinal activity is autoerotic: He directs his sexual impulses toward his own body and discharges them by masturbating. The task of finding a love object belongs to the phallic phase of development. At that time the child discovers the anatomical differences between the sexes, and the pattern is set for later object choices—and for later psychoneuroses. The Oedipus complex—the intense love relationships, rivalries, hostilities, and identifications formed during this period—represents the climax of infantile sexuality. These oedipal strivings must be replaced by adult sexuality if the person is to develop normally. If he clings to oedipal tendencies, he will develop neuroses.

Aggression. At first, Freud equated aggression with sadism. Later, he thought of aggression as self-preservative impulse. But when he saw self-destructive tendencies in depressed patients, self-inflicted injuries among masochistic patients, and wanton destructiveness by small children, he concluded that aggression was often not self-preservative. So Freud gave aggression a separate status as an instinct, noting that the source of the instinct is largely in the skeletal muscles and that its aim is destruction.

The Psychic Apparatus

The Mind. Mental activity takes place on three levels: the unconscious, the preconscious, and the conscious. In the unconscious, personality forces strive for discharge, but strong counterforces block them from conscious awareness.

The preconscious, which develops in childhood, is accessible to both the unconscious and the conscious. Elements in the unconscious reach the conscious only by first reaching the preconscious. One of the functions of the preconscious is to repress or censor certain wishes and desires.

The conscious is the sense organ of the mind. Words, thoughts, impulses, and feelings may be brought to consciousness only with effort and attention, or they may intrude into consciousness unbidden. Keeping some things from becoming conscious and letting other things become conscious involves ego functions. Except for feelings, the things that come into consciousness are associated with symbols or words. The capacity to organize conscious experience in a logical, coherent, reality-oriented way marks the difference between primitive and mature mental functioning.

Structure of the Psychic Apparatus. The psychic apparatus is divided into three provinces: id, ego, and superego. The id, the locus of the instinctual drives, operates in accordance with the pleasure principle, with no regard for reality. The ego, on the other hand, is a coherent organization that controls contact with reality and avoids pain by inhibiting or regulating the discharge of instinctual drives to conform with the demands of the external world. The ego makes use of such defense mechanisms as repression, displacement, reaction formation, isolation, undoing, rationalization, intellectualization, denial, projection, regression, counterphobic mechanisms, withdrawal, and sublimation to oppose the id impulses. The superego, which contains the internalized moral values of parental images also regulates the discharge of id impulses. The aim of the human being is satisfaction of the basic biological influences and adequate adjustment within the environment.

DIAGNOSTIC PROCEDURES

The Psychiatric Interview

The clinical interview, as described by Ripley, whose work forms much of the basis for the discussion that follows, is the psychiatrist's principal diagnostic tool—one that may be supplemented by medical and neurological examinations and by psychological tests. During the interview, the psychiatrist tries to evaluate the patient's developmental history, his present life situation, and his current emotional status and mental capacity.

The psychiatrist begins with signs and symptoms. He listens to the patient's story, subjects him to various types of examinations, and then tries to diagnose his illness. Within this broad framework, the organization of the interview and the techniques employed vary from patient to patient and from one interview to another with the same patient. The therapist's personality, response to the patient, and clinical experience also modify the structure of the interview. Whatever his technique, however, the psychiatrist must focus his attention on the patient, not simply on the manifestations of disease. The psychiatrist must try to understand the disease in terms of the patient's life.

Goals. Before the therapist can make a diagnosis, he must get a description of the patient's symptoms. His symptoms are the focus of the patient's immediate concern, and the therapist must be tolerant of the patient's preoccupation with his symptoms and receptive to his efforts to describe them even if they are not evidence of psychiatric disease. Moreover, the therapist should become aware not only of the symptoms the patient describes but also of those symptoms he minimizes or conceals. The therapist must also understand what the patient says, have some insight into what he is trying to say but is reluctant to put into words, and realize when he is denying the presence of symptoms.

The psychiatrist's second task is to get information about every aspect of the patient's biological, psychological, and social history past and present. With this information, the therapist should be able to identify those factors that helped cause the illness. In addition, he will have a preliminary picture of the patient's personality—his attitudes, character traits, and intrapsychic conflicts and the psychological devices he uses to deal with these conflicts. And the therapist may have some insight into the causes of the patient's symptoms.

At the end of the interview, the therapist may try to make a tentative diagnosis and prognosis. He should also make a preliminary decision about the disposition of the patient. But if the therapist needs more information before he can make even a tentative conclusion about the patient's illness, he may schedule additional diagnostic interviews or recommend other diagnostic procedures—psychological tests and medical or neurological examinations. Once the diagnosis has been made, the therapist may accept the patient for treatment, refer him to another therapist, or recommend some other form of treatment.

The therapist must help the patient understand his illness. The patient who is symptom-free must be made aware of his illness. And the patient with subjective symptoms must learn to accept the fact that he has to change his underlying emotional attitudes.

The interview may be therapeutic as well as diagnostic.

The therapist must try to relieve the patient's immediate suffering by offering reassurance, understanding, and sympathy. Above all, he must empathize with the patient.

The Psychiatrist-Patient Relationship. Whether the psychiatrist achieves his goals depends on how he conducts the diagnostic interview and on the quality of his relationship with the patient.

A satisfactory psychiatrist-patient relationship depends on the psychiatrist's ability to achieve rapport with the patient—to create a feeling of harmonious responsiveness, to make the patient feel that the psychiatrist understands him, accepts him despite his liabilities, and recognizes his assets and that the psychiatrist is someone he can talk to.

Achieving rapport in a clinical setting is contingent on the psychiatrist's ability to understand the patient's symptoms, personality, and behavior on an intellectual level. More important, it is contingent on the therapist's capacity for empathy—his ability to put himself in the patient's place—and for self-examination—his constant awareness of his responses and attitudes toward the patient, and of the psychodynamic factors underlying those responses and attitudes.

The Patient's Attitude toward the Psychiatrist. The patient's reactions to his illness and to the interview as well as his usual ways of dealing with other people will influence the attitude toward the psychiatrist.

The patient's reactions to his illness depend on personal, social, and cultural factors. His personal experiences affect the manifestations of his illness and his affective responses to pathological changes in his personality and behavior. The defenses he mobilizes to deal with these unpleasant feelings reflect his usual way of dealing with such feelings. Social and cultural factors may determine what symptoms he describes to the therapist and what symptoms he conceals, since different cultures have different standards of what is acceptable and what is shameful. Social and cultural factors may also determine when, how, and where the patient goes for help.

Almost all patients approach the first psychiatric interview with some anxiety. The perception of psychiatric symptoms invariably gives rise to fears, realistic and unrealistic, that are as diverse and complex as the forms of psychiatric illness. The patient may express his fears and anxieties verbally or only in his nonverbal behavior. He may deliberately withhold information, give evasive answers, or, in extreme cases, simply refuse to communicate. He may try to charm or endear himself to the psychiatrist, or even behave seductively in an effort to divert him from the real issues. Or, he may use such defense mechanisms as denial and projection.

Some patients place the psychiatrist on a pedestal and endow him with magical powers. The inevitable disillusionment may strengthen their resistance to treatment. They may at times feel that, once they have consulted a psychiatrist, they don't have to do anything else. At other times they may see the seeking of psychiatric help as an act of surrender, an admission of weakness.

The patient often sees the psychiatrist as an authority figure who has the power to control every aspect of his life. This reaction grows out of anxieties and guilt feelings surrounding his illness and also out of his unresolved dependency needs, which may be reactivated during periods of psychological or physical stress and redirected toward an idealized parental figure, such as the psychiatrist.

Finally, the patient's attitude toward the psychiatrist reflects his usual way of relating to other people—aggressive and domineering or dependent and submissive, detached and disinterested or manipulative and seductive.

The Psychiatrist's Attitude toward the Patient. At some time, the patient is negative or ambivalent toward the psychiatrist. The effect of these attitudes on the psychiatrist-patient relationship is minimal if the psychiatrist understands their origins and deals with them appropriately. But if the psychiatrist's attitudes toward the patient are inappropriate, the effects on the psychiatrist-patient relationship, the diagnostic process, and the course and outcome of treatment can be disastrous. So the psychiatrist must be aware of his feelings toward the patient, understand the origins of his countertransference, and work through his inappropriate attitudes. Self-understanding is the key, which is why a personal analysis is considered an essential part of psychiatric training.

The psychiatrist's initial reactions to the patient are based on his first impressions. He may like the patient immediately and feel attracted, or he may automatically dislike him and be repelled by his appearance or behavior. These initial reactions often form part of the basis for a tentative diagnosis.

If the patient is hostile or aggressive, the psychiatrist may perceive such behavior as a personal attack and try to fight back, calling forth more hostility from the patient. Their relationship quickly reaches a stalemate in such a situation. Ideally, of course, the psychiatrist does not overreact. Instead, he evaluates and deals with the patient's attitudes objectively. To do so, he must understand the psychodynamics of the patient's behavior and the psychogenesis of his own response to such behavior.

If the patient's symptoms evoke anxiety, the psychiatrist may ignore them or side-step the patient's efforts to discuss them. Or if the patient's behavior is unorthodox and unexplained by current theories of personality, the psychiatrist may condemn him out of hand. When he reacts with shock or fear, the psychiatrist may try to defend against his feelings. He may adopt a grave, magisterial facial expression that gives the patient the impression that he is being judged or that his condition is worse that it actually is. Or the psychiatrist may put on a cold, expressionless facade that freezes the patient or a pedantic expression that makes him feel like a small child. Whatever form they take, these defensive patterns convey a message of rejection.

A positive reaction that exceeds the proper limits of the therapist-patient relationship can be just as destructive as a negative reaction. If the psychiatrist overempathizes with the patient, he may want to solve his problems and make his decisions for him. Efforts to protect the patient from life can sabotage the psychiatrist's diagnostic and treatment efforts.

The psychiatrist's positive reactions to the patient may also be based on envy, awe of the patient's social or economic status, or admiration of his intellect. If the psychiatrist feels inferior to the patient, he needs to examine the roots of his own feelings. And, he must be alert to any effort by the patient to intimidate or manipulate him.

A written record of the psychiatrist's impressions of attitudes toward, and emotional responses to, the patient can facilitate systematic self-evaluation. A check-list of the variables that may shape the psychiatrist's reactions to the patient is particularly useful.

Number and Duration of Diagnostic Sessions. If, at the end of the initial psychiatric interview, the psychiatrist needs more diagnostic data, he will schedule at least one more diagnostic session. The need for more interviews depends on the skill with which the therapist conducts the initial interview and on factors he cannot control— the nature and severity of the patient's symptoms, the setting in which he is seen, and the time available. How the therapist conducts the initial interview and the quality of the patient-therapist relationship affect the patient's willingness to follow through and cooperate.

As a general rule, the psychiatric interview should last no more than an hour, but it may be extended to an hour and a half, if the patient is particularly alert and receptive. Whatever the length of the interview, the patient should not have the feeling that he is being rushed to produce the kind of information he thinks the therapist wants. Some patients need time to warm up and relax before they can discuss their symptoms. If the patient's anxiety is too great to continue the interview he should be allowed to leave if he wants. Trying to persuade him to stay serves no useful purpose. But the therapist should assure the patient that he is interested and concerned, and that his services are available whenever the patient is ready to discuss his problems.

The Physical Setting. The therapist's office is ideal for the interview, providing privacy, quiet, and seclusion. Such interruptions as telephone calls and the transmission of messages should be kept to a minimum. Sometimes an interruption serves a useful purpose—the patient has a chance to pull himself together and gather the courage to confide some shameful detail—but more often he uses the interval to mobilize his defenses and resistance. Moreover, the therapist has no assurance that the interruption will not occur at a strategic point. And the patient may interpret interruptions as a sign that the therapist is not interested or is hostile toward him.

When the therapist greets the patient he should introduce himself, invite the patient to be seated in a comfortable chair, and try to make him feel at ease. Explaining the purpose of the diagnostic interview is helpful. The therapist might tell a naive patient that he needs to know more about his difficulties if he is to help him. A more sophisticated patient may require a more elaborate explanation and a brief description of the treatment process. Questions about the therapist's professional qualifications should be answered frankly to reassure the patient.

Note-Taking. Notes should be made as unobtrusively as possible so that the patient will not be inhibited. If the patient objects, the therapist may reassure him that the notes are confidential and help to ensure diagnostic accuracy—and proper treatment. If the patient persists in his objections, the therapist should stop taking notes. By contrast, some patients object when the psychiatrist does not take notes. They look on note-taking as a sign of the therapist's interest and recognition of the importance of what the patient is saying.

If the therapist does not take notes during the interview, he can record the relevant data immediately after the patient leaves. But his own reactions may contaminate the patient's record. Sound recordings are a better alternative to note-taking. They are more complete than notes and do not interfere with spontaneous communication.

Observations of the Patient. Observation of specific details of the patient's appearance and behavior begins when the therapist hears the patient's voice on the telephone for the first time or sees him in his waiting room, and it continues throughout the interview. Agitated movements, disturbances in speech, changes in the patient's appearance, or changes in his respiration may give the therapist important clues about the patient's unconscious feelings and attitudes. Such observations may indicate inconsistencies between the emotional reactions the patient reports and those that exist on an unconscious level. In addition, the patient's attire, posture, behavior, and voice may indicate the nature and severity of his illness. Indeed, the therapist's observation of these nonverbal phenomena may be his only diagnostic tool when the patient talks too little, too much about irrelevant matters, or not at all because of his need to avoid discussion of his emotional conflicts.

The therapist should record his observations systematically, under such headings as patient's preinterview behavior, initial response to therapist, attire, body characteristics, facial expression and features, voice and speech, gait and posture, patterns of motor activity.

The patient's behavior in the waiting room, before he is summoned into the private office, gives the therapist his first clues about his mental and emotional status. The patient's behavior when he meets the therapist is an index of his response to his illness and his attitude toward the therapist and may provide insights into the quality of his object relationships.

Excessive fastidiousness in dress may suggest an obsessive-compulsive disorder. Extreme slovenliness may be an early sign of depression or schizophrenia. Seductive dress may indicate a hysterical neurosis. Exhibitionistic attire is worn by certain male homosexuals. Somber, drab clothing may indicate depression, or an effort to discourage sexual interest. Childish patterns of dress may express a regressive clinging to childhood. But the therapist should be aware of dress standards in different cultures—including the teen-age culture. Attire that looks eccentric to the therapist may be acceptable to or even required by the patient's peers.

The patient's physical characteristics may indicate distortions in his body image. He may be excessively preoccupied with particular body parts, feel inferior or proud because of his appearance, or be troubled by problems of sexual identity.

The patient's voice and speech, gait and posture, and pattern of motor activity are clues to his affective state. Increased motor activity—loud speech, chronic restlessness, excessive smoking, irritability—may be part of the anxiety and depression syndrome. Decreased motor activity, abnormal posture and gait, halting speech may express the underlying affects of helplessness and hopelessness found in simple depression.

Some aspects of the patient's behavior and appearance may be only transient phenomena. His increased or decreased motor activity, somber attire, angry or sad facial expression may not be components of his illness but simply his response to his illness and the interview situation.

Interviewing Techniques. The success of the initial interview depends on the therapist's knowledge of what he must find out from the patient and of how he can find it out. The good interviewer, like the good conversationalist, has verbal facility, intuitive tact, and, above all, the ability to listen. In addition, the therapist must have empathy, genuine interest in other people, and tolerance of human frailties.

Opening the Interview. The physical setting and the therapist's observance of the basic social amenities are particularly important at this point. He can use superficial techniques to convey his interest in and acceptance of the patient and his illness and to set the tone for the interview. Then the therapist proceeds to focus on the patient's chief complaint by asking a general question, such as, "What brings you here?" or "What seems to be your trouble?" This approach defines the purpose of the interview and shapes its direction.

Guiding the Interview. Listening is one of the therapist's major tools. By keeping his directive role to a minimum, he can encourage the patient to expand on his thoughts, bring up relevant topics, and lower his resistance.

The therapist's quiet attentiveness can generally lessen the patient's anxiety, blocking, and silences. But at times, he may have to play a more active, directive role. Traumatic, emotionally charged, or painful subjects may cause the patient to fall silent or become angry, tearful, or fidgety; or he may try to change the subject or terminate the interview. These reactions—forms of resistance or blocking—can be attributed to the emergence of a painful emotion, such as anxiety, conflict, shame, embarrassment, or guilt. The therapist can help the patient to overcome or lessen the intensity of these reactions.

If the patient suddenly falls silent, the therapist may ask him one or two direct questions or simply look at him questioningly and nod his head encouragingly. The patient often interprets such activity as a sign of the therapist's interest, which is a potent weapon against resistance.

If the patient remains silent, the therapist may return to the source of the patient's resistance ("You were saying...."). If the patient's pain is clearly apparent, the therapist may find it helpful to put into words what the patient is feeling as a sign that he understands him ("You seem to be feeling depressed [or angry, resentful, anxious, ashamed]"). Or the therapist may interpret the patient's reaction ("You suddenly became upset when you were talking about ..."). Often the therapist tries to allay the patient's anxiety by expressing empathy and sympathy ("That must have been an upsetting experience.").

If the patient summarily drops a subject, the therapist may defer to his wishes and hope that he will resume the discussion at a later date. Or he may openly confront the patient about his reluctance to discuss the subject.

Blocking and emotional reactions are brought on not only by sensitive subjects but also by the patient's reactions to his illness and to the diagnostic situation. If the illness evokes feelings of guilt or shame, the therapist should try to bolster the patient's self-esteem by emphasizing his achievements and positive qualities and the facts that psychiatric illness is not a sign of weakness and that others also have the illness. And if the patient has fears and doubts about the diagnostic situation, the therapist's professional competence, confidentiality, and the treatment process, the therapist can best deal with them by bringing them out into the open.

The therapist must allow the patient to tell the story of his illness in his own words. Only if he is permitted to talk about himself frankly and to express his thoughts and feelings freely, without interruption, can the patient find out about himself. Early in the interview is no time to elicit all the details and the complete factual history. Gaps in the patient's account can be filled in later. Nor should the therapist at this time challenge the patient's statements or correct his misrepresentation or misperception of the facts. These areas can be explored later, when rapport is established.

Questions, however, can be helpful if injected at strategic points in the patient's monologue. When the patient provides appropriate leads, perceptive questions can help the patient develop an understanding of himself. Tactful questioning is indicated when the therapist is not sure what some piece of information means to the patient. And, by discreet questioning, the therapist can get information about intimate topics that the patient may be reluctant to discuss. Topics such as sex can be introduced by asking the patient questions about physical development, for example.

The questions should be open-ended,

somewhat ambiguous, leaving room for explanations and elaborations by the patient. Restrictive questions answered by a "yes" or "no" cannot help the therapist understand the patient or help the patient develop an understanding of himself.

The therapist should avoid leading questions. For example, in asking the patient about his current emotional status, the therapist should not ask him whether he has a bad temper. "How is your temper?" is a more appropriate question.

Excessive questioning should also be avoided. It may overwhelm the patient, interrupt his train of thought, or block his effort to express an emotional reaction. The therapist must overcome any tendency to use precipitate questioning as a way to cope with his own anxiety.

The therapist's questions should be relevant to what the patient is talking about. Questions from out of left field may confuse or inhibit the patient. If the therapist feels that he is belaboring a topic—a sign of resistance—he can change the subject by saying, "There are other important things to cover." As the patient gives his account of his problems, the therapist may ask him whether he had similar problems in the past. This question will bring forth information about the patient's past history, which will give the therapist an insight into the origins of the patient's illness.

Finally, the therapist's vocabulary and the content of his questions and comments should be influenced by the patient's intelligence, level of sophistication, and symptoms. Whenever possible, the therapist should use the patient's own words and phraseology. Doing so assures the patient that the therapist understands him. And the therapist, in turn, minimizes the possibility that the patient will distort what he says.

Concluding the Interview. At this point, the therapist must play a more active and directive role. He must make decisions about the patient's future management, and try to make sure these decisions are carried out.

No matter how little he feels he has accomplished, no matter how frustrated or discouraged he feels, the therapist must give the patient a feeling of optimism and convince him that the diagnostic interview has been useful. But the therapist cannot guarantee a cure or even a favorable response to treatment. Nor can he estimate how much treatment the patient will require.

If no further diagnostic interviews are needed, the therapist may recommend a plan of treatment. If additional interviews are needed, he may tell the patient that there is a need for further discussion, express his continued interest, and suggest that he think about the material covered so far and about the topics he would like to discuss in the next interview. The success of later interviews depends largely on how much the patient cooperates with the therapist.

If the patient cannot face the prospect of treatment or additional interviews, he may convince himself that such procedures are unnecessary, that he only needs to change some aspect of his current life situation—get a new job, earn more money, get divorced or married, take a vacation. The therapist must persuade him that such solutions are rarely effective—and only when the patient's illness is a transient situational disturbance.

During the final phase of the interview, the therapist must tell the patient what he needs to know about his illness. Giving the patient too much information or presenting it improperly may exacerbate the patient's symptoms or create new ones. But obviously withholding information may increase his anxiety by convincing him that the therapist is keeping something from him and that his illness is more serious than he had been led to believe. As a result, the patient's confidence and trust in the therapist are undermined. Generally, it is wise to give the patient whatever information is necessary to enlist his cooperation.

As a rule, the therapist's appraisal is reassuring to the patient. For one thing, it indicates the therapist's recognition and understanding of the patient's illness. Second, when the illness is brought out into the open, it no longer lurks in the realm of the mysterious and frightening unknown.

Later Interviews. The techniques used in subsequent interviews are much the same as those used in the initial interview. The patient is encouraged to continue telling his story and to express his thoughts and feelings freely. And the therapist asks appropriate questions, expresses empathy and understanding, and occasionally interprets the patient's remarks in an effort to help him overcome his reluctance to discuss the emotional conflicts evidenced by blocking and prolonged silences.

One difference is that the therapist usually plays a more directive role in later interviews. Since he scheduled further meetings with the patient to get additional information, the therapist may ask the patient to expand on topics introduced during the first interview, or he may ask about areas that were not discussed at all.

Whatever new information is disclosed, the therapist must maintain his nonjudgmental, understanding attitude, neither condoning nor condemning the patient's behavior and values. His questions may evoke emotional reaction, anxiety, shame, guilt, withdrawal. The therapist must counteract these responses or at least lessen their intensity by reassuring and supporting the patient and by indicating his awareness of the patient's strengths as well as his weaknesses.

Specialized Interviewing Techniques. Interviewing techniques vary according to the patient's personality reactions. The therapist's usual nondirective approach may at times make the patient feel abandoned and anxious. At such times, the therapist must modify, or temporarily abandon, his basic diagnostic technique in favor of guidance and more explicit reassurance.

At other times, the therapist must try to stimulate anxiety so that an apathetic patient experiences enough discomfort to talk about his conflicts. Or the therapist may probe, challenge, and confront the indifferent patient to arouse feelings that will make him participate actively in the diagnostic process.

Interviewing techniques may also vary according to the patient's illness. A depressed patient, for example, generally has a short attention span and should have a relatively brief interview. Moreover, the therapist may have to interrupt because the patient tends to reiterate in a destructive, self-deprecatory way. Often, such a patient does not mention his depression. Instead, he may complain of insomnia, loss of appetite, diurnal changes in feelings, irritability, or difficulty in concentration. The depression is clearly evident, however, in the expressions of futility, hopelessness, self-depreciation, shame, and thinly veiled hostility.

During the interview the therapist should investigate the depressed patient's suicidal tendencies by asking about his interest in life, whether life seems to be worth living, and whether he has thoughts about dying or taking his own life. If the patient has already tried to commit suicide, he should be asked how others reacted and how they would react to his death. If he admits to contemplating suicide, he should be asked what method he would use.

With a delusional patient, the psychiatrist should demonstrate his interest, understanding, and acceptance and should try to convince the patient that he realizes he is expressing thoughts and feelings with a significant meaning, although the meaning may not be clear at the time. But he must not give the impression that he subscribes to the patient's delusions. He should neither agree with nor contradict the patient. A skeptical attitude may help to raise doubts in the patient's mind and make him more receptive to the psychiatrist's efforts to find out more about the delusional thoughts and who he feels is responsible for them.

A withdrawn patient may be so absorbed with his inner world of fantasy that he is unable to talk spontaneously about his feelings, and so the psychiatrist must ask him questions. But the therapist should change the subject when he sees that he has touched on an area of conflict. Shifting to less disturbing subjects helps the patient accept the psychiatrist. If the patient does not respond to any questions, the psychiatrist may express an interest in talking to him again later, emphasize that he is always available, and plan frequent, brief visits.

A manic patient may be so highly excited that the therapist cannot establish rapport with him. The psychiatrist should remain calm and receptive, paying particular attention to the content of what the patient says. Overtalkative, disturbed patients often reveal underlying conflicts that they conceal when they regain control.

Evaluation of Interviewing Techniques. The therapist's interviewing techniques can be considered effective if the patient reacts in certain ways during the interview: He becomes less tense and anxious, more relaxed. His speech becomes more spontaneous and natural, less inhibited and defensive. He shows increased interest in his feelings and in the origins of his symptoms and illness, and he accepts more responsibility for his condition. His feelings of guilt, self-blame, self-contempt, self-hate, and hostility decrease. His despair gives way to hopefulness. He expresses an interest in further diagnostic procedures or in treatment.

Improvement in the patient's symptoms between the initial interview and later interviews may indicate the effectiveness of the therapist's interviewing techniques, or it may be just still another manifestation of the patient's psychopathology. Contact with the therapist may have temporarily satisfied the patient's irrational dependency needs or given rise to unrealistic expectation about treatment. He may have been temporarily removed from external stress and relieved of responsibility, or he may feel relieved of the obligation to try to help himself. Or symptomatic improvement may be a natural evolution of the illness.

The Psychiatric Report

The patient does not usually present diagnostic information in a logical, orderly fashion. But if the therapist prepares a report—whether for his personal use or as a source of information for others—he is compelled to collate and organize the information so that he gets a picture of the patient and a sequential, logical account of the development of his illness. Properly evaluated, this information then enables him to arrive at a preliminary diagnosis, make a prognostic statement, and recommend an appropriate course of therapy.

There is no single correct form for recording the information gathered during the psychiatric interview. But the therapist should follow a prescribed outline, such as the one used below, to make sure important developmental areas are covered and to point up any contradictions in the material presented.

Identification. This section should include the patient's name, age, sex, ethnic and cultural background, marital status, occupation, source of referral, housing situation, and hospitalizations. Identify informants.

Therapist's Personal Impressions. The therapist should give a brief, nontechnical description of the patient's appearance and behavior.

Chief Complaint. If possible, the patient's own words should be used to describe the complaint. He should be encouraged to explain its duration and occurrence, possible causes, intensity, and effects on him.

History of Present Illness. This section should include a chronological account, in the patient's own words, of how his symptoms and signs developed, including a description of his premorbid personality, his life circumstances when his symptoms began, the precipitating stresses or events, and the effects on his behavior, health, attitudes, and personal relationships.

Previous Illnesses. These illnesses may be categorized as emotional or mental disturbances, physiological disorders that may be psychogenic, medical conditions, and neurological disorders.

Personal History. This section should include a separate description of each period in the patient's life—infancy, childhood, adolescence, and adulthood. Gaps may be filled in later, when additional facts emerge during treatment, or information may be gathered from other sources. Also, such gaps may indicate that the patient is repressing particularly stressful or conflictual developmental events.

The personal history gives the psychiatrist an understanding of the patient's development, the environment in which it occurred, the significance of certain people, and the patient's adaptive techniques. The history is also a current commentary. It includes a description of the patient's present environment, of its stresses and sources of pleasure, and of the persons who are significant and influential. For each period of the patient's life, the report should include information about his social, sexual, and vocational functioning, the inhibitions imposed by excessive or inappropriate fear or guilt, and his sources of pleasure.

Family History. This section should include a description of the patient's parents and siblings and anyone else who lived with the family, including their names, ages, occupations, economic and social status, marital records, and major physical and emotional illnesses. Of particular importance are depression, psychiatric hospitalization, suicide, alcoholism, drug addiction, mental retardation, convulsive disorders, and syphilis. This section should also indicate how the patient felt about each relative, what their relationship was like, and what it is like now. Finally, the therapist should include a description of the family's ethnic and religious traditions and the psychological atmosphere in the home.

Mental Status Examination. The mental status examination gives the psychiatrist a precise picture of the patient's emotional status and mental capacity and functioning at the time of the psychiatric interview. The report should be organized in a certain order and according to certain categories, but the examination itself need not be conducted in that order. The psychiatrist may decide to emphasize certain areas of the mental examination, depending on the patient's problem and history, cooperation, and sensorium.

The report's categories might include a general description of the patient's appearance, behavior, and attitude; his speech; his alertness and orientation; his affective state; his level of anxiety; his stream of thought—including verbatim quotations—and content of thought; his memory; his information and intelligence; his ability to count, calculate, and do abstract thinking; his judgment and insight; and his dreams, fantasies, and value systems.

Summary of Positive Findings. The psychiatric report should include the findings derived from medical and neurological examinations and from psychological tests. The report should also list any drugs the patient has been taking, including dosage and duration of intake, since most sedative and hypnotic agents reduce perceptual acuity and motor skills when taken in small amounts and produce somnolence and stupor when taken in large amounts.

Diagnosis. Any diagnosis made after the psychiatric interview must be tentative. Some crucially important information may not have emerged, the patient may have withheld data deliberately, or he may have a severe disorder that is in a state of temporary remission. However, even the psychiatrist's tentative diagnosis should adhere to the standard nomenclature of the American Psychiatric Association.

Prognosis. The report should include the psychiatrist's assessment of the future course and outcome of the patient's illness, taking into account such factors as the particular illness and its natural history; self-limited treatment goals; the patient's assets and liabilities, such as his age, duration of the illness, and his early traumatic experiences; motivations for treatment; accessibility for treatment; and current life situation.

Recommendations for Treatment. After his systematic study of the patient, the psychiatrist should recommend an appropriate course of therapy—or no psychiatric treatment—on the basis of his understanding of the patient's development and the vicissitudes of his life experiences.

Ancillary Diagnostic Procedures

The psychiatrist may need findings derived from medical and neurological examinations and psychological tests to determine whether the patients' symptoms are psychiatric, physiological, or neurological in origin or whether he is suffering from a severe psychoneurosis or a borderline psychosis.

Medical Examination. The central nervous system can react to emotional stress or to physical stress by producing similar symptoms, and these symptoms can be physiological or psychological or both. Diagnostic difficulties arise when a systemic disease produces emotional symptoms. Anxiety, depression, fatigue, headaches, irritability, dizziness, poor or excessive appetite, drowsiness, and insomnia are usually due to psychogenic factors, but they may also be produced by infectious, toxic, metabolic, degenerative, neoplastic, and nutritional disorders. Depression may be an early sign of hepatitis, cirrhosis of the liver, or carcinoma of the pancreas. And fatigue, frequently associated with depression or anxiety, may be caused by a chronic infectious disease.

Neurological Examination. Disorders of perception and apperception, such as depersonalization phenomena or hallucinations, are sometimes caused by lesions or electrical stimulation of the temporal lobe or by certain chemical agents. Similarly, disorders of intellectual function—such as defects in memory, retention, and recall—may be caused by metabolic deficiency or damage to certain brain structures.

Behavioral assessment is a necessary part of neurological evaluation. Psychological tests and clinical observation sample the same aspects of behavior—speed of response, level of comprehension, use of language—but the tests are more reliable and precise. Psychological tests currently used to assess brain damage are summarized in Table 1 (Freedman and Kaplan).

Psychological Tests. Psychological tests are generally used to facilitate assessment of particular aspects of personality function, the nature and extent of psychopathology, the patient's intellectual potential, and possible brain damage. Some commonly used tests—measuring devices, which provide scores and normative standards; behavior samples, which allow qualitative observations within given areas of psychological functioning; and projective techniques—are described in Table 2, which was prepared for Freedman and Kaplan's *Comprehensive Textbook of Psychiatry.*

Psychological tests of personality function are particularly helpful when the psychiatrist needs more information about sensitive areas and he does not want to question the patient directly, lest his probing arouse excessive anxiety. And psychological tests of intellectual function can help the psychiatrist determine whether the patient's impaired functioning is due to cerebral disease, a basic intellectual deficiency, sociocultural factors, or a psychiatric disorder.

Nomenclature

Psychiatric clinical syndromes are currently classified according to the official nosological system of the American Psychiatric Association as published in the *Diag-*

Table 1. *Tests for Assessing Brain Damage**

Category	Subcategories	Remarks
General scales	Wechsler Adult Intelligence Scale (WAIS) Stanford-Binet Wechsler Intelligence Scale for Children (WISC)	Given the availability of adequate normative standards in relation to the patient's educational and cultural background, a performance significantly below expectations should raise the question of cerebral damage. This generalization applies to both adults and children.
Reasoning and problem solving	Abstractions (Shipley) Progressive matrices (Raven) Proverbs (Gorham) Perceptual mazes (Elithorn) Object and color-sorting tests (Goldstein and Scheerer)	Performance level is closely related to educational background and premorbid intellectual level. In general, the clinical application of these tests is more useful in the case of educated patients. If specific language and perceptual defect can be ruled out as determinants of defective performance, failure suggests frontal lobe involvement or diffuse cerebral disease.
Memory and orientation	Immediate auditory memory—repetition of digits Immediate auditory memory—reversal of digits Immediate visual memory (Benton, Graham-Kendall) Recent auditory memory—words or stories Recent visual memory—words or pictures Temporal orientation (Benton, Van Allen, and Fogel)	For complete assessment, a number of memory tasks (auditory vs. visual, verbal vs. nonverbal, immediate vs. recent) should be given. Minor defects in temporal orientation may be elicited and suggest weakness in recent memory.
Visuoperceptive and visuoconstructive	Identification of hidden figures (Teuber-Weinstein-Rudel) Identification of fragmented figures (Street-Gestalt) Block design construction (Kohs, Goldstein-Scheerer, Wechsler) Stick arranging (Goldstein-Scheerer) Copying designs (L. Bender, Benton visual retention) Three-dimensional block construction (Benton-Fogel) Inkblot interpretation (Rorschach, Holtzman) Perceptual mazes (Elithorn) Responsiveness to double visual stimulation (M. B. Bender)	These types of task are relatively sensitive indicators of the presence of cerebral disease. Analysis of qualitative features of performance and comparison of performance level with the status of language and reasoning abilities often provide indications with regard to locus of the lesion.
Somatoperceptual	Tactile recognition (Parker, Ross) Finger recognition (Benton) Right-left orientation (Benton) Responsiveness to double tactile stimulation (M. B. Bender)	Frequently useful indicators of the presence and locus of cerebral disease.
Language	Token test (De Renzi-Vignolo) Abstractions (Shipley) Proverbs (Gorham) Word fluency (Benton-Spreen-Fogel) Illinois test of psycholinguistic abilities (Kirk-McCarthy)	Test performance is dependent on educational background, and it is essential that clinical interpretation allow for this and other possibly significant factors. In adult patients, defective performance (particularly in relation to other abilities) suggests dysfunction of the cerebral hemisphere that is dominant for language. In children, defective performance does not have this localizing significance but does raise the question of the presence of cerebral damage.
Attention, concentration, and motor abilities	Continuous performance test (Rosvold) Visual vigilance (McDonald-Burns) Reaction time (Blackburn-Benton-Joynt) Motor impersistence (Garfield) Imitations of actions (Bergès-Lézine)	Valuable behavioral indicators of the presence (and sometimes locus) of cerebral disease that deserve more extensive clinical application.

* Adapted from *Comprehensive Textbook of Psychiatry*, edited by A. M. Freedman and H. I. Kaplan, Williams & Wilkins, Baltimore, 1967. Chart by Arthur Benton, Ph.D.

Table 2. Some Instruments Commonly Used by Clinical Psychologists*

Instrument	Description	Comments
Measuring Devices Benton Visual Retention Test	An individually administered test designed to measure visual memory, used for subjects 8 years of age and older.	This is one of a class of instruments used to investigate memory functions. It is most useful in differential diagnosis and in the evaluation of brain damage.
Cattell Infant Intelligence Scale	A downward extension of the Stanford-Binet test to cover ages 3 to 30 months.	This test has little predictive value for future intellectual level, particularly in the early ages. However, it does yield a good description of current functioning and is useful for the early diagnosis of mental retardation and brain damage.
Gesell Developmental Schedule	A scale based on behavioral observations, to measure development in different areas from the age of 4 weeks to 6 years.	Although the scale yields poor predictions for later developmental quotients, particularly during the early ages, it does yield a satisfactory picture of current functions. Clinically, it is most useful as a supplement to other data or when successive measurements are taken over a period of time.
Minnesota Multiphasic Personality Inventory	A questionnaire type of personality test for ages 16 years and over. May be administered individually or in groups. Yields 14 scores in scales representing diagnostic categories (such as hysteria, schizophrenia) and test-taking behavior (such as lying).	Besides the scales noted in the test manual, other scales, such as ego strength, have been reported in the literature. Although the administration and scoring of this test are quite simple, the interpretation of the score profiles may become rather complex and requires considerable experience.
Stanford-Binet Intelligence Scale, Form L-M, 1960	An individually administered age scale intelligence test designed to range from 2 years up. This is a revision based on the 1937 Forms L and M. It yields a mental age and a deviation I.Q.	This scale presents a wide variety of items and item difficulty. It is organized by item difficulty (i.e., age level). The choice between this scale and the WISC is often a matter of the preference of the individual clinician, with the Stanford-Binet usually being the most helpful at the lower age levels and at the extremes of intelligence.
Wechsler Adult Intelligence Scale (WAIS)	An individually administered intelligence test for ages 16 years and over. It yields scores for 11 subtests as well as verbal, performance, and full-scale I.Q.'s.	The items of this scale are organized according to the task presented, with a separate score for each type of task. Besides yielding information concerning the intellectual and cognitive functions, analysis of the pattern of subtest scores and qualitative examination of the protocol may yield information concerning the impact of psychopathology in these areas.
Wechsler Intelligence Scale for Children (WISC)	A downward extension of an earlier form of the WAIS to cover the ages below 16 years. Yields scores similar to the WAIS (one additional optional test) but with subtest scores based on chronological age; covers ages to 16 years.	As with the WAIS, the scale is often used for more than the determination of level of intelligence. The grouping of items by type of task involved makes it easier for the clinician in actual practice to use it as an instrument to investigate the impact of pathology in the intellectual and cognitive areas.

Table 2—Continued

Instrument	Description	Comments
Vineland Social Maturity Scale	An individual interview schedule aimed at determining rate of development. An age scale, it covers from birth to maturity. It yields a development quotient (D.Q.), which is the ratio of developmental age to chronological age.	This scale is simpler to administer and to score than is the Gesell scale, but it is based on reports rather than on direct observation. It does furnish a helpful picture of current developmental status, and it is strongest when used to supplement other data or to provide successive measures over time.
Behavior Samples Bender-Gestalt Test	An elicitation of visual-motor behavior by having the patient copy a set of geometric designs. Various modifications of administration may be introduced, such as having the designs redrawn from memory.	Although several scoring systems have been developed for this test, it is usually used qualitatively. Deficits in this area are often associated with brain damage, and the test is most used for differential diagnosis of brain damage. It may also be used to investigate developmental and intellectual levels in children and the characteristics of ego functions in adults. A number of clinicians use the instrument as a projective technique.
Examining for aphasia (Eisenson)	A systematic survey of the ability to receive and to express meaning through different modalities. It includes the aphasias, agnosias, and apraxias.	This instrument provides for behavior samples in various areas of language and symbolic function and at several levels within each area. As a quick survey, it is extremely useful where brain damage is suspected. However, further examination is usually necessary for treatment planning.
Goldstein-Scheerer Tests of Abstract and Concrete Thinking	A battery of five tests (cube test, color sorting, object sorting, color form sorting, stick test) to examine the ability to attain and to maintain the abstract attitude.	These tests afford opportunities to observe the patient attempting to solve problems that require abstraction and shifts in abstractions. Although other thought disorders, such as schizophrenic thinking, may be elicited, concrete thinking tends to be highlighted. The tests are most used for the diagnosis and the evaluation of brain damage.
Concept Formation Test (Kasanin and Hanfman)	A complex problem of grouping the Vigotsky Blocks is presented. Clues given and explanations of groupings are questioned.	The attempts to solve the complex problem provides opportunity to observe the patient's modes of thinking. The test is particularly useful in revealing patterns of schizophrenic thinking.
Projective Techniques Blacky Pictures	A series of 11 cartoons about a dog (Blacky) and his/her family. The patient makes up stories, answers more structured questions, and indicates like-dislike for the pictures.	The stimulus pictures depict different stages of psychosexual development. Its major use is with children, but it can be used with adults. Some writers suggest the following sequence: Blacky with younger children, CAT with older children and adolescents; TAT with adults. This, however, is very much at the discretion of the individual clinician.

Table 2—Continued

Instrument	Description	Comments
Draw a Person	The basic instruction is simply to draw a person, then to draw a person of the opposite sex. Many elaborations exist, including interviews about figures drawn.	This is one of a number of drawing projective techniques, including the drawing of a house, tree, person; of the family; of animals. The figure drawings, in general, may be interpreted as yielding data concerning self-concept, perception of significant figures, problem and conflict areas, mood, affect, and anxiety.
Rorschach	A series of 10 symmetrical ink-blots. The patient tells what he sees in each. This is followed by an inquiry concerning the responses. Different sets of stimulus cards are available, but the original Rorschach plates are by far the most frequently used.	This is the most useful single instrument of the clinical psychologist. Through analysis of perception, cognition, and content, information concerning almost every aspect of psychological organization may be revealed.
Sentence Completion Test	Incomplete sentences are completed by patient (e.g., "My mother . . . ."). Sentences may be aimed at specific potential conflict areas. Standard forms, such as the one by Rotter, are available.	This technique may be used at different levels from the prediction of overt behavior to the uncovering of deep personality dynamics. It yields data concerning conflict areas and emotional attitudes. This technique has the advantage of flexibility, for the skilled clinician may devise incomplete sentences tailored for a specific patient.
Thematic Apperception Test (TAT)	Patient makes up stories about stimulus pictures. Some pictures are specially designed for girls, boys, women, or men. Other sets of stimulus cards for special groups are available, such as the Children's Apperception Test (CAT), which uses pictures of animals.	This test helps to furnish the content of the patient's inner life. It may be said with some truth that the Rorschach furnishes the skeleton on which to hang the flesh and blood of the TAT. It yields data concerning, among other things, needs, pressures, self-concept, motives, fantasies, attitudes, and feelings.

* Adapted from *Comprehensive Textbook of Psychiatry*, edited by A. M. Freedman and H. I. Kaplan, Williams & Wilkins, Baltimore, 1967. Chart by Herbert Fensterheim, Ph.D.

nostic and Statistical Manual of Mental Disorders (*DSM-II*) and as outlined in Table 3. This system of nosology is not entirely satisfactory, chiefly because the causes of many psychiatric disorders are not yet fully understood. The system is, therefore, based on superficial characteristics and must be considered artificial. But an artificial system is far better than none at all, and so it is generally used.

More than one category of disturbance may be seen in a patient, and so the first edition of the manual (*DSM-I*), published in 1952, supported the concept of multiple diagnoses, but certain combinations of diagnoses were not permitted. For example, Alcoholism could not be listed as a separate diagnosis when it was associated with an underlying disorder. In contrast *DSM-II* encourages clinicians to diagnose every disorder present, even if one is the symptomatic expression of another. Also, *DSM-II* makes greater use of qualifying phrases—acute and chronic, not psychotic, in remission, mild, moderate, and severe.

Table 3. *Classifications of Mental Disorders According to DSM-II**

I. Mental Retardation—subnormal intellectual functioning. Retardation begins during the developmental period and is associated with impairment in maturation or in learning and social adjustment or both.

Borderline: I.Q. of 68 to 85
Mild: I.Q. of 52 to 67
Moderate: I.Q. of 36 to 51
Severe: I.Q. of 20 to 35
Profound: I.Q. under 20

Clinical Subcategories of Mental Retardation:

After Infection and Intoxication (congenital cytomegalic inclusion body disease, rubella, syphilis, toxoplasmosis; encephalopathy associated with other prenatal infections, due to postnatal cerebral infection, associated with maternal toxemia of pregnancy, bilirubin, and postimmunization).

After Trauma or Physical Agent (encephalopathy due to prenatal injury, mechanical injury at birth, asphyxia at birth, and postnatal injury).

Associated with Disorders of Metabolism, Growth, or Nutrition (cerebral lipoidosis, lipid histiocytosis, phenylketonuria, hepatolenticular degeneration, porphyria, galactosemia, glucogenosis, and hypoglycemosis).

Associated with Gross Brain Disease, postnatal (neurofibromatosis, trigeminal cerebral angiomatosis, tuberous sclerosis, encephalopathy associated with diffuse sclerosis of the brain).

Associated with Diseases and Conditions Due to Unknown Prenatal Influence (anencephaly, malformations of the gyri, congenital porencephaly, multiple congenital anomalies of the brain, craniostenosis, congenital hydrocephalus, hypertelorism, macrocephaly, primary microcephaly, and Laurence-Moon-Biedl syndrome).

Associated with Chromosomal Abnormality.

Associated with Prematurity.

After Major Psychiatric Disorder.

Associated with Psychosocial Factors (environmental deprivation).

II. Organic Brain Syndromes—disorders characterized by impairment of brain tissue function and resulting in impairment of orientation, memory, intellectual functions, and judgment and in shallow affects (the acute form is reversible; the chronic form is permanent).

A. Psychoses Associated with Organic Brain Syndromes:

Senile Dementia—occurs with senile brain disease in old people; manifested by self-centeredness, childish emotionality, difficulty in assimilating new experiences, and deterioration—sometimes to the point of vegetative existence.

Presenile Dementia—covers cortical brain diseases similar to senile dementia but occurring in younger people; examples include Alzheimer's and Pick's diseases.

Delirium Tremens—acute brain syndrome caused by alcohol poisoning and characterized by delirium, visual hallucinations, and coarse tremors.

Korsakov's Psychosis—(alcoholic) chronic brain syndrome caused by long-time alcohol poisoning and characterized by confabulation, memory impairment, disorientation, and peripheral neuropathy.

Other Alcoholic Hallucinosis—hallucinosis caused by alcohol but not categorized as delirium tremens, alcoholic deterioration, or Korsakov's psychosis. The patient may have threatening auditory hallucinations, while his sensorium is relatively clear.

Alcohol Paranoid State—paranoid state in chronic alcoholics characterized by excessive jealousy and delusions of the spouse's infidelity.

Acute Alcohol Intoxication—covers acute brain syndromes caused by alcohol and of psychotic proportion but not categorized as delirium tremens, acute hallucinosis, or pathological intoxication.

Alcoholic Deterioration—covers chronic brain syndromes caused by alcohol and of psychotic proportion but not categorized as Korsakov's psychosis.

Pathological Intoxication—acute brain syndrome of psychotic proportion after a small intake of alcohol.

Psychosis Associated with Intracranial Infection, General Paralysis—psychosis characterized by signs and symptoms of parenchymatous syphilis of the nervous system and usually by positive serology.

Table 3—Continued

Psychosis with Other Syphilis of Central Nervous System—covers all other psychoses caused by intracranial infection by *Spirochaeta pallida*.

Psychosis with Epidemic Encephalitis (von Economo's Encephalitis)—disorder caused by post-World War I viral epidemic encephalitis.

Psychosis with Other and Unspecified Encephalitis—includes disorders caused by encephalitic infections other than epidemic encephalitis and encephalitis not otherwise specified.

Psychosis with Other and Unspecified Intracranial Infection—covers acute and chronic conditions caused by nonsyphilitic and nonencephalitic infections, including meningitis and brain abscess.

Psychosis with Cerebral Arteriosclerosis—chronic disorder caused by cerebral arteriosclerosis; it may coexist with senile dementia or presenile dementia.

Psychosis with Other Cerebrovascular Circulatory Disturbance—disturbances such as cerebral thrombosis, cerebral embolism, arterial hypertension, cardiac disease, and cardiorenal disease.

Psychosis with Epilepsy—condition associated with idiopathic epilepsy; the patient's consciousness may be clouded or he may be dazed, confused, bewildered, and anxious; on occasion he may have an episode of excitement, hallucinations, fears, and violent outbreaks.

Psychosis with Intracranial Neoplasm—includes primary and metastatic neoplasms.

Psychosis with Degenerative Disease of the Central Nervous System.

Psychosis with Brain Trauma—covers posttraumatic chronic brain disorders and disorders that develop immediately after a severe head injury or brain surgery and that produce significant changes in sensorium and affect.

Psychosis with Endocrine Disorder—covers disorders caused by complications of diabetes and by disorders of the endocrine glands.

Psychosis with Metabolic or Nutritional Disorder—covers disorders caused by pellagra, avitaminosis, and metabolic disorders.

Psychosis with Systemic Infection—covers disorders caused by such severe general systemic infections as pneumonia, acute rheumatic fever, typhoid fever, and malaria.

Psychosis with Drug or Poison Intoxication (other than alcohol)—covers disorders caused by drugs such as psychedelic drugs and by hormones, gases, heavy metals, and other intoxicants except alcohol.

Psychosis with Childbirth—not used unless all other possible diagnoses have been eliminated.

Psychosis with Other and Undiagnosed Physical Condition—covers psychoses caused by physical conditions not already listed and brain syndromes caused by physical conditions not yet diagnosed.

B. Nonpsychotic Organic Brain Syndromes—children with mild brain damage often show hyperactivity, short attention span, easy distractibility, and impulsiveness; they are sometimes withdrawn, listless, perseverative, and unresponsive; a few have difficulty in initiating action. Subcategories include nonpsychotic organic brain syndromes with intracranial infection; with drug, poison, or systemic intoxication; with brain trauma; with circulatory disturbance; with epilepsy; with disturbance of metabolism, growth, or nutrition; with senile or presenile brain disease; with intracranial neoplasm; and with degenerative disease of central nervous system.

III. Psychoses Not Attributed to Physical Conditions Listed Previously:

A. Schizophrenia—covers disorders manifested by disturbances of thinking (alterations of concept formation that may lead to misinterpretation of reality and sometimes to delusions and hallucinations), mood (ambivalent, constricted, and inappropriate responsiveness and loss of empathy with others), and behavior (withdrawn, regressive, and bizarre).

Simple Type—schizophrenia characterized by slow reduction of external attachment and interests, by apathy and indifference, by impoverishment of interpersonal relations, by mental deterioration, and by a low level of functioning.

Hebephrenic Type—schizophrenia characterized by disorganized thinking, unpredictable giggling, shallow and inappropriate affect, silly and regressive behavior and mannerisms, frequent hypochrondriacal complaints, and, occasionally, transient and unorganized delusions and hallucinations.

Catatonic Type—the excited subtype is characterized by excessive and sometimes violent motor activity; the withdrawn subtype is characterized by generalized inhibition—stupor, mutism, negativism, waxy flexibility, or, in some cases, a vegetative state.

Paranoid Type—schizophrenia characterized by persecutory or grandiose delusions and sometimes by hallucinations or excessive religiosity; the patient is often hostile and aggressive.

Table 3—Continued

Acute Schizophrenic Episode—condition characterized by acute onset of schizophrenic symptoms and confusion, emotional turmoil, perplexity, ideas of reference, dreamlike dissociation, excitement, depression, or fear.

Latent Type—schizophrenia characterized by clear symptoms but no history of a psychotic schizophrenic episode; sometimes called incipient, prepsychotic, pseudoneurotic, pseudopsychopathic, or borderline schizophrenia.

ₗ*Residual Type*—covers patients with signs of schizophrenia after a psychotic schizophrenic episode but who are no longer psychotic.

Schizo-affective Type—covers patients with a mixture of schizophrenic symptoms and pronounced elation (excited subtype) or depression (depression subtypes).

Childhood Type—schizophrenia that appears before puberty. It is characterized by autistic, atypical, and withdrawn behavior; failure to develop identity separate from the mother's; and general unevenness, gross immaturity, and inadequacy in development.

Chronic Undifferentiated Type—schizophrenia with mixed symptoms or with definite schizophrenic thought, affect, and behavior not categorized elsewhere.

Other and Unspecified Types—schizophrenia not previously described.

B. Major Affective Disorders—psychoses characterized by a single disorder of mood—extreme depression or elation—that dominates the patient's mental life and is responsible for loss of contact with his environment but that is not precipitated by any life experience.

Involutional Melancholia—psychosis occurring during the involutional period and characterized by anxiety, agitation, worry, and severe insomnia and frequently by somatic preoccupations and feelings of guilt.

Manic-Depressive Illnesses—psychoses marked by severe mood swings and by remission and recurrence.

Manic Type—manic-depressive illness that consists of manic episodes only—excessive elation, talkativeness, irritability, flights of ideas, and accelerated motor activity and speech.

Depressive Type—manic-depressive illness that consists of depressive episodes only—severely depressed mood, mental and motor retardation, and sometimes apprehension, uneasiness, perplexity, agitation, illusions, hallucinations, and delusions of guilt.

Circular Type—manic-depressive illness characterized by at least one attack of a depressive episode and of a manic episode.

Other Major Affective Disorder—psychosis with no more specific diagnosis or mixed manic-depressive illness, in which manic and depressive symptoms appear almost simultaneously.

C. Paranoid States—psychotic disorders in which a persecutory or grandiose delusion is the essential abnormality.

Paranoia—a rare condition characterized by gradual development of an elaborate paranoid system based on an actual event; the patient often considers himself unique and superior; the chronic condition rarely interferes with his thinking and personality.

Involutional Paranoid State—paranoid psychosis characterized by delusional formation in the involutional period.

Other Paranoid State—covers paranoid psychotic reactions not previously classified.

D. Psychotic Depressive Reaction—psychosis characterized by a depressive mood caused by a real experience but with no history of repeated depressions or mood swings.

IV. Neuroses—disorders characterized by anxiety but not by gross personality disorganization or gross distortion or misinterpretation of external reality.

Anxiety Neurosis—neurosis characterized by anxious overconcern to the point of panic; often associated with somatic symptoms.

Hysterical Neurosis—neurosis characterized by involuntary psychogenic loss or functional disorder; symptoms begin and end suddenly in emotionally charged situations symbolic of underlying conflict.

Conversion Type—hysterical neurosis in which the special senses or voluntary nervous system is affected, causing blindness, deafness, anosmia, anesthesias, paresthesias, paralyses, ataxias, akinesias, or dyskinesias; the patient often shows inappropriate lack of concern and may derive some benefits from his symptoms.

Dissociative Type—hysterical neuroses in which alterations in the patient's state of consciousness or his identity produce amnesia, somnambulism, fugue, or multiple personality.

Table 3—Continued

Phobic Neurosis—neurosis characterized by intense fear of an object or situation that the patient knows is no real danger to him but that causes faintness, palpitations, perspiration, nausea, fatigue, tremor, and panic.

Obsessive-Compulsive Neurosis—neurosis characterized by the involuntary and persistent intrusion of thought, urges, or actions and often accompanied by anxiety and distress.

Depressive Neurosis—neurosis marked by excessive depression caused by an internal conflict or an identifiable event or loss.

Neurasthenic Neurosis—neurosis characterized by complaints of chronic weakness, easy fatigability, and exhaustion, which distress the patient.

Depersonalization Neurosis—syndrome characterized by a feeling of unreality and estrangement from the body, self, or surroundings.

Hypochondriacal Neurosis—condition marked by preoccupation with the body and persistent fears of presumed disease.

Other Neurosis—covers psychoneurotic disorders not classified previously.

V. Personality Disorders and Certain Other Nonpsychotic Mental Disorders:

A. Personality Disorders—disorders characterized by deeply ingrained, generally life-long maladaptive patterns of behavior that are usually recognizable by adolescence or earlier.

Paranoid Personality—behavioral pattern characterized by unwarranted suspicion, hypersensitivity, jealousy, envy, rigidity, excessive self-importance, and a tendency to blame and ascribe evil motives to others—symptoms that often interfere with ability to maintain satisfactory interpersonal relations.

Cyclothymic Personality—behavior pattern characterized by recurring and alternating periods of elation (marked by optimism, ambition, high energy, warmth, and enthusiasm) and depression (marked by pessimism, low energy, worry, and a sense of futility)—moods that are not attributable to external circumstances.

Schizoid Personality—behavior pattern characterized by shyness, oversensitivity, seclusiveness, avoidance of close or competitive relationships, and eccentricity and sometimes by autistic thinking without loss of capacity to recognize reality, by daydreaming, and by inability to express hostility and aggression.

Explosive Personality—behavior pattern characterized by sudden, gross outbursts of aggressiveness or rage that differ strikingly from the patient's usual behavior.

Obsessive-Compulsive Personality—behavior pattern characterized by excessive concern with conformity and standards of conscience; patient may be rigid, overconscientious, overdutiful, overinhibited, and unable to relax.

Hysterical Personality—behavior pattern characterized by emotional instability, excitability, overreactivity, vanity, immaturity, dependence, and self-dramatization that is attention-seeking and seductive.

Asthenic Personality—behavior pattern characterized by low energy, easy fatigability, lack of enthusiasm, inability to enjoy life, and oversensitivity to stress.

Antisocial Personality—covers unsocialized persons in conflict with society—persons who are incapable of loyalty, selfish, callous, irresponsible, impulsive, unable to feel guilt or learn from experience, with a low level of frustration tolerance and a tendency to blame others.

Passive-Aggressive Personality—behavior pattern characterized by both passivity and aggressiveness, which is often expressed passively in obstructionism, pouting, procrastination, inefficiency, and stubbornness.

Inadequate Personality—behavior pattern characterized by ineffectual responses to demands—by ineptness, poor judgment, social instability, inadapatbility, and lack of stamina.

Other Personality Disorders of Specified Types.

B. Sexual Deviations—covers persons whose sexual interests are primarily directed toward objects other than people of the opposite sex, toward sexual acts not usually associated with coitus, or toward coitus performed under bizarre circumstances. Included are such deviations as homosexuality, fetishism, pedophilia, transvestitism, exhibitionism, voyeurism, sadism, and masochism.

C. Alcoholism—covers patients whose alcohol intake damages their physical health or personal or social functioning and those to whom alcohol is essential.

Table 3—Continued

Episodic Excessive Drinking—condition when alcoholism is present and person becomes intoxicated at least four times a year.

Habitual Excessive Drinking—condition when alcoholic becomes intoxicated (impaired speech, coordination, or behavior) more than 12 times a year or is recognizably under the influence of alcohol more than once a week, though not intoxicated.

Alcohol Addiction—condition when patient is dependent on alcohol—suffers withdrawal symptoms.

D. Drug Dependence—covers patients addicted to or dependent on drugs other than alcohol, tobacco, and caffeine beverages. Patient may be dependent on opium, opium alkaloids, and their derivatives; synthetic analgesics with morphinelike effects; barbiturates; other hypnotics, sedatives, or tranquilizers; cocaine; *Cannabis sativa* (hashish and marijuana); other psychostimulants such as amphetamines; and hallucinogens.

VI. Psychophysiological Disorders—disorders characterized by physical symptoms caused by emotional factors and involving a single organ system, usually under autonomic nervous system control.

Psychophysiological Skin Disorder—covers reactions like neurodermatosis, pruritis, atopic dermatitis, and hyperhydrosis, caused by emotional factors.

Psychophysiological Musculoskeletal Disorder—covers disorders like backache, muscle cramps, myalgias, and tension headaches caused by emotional factors.

Psychophysiological Respiratory Disorder—covers disorders like bronchial asthma, hyperventilation syndromes, sighing, and hiccoughs, caused by emotional factors.

Psychophysiological Cardiovascular Disorder—covers disorders like hypertension, vascular spasms, paroxysmal tachycardia, and migraine caused by emotional factors.

Psychophysiological Hemic and Lymphatic Disorder—covers any hemic and lymphatic disturbances caused by emotional factors.

Psychophysiological Gastrointestinal Disorder—covers such disorders as peptic ulcer, constipation, chronic gastritis, ulcerative and mucous colitis, hyperacidity, pylorospasm, heartburn, and irritable colon caused by emotional factors.

Psychophysiological Genitourinary Disorder—covers such disorders as dyspareunia, impotence, and disturbances in menstruation and micturition that are caused by emotional factors.

Psychophysiological Endocrine Disorder—covers endocrine disorders caused by emotional factors.

Psychophysiological Disorder of Organ of Special Sense—covers any disturbance, except conversion reactions, in the organs of special sense that are caused by emotional factors.

VII. Special Symptoms Not Elsewhere Classified—covers psychopathologies manifested by a single specific symptom that is not the result of an organic or other mental disorder. Included are speech disturbance, specific learning disturbance, tic, other psychomotor disorder, sleep disorder, feeding disturbance, enuresis, encopresis, and cephalalgia.

VIII. Transient Situational Disturbances—temporary disorders of any severity that occur without any apparent underlying disorder and that are acute reactions to environmental stress. Disorders are classified as adjustment reaction of infancy, childhood, adolescence, adult life, or late life.

IX. Behavior Disorders of Childhood and Adolescence—disorders that are more stable, internalized, and resistant to treatment than transient situational disturbances but less so than psychoses, neuroses, and personality disorders. Characteristic symptoms include overactivity, inattentiveness, overaggressiveness, delinquency, shyness, feeling of rejection, and timidity.

Hyperkinetic Reaction of Childhood or Adolescence—disorder characterized by overactivity, restlessness, distractibility, and short attention span, especially in young children.

Withdrawing Reaction of Childhood or Adolescence—disorder characterized by shyness, timidity, seclusiveness, detachment, sensitivity, and inability to form close interpersonal relationships.

Overanxious Reaction of Childhood or Adolescence—disorder characterized by chronic anxiety, sleeplessness, nightmares, excessive and unrealistic fears, and exaggerated autonomic responses. The patient is usually immature, self-conscious, conforming, inhibited, dutiful, lacking in self-confidence, approval seeking, and apprehensive in new situations and places.

Runaway Reaction of Childhood or Adolescence—covers patients who characteristically run away from home for a day or more to escape threatening situations, who steal furtively, who are immature and timid, and who feel rejected at home, friendless, and inadequate.

Table 3—Continued

Unsocialized Aggressive Reaction of Childhood or Adolescence—disorder characterized by hostile disobedience, aggressiveness, quarrelsomeness, vengefulness, destructiveness, temper tantrums, solitary stealing, lying, and hostile teasing of other children. The patients usually have no consistent parental discipline or acceptance.

Group Delinquent Reaction of Childhood or Adolescence—covers patients, usually boys, who accept the values, behavior, and skills of their gang, with whom they steal, skip school, and stay out late at night.

Other Reaction of Childhood or Adolescence—covers children and adolescents with disorders not previously categorized.

X. Conditions without Manifest Psychiatric Disorder and Nonspecific Conditions:

A. Social Maladjustments without Manifest Psychiatric Disorder—covers persons who are psychiatrically normal but who have severe problems.

Marital Maladjustment—covers normal persons with significant conflicts in marriage.

Social Maladjustment—covers culture shocks and conflicts caused by loyalties to two cultures.

Occupational Maladjustment—covers normal persons who are grossly maladjusted in their work.

Dyssocial Behavior—covers persons who follow criminal pursuits but are not categorized as antisocial personalities.

B. Nonspecific Conditions—covers conditions not classified under any other category.

---

* This table is based on the American Psychiatric Association's *Diagnostic and Statistical Manual of Mental Disorders*, second edition (DSM-II).

REFERENCES

American Psychiatric Association. *Diagnostic and Statistical Manual of Mental Disorders*, ed. 2 (DSM-II). American Psychiatric Association, Washington, 1968.

Blum, R. H. *The Management of the Doctor-Patient Relationship*. McGraw-Hill, New York, 1960.

Deutsch, F., and Murphy, W. F. *The Clinical Interview*, vol. 1. International Universities Press, New York, 1955.

Finesinger, J. E. Psychiatric interviewing: principles and procedure in insight therapy. Amer. J. Psychiat., *105*: 187, 1948.

Freedman, A. M., and Kaplan, H. I., editors. *Comprehensive Textbook of Psychiatry*. Williams & Wilkins, Baltimore, 1967.

Freud, S. The dynamics of the transference. In *Collected Papers*, vol. 2, p. 312. Hogarth Press, London, 1946.

Freud, S. Fragment of an analysis of a case of hysteria. In *Collected Papers*, vol. 3, p. 13. Hogarth Press, London, 1946.

Gill, M., Newman, R., and Redlich, F. C. *The Initial Interview in Psychiatric Practice*. International Universities Press, New York, 1954.

Lewin, B. D. Counter-transference in the technique of medical practice. Psychosom. Med., *8:* 195, 1946.

Lewis, N. D. C. *Outlines for Psychiatric Examination*, ed. 3. State Hospitals Press, Utica, N. Y., 1943.

Menninger, K. *A Manual for Psychiatric Case Study*. Grune & Stratton, New York, 1952.

Ripley, H. Psychiatric interview. In *Comprehensive Textbook of Psychiatry*, p. 491, A. M. Freedman and H. I. Kaplan, editors. Williams & Wilkins, Baltimore, 1967.

Rogers, C. R. *Client-Centered Therapy*. Houghton Mifflin, Boston, 1951.

Sullivan, H. S. *The Psychiatric Interview*. W. W. Norton, New York, 1954.

Whitehorn, J. C. Guide to interviewing and clinical personality study. Arch. Neurol. Psychiat., *52:* 197, 1944.

6

Selection of Patients and the Dynamic and Structural Organization of the Group

Benjamin J. Sadock, M.D. and Harold I. Kaplan, M.D.

SELECTION OF PATIENTS

When the group concept is used as the psychotherapeutic vehicle for change in personality functioning, careful selection of patients and careful group organization is an essential clinical responsibility. Group psychotherapy cannot be applied as a blanket form of psychiatric treatment suitable for all types of emotional disorders, even though a great variety of patient populations have been exposed to the method. For instance, the patient who has had destructive relationships with his peer group or one who has been extremely isolated from peer-group contact (such as the schizoid personality) generally reacts negatively or with increased anxiety when placed in the group setting. On the other hand, patients whose major problem is in their sibling relationship may have a corrective emotional experience. These patients act out their feelings toward the other members and, if properly handled by the therapist, they are subject to analysis and objective understanding. The reality of having other patients with whom to interact often leads to more insight than a verbal reconstruction obtained in individual psychotherapy.

DYNAMIC ORGANIZATION OF THE GROUP

Once having decided that a particular patient is suitable for group psychotherapy, it is necessary to place him in a group where he can freely communicate with others, including the therapist. The proper organization of the group is crucial if a therapeutic atmosphere, conducive to personality change, is to occur for all the participants. This requires that a number of parameters (discussed below) be considered.

It should be noted that even with the most careful thought being given to its organization, each group will develop a unique ambiance that cannot be replicated. As each individual is unique, so is each group. The challenge of proper group organization is for the therapist to be as aware as possible of the potential varieties of interaction that are to unfold. The better the clinician's ability to postulate a hypothesis about the interaction between patient A and patient B and the constructive potential in that interaction, the more assured he can be about his having organized the group properly. The gratification in group work is to be able to help the participants achieve emotional growth and development as a result of their collective interaction. To organize a group at random by taking patients into a group simply on the basis of their presenting themselves for treatment—unless particular research issues are being investigated—is to do the patients and the modality a disservice.

Authority Anxiety

Those patients whose primary problem centers about their relationship to authority and who are extremely anxious in the presence of authority figures often do better in the group setting than in the dyadic or one-to-one setting. They gain support from the peer group and are thus aided in dealing with the therapist more realistically. Able to identify with others in the group who may have less difficulty in this area, they are eventually better able to perceive the therapist as less punitive or authoritarian than they had believed him to be.

Defense Mechanisms

Projection. The positive indications for group psychotherapy include those patients who use projection as a way of attributing to others impulses they find unacceptable in themselves. Such patients persistently blame others for their own inadequacies and failures and distort the realities of the outside world. They are reluctant to talk about their own motives and avoid introspection, which they fear might lead to an uncovering of their own unwanted, shameful, and guilt-ridden thoughts. In the one-to-one setting those patients may be unable to establish a working relationship with the therapist because of their tendency to project onto him thoughts and feelings (generally negative ones) which interfere and are not available for reality-testing.

In the group setting, this particular defense mechanism can be effectively dealt with by the other group members, who constantly confront such a patient with his distortions as they are directed toward them or the therapist. Such group processes force introspective analysis to occur, and the projective mechanism is thereby eroded. One of the problems to be faced by the therapist is that often the patient using this defense may make accurate observations of others, since he may be especially sensitive to finding in them the same faults he himself possesses. Thus, his observations about others may be accurate. Accordingly, the therapist cannot always assume the observation to be incorrect; but he must make certain that the projecting member take responsibility for the same character trait in himself that he notes in others.

Repression, Denial, and Suppression. These defenses are among the most common. They are characterized by the individual's eliminating from consciousness all thoughts, feelings, memories, strivings, impulses, and other mental experiences that constitute a threat to the person's self-image and the image he wishes others to have of him or her. Repression relates to denial except that, in the latter, it is external reality rather than internal reality that is transformed so as not to be painful. Suppression—not to be confused with repression, which occurs outside of the person's awareness—is a conscious attempt to withhold painful material.

Repression, denial, and suppression are particularly well-suited for examination in group psychotherapy. Where these defenses are delineated in the screening interview, the clinician should consider the advantages of group treatment. Without losing sight of the important distinctions between these different but related defenses, they can be considered together for purposes of discussion.

When denial is the major mental mechanism employed by the patient who finds an aspect of his external life situation too painful to see realistically, the group is not only able to correct the distortion but is capable of helping the patient examine a variety of ways in which the situation can be coped with more effectively. The well-organized group will have within it a diverse membership capable of providing role-models that enable each to learn from the other. Finally, where denial of illness is the major problem, feedback from others in the group may be the first step in getting the patient to recognize that emotional disturbance exists.

Transference

One of the characteristics of all in-depth psychotherapies—particularly those that are psychoanalytically oriented—is a close examination of the distortions that exist in the feelings of the patient to the therapist. Such transference examination rests on the premise that the patient will react to the therapist in the same way that he reacted to significant figures in his past life and, as this is analyzed, emotional growth and development will occur. But sometimes the intensity of the transference is such that it cannot be analyzed in the one-to-one relationship, either because it takes on such negative aspects that the patient can no longer tolerate the feelings and leaves treatment entirely, or it becomes fixed. Wolf has called the fixed transference, the "transference psychosis." This differs from the transference neurosis, which is the more flexible, analyzable state. The fixed transference is not always negative; it can be positive to the extent that it becomes an erotic fixation on the therapist, a condition which is equally resistant to interpretation and change.

Patients who are likely to develop a psychotic transferential reaction to the therapist (either positive or negative) are best placed in a group in addition to or in place of individual therapy. Where the transference is negative, the patient has the opportunity to observe his or her co-patients react to the therapist in a distinctly different manner. This aids his or her reality-testing because it becomes difficult to maintain irrational negative attitudes in the face of most, if not all, of the group members having a different perceptual framework. Where the transference is positive, the group setting provides the opportunity for certain elements of the transference to be diluted into other members. It also does not allow the patient to harbor the fantasy (common in this condition) that he or she is the only patient of the therapist's. The fact that the therapist directs his attention to other patients in the group is an inherent reality-testing function built into the group situation.

DIAGNOSTIC FACTORS IN SELECTION

The diagnosis of the patient's disorder is important in determining the best thera-

peutic approach for a particular case as well as in evaluating the motivation for treatment, the capacity for change, and the strengths and weaknesses of the personality structure. Diagnosis is more than nosological pigeonholing. Those workers who suggest the diagnosis is unimportant in group therapy take too simplistic a view of the diagnostic process, which includes, routinely, an extensive examination of the patient's chief complaint along with a detailed evaluation of the past developmental history, including a review of the levels of functioning in various life areas—vocational, familial, social, marital, sexual, etc. The mental status provides clues to the psychopathological processes at work currently, in the past, and under stress, and it also serves as a predictor to the patient's characteristic response to stress.

Schizophrenia

This large category includes a group of disorders characterized by disturbances of thinking, mood, and behavior which may or may not have the secondary symptoms of hallucinations, illusions, and delusions. The schizophrenic generally has a history of severe emotional deprivation, and may be in poor control of his or her impulses and be in a chronic state of anxiety and agitation. The fear of a loss of reality-testing can be omnipresent, and most schizophrenics display mistrust of others, thus leading an isolated, socially withdrawn type of existence.

Accordingly, the group experience for the schizophrenic patient requires a therapeutic atmosphere which supports reality-orientation and encourages a sense of relating to others to combat the feelings of fear and distrust. The emphasis on reality-testing diminishes the concentration on unconscious material to the extent that the therapist would attempt such exploration with the psychoneurotic disorders. Additionally, the group is geared to be socially supportive and, toward this end, outside group contact has been advocated by certain workers, because for many patients the group provides their only socialization experience in an otherwise bleak and dreary existence.

If there is a contraindication to be found, it is in certain technical procedures rather than in the group modality. Thus, other patients in the group may interact and interpret in ways that threaten a particular patient's defense system. Skillful handling by the therapist is necessary to overcome this difficulty, although there is some safety in the fact that the schizophrenic in group is much more leader-oriented than peer-oriented and will be more susceptible to interpretation and direction offered by the leader.

Affective Disorders

This category of illness includes the involutional depressions as well as the manic-depressive disorders. These patients have the least successful outcome in group psychotherapy. Where depression is the major symptom and suicide represents a real risk, hospitalization is preferable to outpatient treatment of any kind. The depressed patient especially, who requires a high degree of emotional support and nurturance, may have his symptoms aggravated by placement in a group because of the immediate dilution of the nurturance factor, which he or she seeks primarily from the leader. If the patient had been previously integrated into a group and the onset depression occurs after he or she has been an active participant, the group can provide a great deal of emotional gratification. But the severely depressed, suicidal patient should not be placed as a new member in group on an outpatient basis.

Manic patients, who do not necessarily suffer from conscious suicidal ideas, are nonetheless extremely difficult patients to manage in the group setting. Their illness, characterized by excessive elation, talkativeness, and irritability, often antagonizes both the group members as well as the leader, and the group is often unable to control these patients' accelerated speech and motor activity.

Paranoid States

This category includes patients considered psychotic because of delusional manifestations. Such patients generally are resistant to most forms of psychotherapy. Where there is a risk of the patient incorporating the group into his paranoid delusion, it is unlikely that effective reality-testing will be possible. But when the illness is less severe, as in the paranoid personality who is still capable of being influenced by the consensual validation of the group, such treatment may be quite effective and superior to the one-to-one therapeutic situation. The major defense mechanism employed by the paranoid personality, which accounts for his suspicion, jealousy, and tendency to blame others, is projection, and, as mentioned earlier, the projective defense leads itself to accurate and effective interpretation by the group as a whole. These patients often have extremely poor interpersonal relationships and in large measure the group is a laboratory in which they can use the feedback from peers to learn new adaptive patterns that contribute to improved social relationships as well as to an understanding of the life stresses that caused the particular paranoid pattern to develop.

Neuroses

Traditionally, the neurotic patient is aware of his difficulty, which is mainly manifested by anxiety. The patient is generally well-motivated to obtain relief from his symptoms, and most group psychotherapy approaches—as well as individual psychotherapy approaches—have been attempted with this patient population. Every category of neurosis has been treated with some degree of success. While the majority of psychoneurotic conditions have been treated in psychoanalytically oriented group psychotherapy, in recent years behavioral group therapy has been used with increasing success for the phobic disorders via operant conditioning and desensitization procedures.

Where the depressive neurosis exists, care should be taken in placing such a patient into a group as the first therapeutic intervention. The therapist should have a clear understanding of the precipitating factors behind the depressive condition, and an accurate determination of suicide potential, if any, should be ascertained. Generally, the episodically depressed patient who does not require hospitalization will do best in group after he has established a warm, supportive relationship with the therapist. In an ongoing group, episodes of depression in one of the members can usually be handled quite well by exploring the genesis and dynamics of the depression while the patient is supported in these efforts by a group with whom he has already established empathic ties.

Personality Disorders

This group of disorders is characterized by life-long patterns of maladaptive behavior about which the patient may be completely unaware except for vague feelings of dissatisfaction with his life. Many workers consider group psychotherapy the treatment of choice for this category of illness, because most patients tend to deny or rationalize their maladaptive behavior. Their characteristic behavioral patterns manifest themselves in the group, which then reflects back to the patient the effects of these patterns on his interpersonal relationships, which have either been chaotic or nonexistent. Such vigorous confrontations force the patient to examine his behavior, and, once recognizing it as pathological, he is then able to gain some insight into its development and ways to change it. Certain modifications in technique or frank contraindications to group treatment exist with some of the following sub-groups classified as personality disorders.

Schizoid Personality

These patients require an extremely supportive group milieu in that they are generally shy, oversensitive, and avoid close or competitive relationships with others. The group therapist must be constantly alert to the feelings of rejection experienced by these patients without any apparent cause and about which they tend to remain silent.

They are seclusive and nonparticipating in therapy, and efforts must be made to include them in group interaction. A well-functioning established group will recognize the withdrawal pattern in one of its members, as will an alert leader, but there is a risk that the more verbal, healthier patient will tend to overshadow the schizoid member. Accordingly, specific techniques, such as the go-round, may have to be employed to engage his or her active participation in the group. There is no doubt, however, about the efficacy of the group experience for the schizoid personality pattern. For a clinician to deny such an experience to a schizoid patient is to do the patient a great disservice.

Explosive-Aggressive Personality

The personality pattern marked by gross outbursts of physical or verbal aggressiveness creates a specific problem for the group therapist. These patients chronically overreact and are often incapable of controlling their outbursts. These manifestations may represent a physical risk to the other participants in the group, for whom the therapist has taken on equal responsibility. Where there is a real danger that a person will act out aggressive impulses, it is best not to include him or her in a therapy group. The emotional interaction in groups is often heightened by such a person, and control of aggressive impulses is a necessary prerequisite for group membership. Such patients need to develop internal controls of their tendency to act out and, while some may be able to adhere to external controls established by either the therapist or the group, the explosive personality is generally unable to curb his excitability.

The importance of accurately assessing a patient's ability to control impulses—to verbalize them rather than act on them—is perhaps even more important today than ever before. Various techniques from the encounter movement, for example, which encourage the acting out of impulses, may be extremely useful for certain obsessive-compulsive personalities who are excessively concerned with conformity and adherence to standards of conscience. But applied indiscriminately to those whose real need is to develop controls, they are anti-therapeutic (as with the explosive patient) and potentially dangerous to the group as a whole.

Passive-Aggressive Personality

This personality disorder is characterized by either passivity or aggressiveness. In the former pattern, the individual is unable to assert himself, and assumes a role of chronic submissiveness and compliance. But beneath the unassuming façade there may be a great deal of underlying hostility and resentment. Group therapy is especially favorable in the treatment of the passive patient on a number of levels. It allows the patient to become consciously aware of his passivity, which may have been subject to denial and or rationalization and thus closed off from individual analysis. Confrontations by group members whenever the passive mode is demonstrated encourage the patient to become more outgoing and to react more spontaneously with a true expression of feelings. And finally, if the group is properly organized, the passive member will find effective role-models to identify with and thus learn new and more well-adapted ways in which to make his needs known.

The behavioral group-therapy approaches have been particularly successful in treating the passive patient via assertive training methods. Specific techniques which reinforce the expression of appropriately assertive behavior are used, and the group becomes the testing ground for the change in response brought about.

In the aggressive pattern the patient does not overtly express angry feelings but rather expresses them covertly by being stubborn, obstructionistic, or intentionally inefficient. These disguised expressions of anger generally create a reactive hostility on the part of the group. In this way the patient is made aware of the effects of his passive-aggressive behavior on others. In general, a group will refuse to tolerate the persistent pouting, procrastination, and stubbornness that such patients demonstrate; but rather than react by overt rejection of the patient (as generally happens outside of the group), the co-patients try to be of help, even though they may disapprove of the antagonistic or disruptive behavior.

Underlying the passive-aggressive personality pattern are deep dependency needs which are usually not being gratified by the external environment, thus leading to disappointment and resentment. The multiple relationships established within the group provide substitute dependency objects and tend to eventually diminish anxiety and the need for the maladaptive behavior pattern. As group therapy progresses, the excessive dependency striving can be examined. But it is first necessary to cause a dissolution of the predominant character structure. which can be done most successfully by the peer group. In the one-to-one situation, it requires more time before the therapist is in a position to assail the ingrained behavioral patterns, and even then the patient may feel unduly criticized, have his dependency needs undermined, and terminate as a result. In the group setting, the therapist, or one or more of the other members. may provide the necessary support while the removal of the character armor takes place.

Antisocial Personality

These individuals are characterized by patterns of behavior that often result in legal or social offenses. They are incapable of significant loyalty to individuals or groups and are irresponsible and unable to learn from experience. Accordingly, they are resistant to all forms of psychotherapy but are particularly difficult to manage in group psychotherapy, as they do not constructively assimilate the interpretations made by other group members or by the therapist. Because of their inability to adhere to group standards of any sort, they may not be able to maintain the confidentiality of the group and. if for no other reason, should be excluded from the group.

It should be noted, nonetheless, that attempts have been made to work with the antisocial personality in group settings with some success. But these attempts have generally been carried out in penal settings where marked external pressure has been exerted to ensure their participation. In the group usually composed solely of these patients, massive confrontation techniques by the members toward one another may be sufficient at times to mobilize introspective attempts on the part of some.

Other Disorders

Homosexuals. With certain categories of illness, such as homosexuality, the group may be organized unisexually. Advocates of this approach, such as Bieber, point out that the homosexual's anxiety in discussing and examining the genesis and dynamics of his or her situation may be too great—especially in view of societal pressures against this form of behavior—where other members do not have a similar problem. One must also distinguish the therapeutic goal involved—conversion to heterosexuality or better adaptation to homosexuality—in determining whether to place a practicing homosexual in a mixed group. In general, most heterosexually oriented groups, while tolerant of the deviant sexual behavior, will tend to place pressure on the homosexual patient to change his or her orientation. If this is consonant with the patient's goal, placement in a mixed group may be indicated. But the therapist must be aware that such group pressure may be premature or ill-timed and serve only to raise the patient's anxiety level. Where the patient is unwilling to become heterosexual and desires a more effective adaptation to homosexuality, the mixed group may not be willing to work with the patient toward that end. Thus, while there is no firm contraindication to placing the homosexual patient in a mixed group, these pitfalls should be kept in mind. Or, as Bieber suggests, begin the treatment of the homosexual in homogeneous groups and, depending on the progress of a particular member, consider transfer to a mixed group at a later stage in therapy.

Adolescents

The adolescent characteristically shows fluidity of behavior in his or her attempts to consolidate the identity crisis (Erikson's postulate) during this stage of development. Where there is psychopathology it may take a variety of forms: irritability, withdrawal, depression, brooding, shyness, anxiety, or delinquency, etc. In addition, there is often a common fear of authority. The group setting allows the adolescent to explore attitudes toward authority more effectively than the dyadic situation because of the support of peers. It is considered by many to be the treatment of choice for most adolescent disorders, because it also provides a peer experience that the disturbed adolescent may have been denied. Sullivan has suggested that unless such a peer experience occurs during this stage, there is a higher risk of overt schizophrenia developing. In this sense, group treatment for this age span may also be preventative.

STRUCTURAL ORGANIZATION OF THE GROUP

Size

The size of the psychotherapy group is not fixed. Group therapy has been successful with as few as three members or as many as 15—but most therapists consider eight to ten members optimal. With fewer members there may be too little interaction —unless they are especially verbal. With a larger group the interaction may be too great for the members or the therapist to follow.

For each group therapist, the number of patients that he can observe adequately also varies. With experience, the range of emotional interaction the therapist can integrate adequately increases to its optimum. And depending on the variables of leadership style and theoretical orientation, the size of the group may also vary.

At times the composition of the group may determine its size. If, for example, a group contains an extremely verbal, aggressive, dominating member, it may be necessary to increase the size to provide counterforces to offset the monopolist. Similarly, a group composed primarily of withdrawn, schizoid members may require additional members to heighten the level of interaction. Ideally, the group should maintain a constancy, however, and within a relatively limited range the personality makeup of the individual members should be able to provide checks and balances to produce effective interaction.

Frequency of Sessions

Most group psychotherapists conduct group sessions once weekly, although Wolf, adhering to a more classical psychoanalytic procedure, has conducted three to five group sessions per week. It is important to maintain continuity in sessions so that themes from a previous session may be carried over, as necessary, to the next without too great a time lag between. The authors consider group psychotherapy inefficient if sessions are dropped for any reason whatsoever. Thus they advocate "summer sessions" which meet even though the therapist may be on vacation. Where alternate sessions are used, the group will meet twice a week—once with the therapist and once without him.

At times it may be necessary to increase the frequency of sessions during a particular period. But this should be done for specific reasons: A member of the group may be undergoing a life stress of sufficient magnitude that he or she requires the more frequent meeting of the group to provide him or her with the necessary support. Or, the group as a whole may be in crisis—a member may have died, for example—such that only increased numbers of meetings provide sufficient opportunity for the crisis to be worked through. Certainly, increased frequency should not be capricious but based on a sound appraisal of the needs of a particular member or of the group.

One of the advantages of co-therapists is that of assuring continuity of sessions. If one member of the co-therapy team is absent, the other can carry the group. Where a single therapist conducts the group, the members may be encouraged to meet even though circumstances prevent the leader from attending a particular session.

Length of Sessions

In general, group sessions last anywhere from one to two hours, with the average length being one and one-half hours. The time limit set, however, should be constant. This allows for the group to become aware of patterns that may be of significance—such as a particular member always bringing up a topic meaningful to him just prior to the group's ending, or the group as a whole reacting in a similar manner. If the group session is too short, there may be insufficient time for necessary emotional interaction to develop, and "warm-up" procedures have been described by some therapists to counteract this process when it occurs. Conversely, if the session is too long, the level of emotional interaction may be too heightened to be assimilated cognitively by either the members or the therapist.

The fixed time limit to the session also has the practical advantage of allowing both the patients and the leader to adhere to the commitments of their everyday life. It places an optimum value on the necessity to use the time available for group work as effectively as possible. And for certain patients, such as those who have difficulty controlling impulses, the fixed group time serves as a model for the setting of limits. This can be reassuring for those patients who fear a loss of control.

Homogeneous vs. Heterogeneous Factors

There has been some controversy as to whether or not the therapy group should be homogeneous or heterogeneous—that is, composed of one sex, age, race, socioeconomic level, symptom, or category of illness as opposed to varying these factors within the same group. In general, however, most therapists support the view that the group be as heterogeneous as possible to ensure that maximum interaction occurs. Thus the group should be composed of members drawn from different categories of illness, with varied behavioral patterns, and from all races, social strata, and educational backgrounds as well as of varying ages and of both sexes.

In the heterogeneous group the individual receives greater stimulation and is forced to examine and understand what is different about his fellow group members. There is a tacit group standard to accept that which is different, and the adaptive capacity of the individual to be tolerant of difference is tested and reinforced. In addition, the heterogeneous group provides greater opportunities for more effective reality-testing, in that malfunctioning in one area of living by a particular member may be offset by effective functioning in the same area by another member.

It should be noted that even if the group is homogeneous, such as in the categories of illness mentioned earlier (adolescent adjustment problems, antisocial personality disorders, certain sexual deviations, among others), the concept of heterogeneity still exists to some degree. For, regardless of diagnosis, the etiologic, genetic, and dynamic factors, as well as the life styles within any diagnostic category will differ considerably.

The concept of organizing a group along heterogeneous lines is not served by haphazard composition, however. Certain parameters can be set for proper group organization.

Diagnostic Factors

As already discussed, certain borderline states can be placed in the same group with a variety of psychoneurotic disorders. The schizophrenic, who is more vulnerable to the evocation of unconscious processes, can pro-vide the neurotic with the necessary stimulation to break through repressive barriers, which are usually more intact in the neurotic. Conversely, the neurotic can provide a high degree of reality-testing and support for certain ego defenses that may have become weakened in the schizophrenic.

Where the schizophrenic process is more severe and the patient is delusional or hallucinatory, it is inadvisable to place such patients in neurotic groups. This is not to say that such patients cannot be treated in group therapy. Provided there is heterogeneity, the delusional patient will be able to provide effective reality-testing to the hallucinating patient, and vice versa.

A clinical example will illustrate the aforementioned point. In a group composed of overtly psychotic, schizophrenic patients, a 41-year-old man complained of how he was being followed by a variety of persecutors who were spying on him constantly. As he was attempting to convince the group of the injustices he suffered as a result, a woman interrupted his story, telling him that he was "crazy" in harboring such ideas. Others in the group supported her position. However, the woman in question believed that she was the Virgin Mary. Her delusional system, at variance with the man's, enabled her to mobilize the group in an attempt to provide reality-testing for him. She, in turn, was subject to the same group process when she attempted to convince the group of her false beliefs. Had the group been composed of patients with similar beliefs, this process could not have occurred, since each should have reinforced the delusion of the other. Such collective delusional systems in a group are not uncommon when the organization of the group is not carefully thought out beforehand.

Dynamic Constructs

When the therapist has a sound understanding of the psychodynamics of a variety of patients, he can organize a group most efficiently. If the oedipal conflict is used as a basis of organization, for example, a broad range of effective interactional potentials can be considered: A patient who is competitive with his father can be placed in the same group with a man who competes with his son. The patient subjected to an overprotective or seductive mother can be placed into a group in which such a close-binding mother is included. The varieties of group organization revolving about this dynamic constellation are almost endless; but each patient should be the mirror image of the other—in this case, complementary with regard to the oedipal nuclear conflict. But regardless of the theoretical dynamic construct to which he adheres, the therapist should be able to predict with a fair degree of accuracy how patients will interact within the group.

When considering the dynamic constructs of the group, diagnosis per se may be misleading, as in the case of depression. Depression can be the result of a real loss—the actual death of a loved one. It can also result from a threatened loss—impending divorce. Or it can result from an imagined loss—the fear that a loved one has left. In a group of patients demonstrating these varieties of psychodynamic formulations, it would be desirable to have an admixture accounting for the depressive symptom in order to provide a richness to the potential interaction among the members. Again, this requires a high degree of clinical sophistication, reflecting the therapist's ability to define symptoms psychodynamically.

Behavioral Patterns

An examination of the patients' life styles and behavioral patterns can also be used effectively to organize a group. In so doing, the therapist should attempt to vary such patterns among the membership as much as possible. The patient whose life style is marked by isolation, withdrawal, and a fear of close relationships is ideally suited to group therapy. Such a patient should be exposed to another whose life style is marked by an extrovertive or pathologically outgoing personality organization. The patient who is helpless, indecisive, and

overly dependent should be matched with one who is impulsive, quick to make decisions—however wrong they may be—and overly independent. By so organizing the group, patients are mutually exposed to different patterns of behavior, and each can learn from the other.

Similarly, life experiences in conflict or in the process of resolution can be a further basis on which to organize a group. A member dealing with reactions stemming from having moved out of the parental home can be matched with one who is contemplating such a move or one who has successfully handled this event. A patient anxious about an impending marriage—or divorce—can be placed into the same group with one having gone through either experience. As varied as life styles and behavioral patterns may be, so are the infinite varieties of potential group membership along these parameters, providing the concept of complementary patterning is kept in mind.

Sexual Patterns

There are few patients who present themselves for psychotherapy who do not suffer from some sexual disorder as part of their psychopathology, irrespective of diagnosis and regardless of whether or not this is the primary complaint. It has become increasingly apparent that many of the sexual conflicts that exist stem not only from psychological conflict but also from educational deficiencies. The interrelationship between the two is exceedingly complex and the group setting provides a unique opportunity for both the patients and the therapist to gain a clearer understanding of which problem is the result of faulty education, psychological problems, or a combination of both.

For example, in spite of many individuals having an intellectual awareness that masturbation is a normal function, it is almost ubiquitous that a patient will suffer some degree of guilt over this activity. In part it can be culturally induced, in part it may be the result of specific traumata suffered in life that were associated with masturbatory activity, or, among other causes, it may be related to specific and pathological masturbatory fantasies. But regardless of the causes—only some of which have been mentioned—the verbalization of masturbatory experiences can have an almost immediate guilt-reducing effect. The same can be said for other varieties of sexual experiences, both normal and abnormal. It is quite common for a group member to harbor the feeling that a particular sexual act is pathological, only to discover that others are acquainted with the act in question and view it with equanimity.

Furthermore, there is a great difference in being reassured by the therapist in the dyadic relationship that a particular sexual experience is no cause for alarm, and to hear others in one's group take a similar position. In the former situation, the patient may see the reassurance being offered as a particular technical maneuver on the part of the therapist. In the latter, the group members openly share with a particular member similar acounts of their sexual activities, which serve more effectively as peer reassurance. The sharing of experiences also has an educational purpose, and where a patient is unable to assimilate accurate data about sexual functioning, the block to learning can more clearly be traced to psychological inhibition.

Accordingly, effective group organization should take these aspects of sexual experiences and patterning into account. To organize a group, for example, where all of the men suffer from impotence, or where all of the women suffer from frigidity, may serve to diminish the initial embarrassment and anxiety that a presentation of this complaint may entail—everyone else suffers from the same affliction—but it ultimately will do little to further the therapeutic progress of the members because of the lack of understanding about more adequate sexual functioning. And it is unwise for the therapist to believe himself to be the sole repository of all information about sexual functioning and to assume the task of correcting the varieties of sexual mal-

functioning with which he will be presented. Such a stance replicates the one-to-one situation and does not make use of the inherent value of peer exchange regarding sexual information. Rather, the group should contain members who are sexually repressed and members who are sexually uninhibited, members who are revolted by cunnilingus or fellatio and members who are addicted to it, members who are virginal and members who are promiscuous—and so on, until the range of sexual behavior is discussed as much as possible within the same group.

It follows then that men and women should be placed in the same group so that attitudes toward sex can be examined more effectively. And even though there may be initial inhibitions to a frank and open discussion of sexual matters in the mixed group, such exchanges will eventually occur as the members establish mutual trust and the anxieties attached to such interchanges are fruitfully examined.

In addition, the placement of men and women is the more normative situation, and behavior—both sexual and nonsexual—can be explored more realistically. Patients become aware of how they are perceived by members of the opposite sex and each can react in the microcosm of the group as they would outside of the therapeutic situation. The mixed group also allows for a variety of familial surrogates—mother, father, brother, sister, etc.—to be replicated, and insights into past relationships motivating present behavior toward the opposite sex can be gained more quickly.

Socioeconomic and Ethnic Factors

Consonant with the idea of heterogeneity being desirable in most instances, patients of different socioeconomic levels can be integrated into the same group with salutary effects. If, for example, one places a patient who has achieved financial success but who is anxious about not having received a college degree, with a patient anxious about his limited financial means but having received a college degree, one can predict the potential value of their interaction, which otherwise would have been lost had a college degree been a prerequisite for group membership. Similar juxtapositions of a great variety of different social and economic factors are available, and can be used successfully to heighten the psychological awareness of the group members.

Similarly, racial, religious, and ethnic variations in group composition can be utilized effectively. Where this is done it is desirable to include at least one other member of a similar background to provide mutual support and identification and so enable the patient to tolerate the minority position. For example, this applies whether one is working with blacks in a predominately white group or whites in a predominately black group. A statement of policy by the therapist should be made to the effect that one of the group standards is to respect the differences between members. It has been shown that such a statement made by a leader is an important prerequisite for modifying attitudes toward minority ethnic groups.

Of particular relevance is group work with the poor conducted by a therapist of a different socioeconomic position. Where this occurs, the members may see the therapist as unable to understand their situation—and sometimes this may be so. The group setting is particularly advantageous in that the members gain support and understanding from one another while, at the same time, the therapist is in a position to separate the very real stresses produced by adverse socioeconomic factors from those that are truly psychological in nature. In individual therapy the cultural gap between patient and therapist may be too great for this process to occur.

Age Range

For adult psychotherapy groups, age ranges are extremely broad and patients between 20 and 50 can be integrated in the same group effectively.

A clinical example follows. A 22-year-old man was included in a group with a man of 49. The older patient had adopted a stern, authoritarian position with his son—particularly over the length of his hair—that resulted in their complete alienation. The younger patient had not spoken to his father in three years because of a similar family constellation. Both group members were able to work through feelings toward their own son and father, respectively, via the interaction between them in the group, which was, as expected, stormy at times.

Age differences support the development of parent-child and brother-sister models (among others) for patients, and the opportunity to relive and rectify interpersonal difficulties that might otherwise have appeared to be insurmountable. In organizing the adult group, the therapist should be cautious in not having only one member representative of the extreme age group. It is likely, for example, that a woman of 50 in a group of adults aged 20 to 25 would be subject to a variety of transferential mother-surrogate reactions on the part of the younger members. While this could be tolerable and therapeutic for all concerned, it might be intolerable and antitherapeutic if the group were so organized that all of the younger patients had mothers whom they despised.

Both the child and the adolescent are best treated in groups that are composed of their own age group, as mentioned earlier. This is not to exclude all adolescents from adult groups; but before placement, the therapist should assess the adolescent's prior peer experience. If deficient, the patient should be given adolescent group placement.

CONCLUSION

In spite of the outlined parameters about patient selection and group organization, the issues are not as clear-cut as one might wish. The organization of the group along behavioral and dynamic lines allows for an infinite variety of interactional events, and the groups will unfold as therapy proceeds in ways that could not have been anticipated. The task of the therapist is to pay continuous attention to the interactions that develop and by so doing facilitate those processes which will allow each member to benefit from the group psychotherapy experience.

REFERENCES

Erikson, E. H. *Childhood and Society.* W. W. Norton, New York, 1950.

Geller, J. J. Concerning the size of therapy groups. Int. J. Group Psychother. *1*: 1, 1951.

Slavson, S. R. Criteria for selection and rejection of patients for various types of group psychotherapy. Int. J. Group Psychother. *5*: 3, 1955.

Sullivan, H. S. *Clinical Studies in Psychiatry.* W. W. Norton, New York, 1956.

Wolf, A. and Schwartz, E. K. *Psychoanalysis in Groups.* Grune & Stratton, New York, 1962.

Yalom, I. D. A study of group therapy dropouts. Arch. Gen. Psychiat. *14*: 393, 1966.

Glossary*

Aberration, mental. Pathological deviation from normal thinking. Mental aberration is not related to a person's intelligence. *See also* Mental illness.

Abreaction. A process by which repressed material, particularly a painful experience or a conflict, is brought back to consciousness. In the process of abreacting, the person not only recalls but relives the repressed material, which is accompanied by the appropriate affective response. *See also* Catharsis.

Accelerated interaction. An alternate term for marathon group session that was introduced by one of its co-developers, Frederick Stoller. *See also* Group marathon.

Accountability. The responsibility a member has for his actions within a group and the need to explain to other members the motivations for his behavior.

Acid. Slang for lysergic acid diethylamide (LSD).

Acrophobia. Fear of high places.

Acting out. An action rather than a verbal response to an unconscious instinctual drive or impulse that brings about temporary partial relief of inner tension. Relief is attained by reacting to a present situation as if it were the situation that originally gave rise to the drive or impulse. *See also* Therapeutic crisis.

Actional-deep approach. Group procedure in which communication is effected through various forms of nonverbal behavior as well as or in place of language to produce character change. It is a technique used in psychodrama. *See also*

---

* Edited by Ernesto A. Amaranto, M.D.

Actional-superficial approach, Activity group therapy, Verbal-deep approach, Verbal-superficial approach.

Actional-superficial approach. Group procedure in which specific activities and verbal communication are used for limited goals. Verbal interchange and patient-to-patient interaction are of relatively minor therapeutic significance, and the groups are usually large. *See also* Actional-deep approach, Verbal-deep approach, Verbal-superficial approach.

Action group (A-group). Group whose purpose is to discuss a problem—community, industrial, or organizational—and to formulate a program of action. Emphasis is put on problem-solving rather than on developing awareness of self and group process. *See also* T-group.

Active therapist. Type of therapist who makes no effort to remain anonymous but is forceful and expresses his personality definitively in the therapy setting. *See also* Passive therapist.

Activity group therapy. A type of group therapy introduced and developed by S. R. Slavson and designed for children and young adolescents, with emphasis on emotional and active interaction in a permissive, nonthreatening atmosphere. The therapist stresses reality-testing, ego-strengthening, and action interpretation. *See also* Actional-deep approach; Activity-interview method; Bender, Lauretta; Play therapy.

Activity-interview method. Screening and diagnostic technique used with children. *See also* Activity group therapy.

Actualization. Process of mobilizing one's potentialities or making them concrete. *See also* Individuation.

I

Adaptational approach. An approach used in analytic group therapy. Consonant with Sandor Rado's formulations on adaptational psychodynamics, the group focuses on the maladaptive patterns used by patients in the treatment sessions, on how these patterns developed, and on what the patients must do to overcome them and stabilize their functioning at self-reliant, adult levels. New methods of adaptation are practiced by the group members in the therapeutic sessions and later in their regular interpersonal relationships. *See also* Social adaptation.

Adapted Child. In transactional analysis, the primitive ego state that is under the parental influence. The adapted Child is dependent, unexpressive, and constrained. *See also* Natural Child.

Adler, Alfred (1870–1937). Viennese psychiatrist and one of Freud's original followers. Adler broke off from Freud and introduced and developed the concepts of individual psychology, inferiority complex, and overcompensation. A pioneer in group psychotherapy, he believed that the sharing of problems takes precedence over confidentiality. He also made contributions in the understanding of group process. *See also* Individual psychology, Masculine protest.

Adolescence. Period of growth from puberty to maturity. The beginning of adolescence is marked by the appearance of secondary sexual characteristics, usually at about age 12, and the termination is marked by the achievement of sexual maturity at about age 20. *See also* Psychosexual development.

Adult. In transactional analysis, an ego state oriented toward objective, autonomous data-processing and estimating. It is essentially a computer, devoid of feeling. It is also known as neopsychic function.

Affect. Emotional feeling tone attached to an object, idea, or thought. The term includes inner feelings and their external manifestations. *See also* Inappropriate affect, Mood.

Affect, blunted. A disturbance of affect manifested by dullness of externalized feeling tone. Observed in schizophrenia, it is one of that disorder's fundamental symptoms, according to Eugen Bleuler.

Affection phase. Last stage of group treatment. In this phase the members experience reasonable equality with the therapist and dwell on affectionate contact with each other in a give-and-take atmosphere rather than dwelling on dependency or aggression. *See also* Inclusion phase, Power phase.

Affective interaction. Interpersonal experience and exchange that are emotionally charged.

Affectualizing. In transactional analysis, the expression of emotions or feelings in group or individual treatment as part of a pasttime or game. It is distinguished from the expression of authentic feelings, which are characteristic of intimacy.

Afro-American. American Negro of African ancestry. This term has significance for blacks who seek a deeper and more positive sense of identity with their African heritage. *See also* Black separatism.

After-session. Group meeting of patients without the therapist. It is held immediately after a regular therapist-led session. *See also* Alternate session, Premeeting.

Agency. The striving and need to achieve in a person. Agency manifests itself in self-protection, the urge to master, self-expansion, and repression of thought, feeling, and impulse. *See also* Communion.

Aggression. Forceful, goal-directed behavior that may be verbal or physical. It is the motor counterpart of the affects of rage, anger, and hostility.

Aggressive drive. Destructive impulse directed at oneself or another. It is also known as the death instinct. According to contemporary psychoanalytic psychology, it is one of the two basic drives; sexual drive is the other one. Sexual drive operates on the pleasure-pain principle, whereas aggressive drive operates on the repetition-compulsion principle. *See also* Aggression, Libido theory.

Agitation. State of anxiety associated with severe motor restlessness.

Agnosia. Disturbance of perception characterized by inability to recognize a stimulus and interpret the significance of its memory impressions. It is observed in patients with organic brain disease and in certain schizophrenics, hysterics, and depressed patients.

Agoraphobia. Fear of open places. *See also* Claustrophobia.

Agranulocytosis. A rare, serious side effect, occurring with some of the psychotropic drugs. The condition is characterized by sore throat, fever, a sudden sharp decrease in white blood cell count, and a marked reduction in number of granulocytes.

A-group. *See* Action group.

Alcoholics Anonymous (A.A.) An organization of alcoholics formed in 1935. It uses certain group methods, such as inspirational-supportive techniques, to help rehabilitate chronic alcoholics.

Algophobia. Fear of pain.

Allergic jaundice. *See* Jaundice, allergic.

Alliance. *See* Therapeutic alliance, Working alliance.

Allport's group relations theory. Gordon W. Allport's theory that a person's behavior is influenced by his personality and his need to conform to social forces. It illustrates the interrelationship between group therapy and social psychology. For example, dealing with bigotry in a therapy group enhances the opportunity for therapeutic experiences because it challenges the individual patient's need to conform to earlier social determinants or to hold on to familiar but restrictive aspects of his personality.

Alternate session. Scheduled group meeting held without the therapist. Such meetings are held on a regular basis in between therapist-led sessions. Use of this technique was originated by Alexander Wolf. *See also* After-session, Premeeting.

Alternating role. Pattern characterized by periodic switching from one type of behavior to another. For example, in a group, alternating role is observed among members who switch from the role of the recipient of help to the giver of help.

Alternating scrutiny. *See* Shifting attention.

Altruism. Regard for and dedication to the welfare of others. The term was originated by Auguste Comte (1798–1857), a French philosopher. In psychiatry the term is closely linked with ethics and morals. Freud recognized altruism as the only basis for the development of community interest; Bleuler equated it with morality.

Ambivalence. Presence of strong and often overwhelming simultaneous contrasting attitudes, ideas, feelings, and drives toward an object, person, or goal. The term was coined by Eugen Bleuler, who differentiated three types: affective, intellectual, and ambivalence of the will.

Amnesia. Disturbance in memory manifested by partial or total inability to recall past experiences.

Amphetamine. A central nervous system stimulant. Its chemical structure and action are closely related to ephedrine and other sympathomimetic amines. *See also* Sympathomimetic drug.

Anal erotism. *See* Anal phase.

Anal phase. The second stage in psychosexual development. It occurs when the child is between the ages of one and three. During this period the infant's activities, interests, and concerns are centered around his anal zone, and the pleasurable experience felt around this area is called anal erotism. *See also* Genital phase, Infantile sexuality, Latency phase, Oral phase, Phallic phase.

Analysis. *See* Psychoanalysis.

Analysis in depth. *See* Psychoanalysis.

Analysis of transference. *See* Psychoanalysis.

Analytic psychodrama. Psychotherapy method in which a hypothesis is tested on a stage to verify its validity. The analyst sits in the audience and observes. Analysis of the material is made immediately after the scene is presented.

Anchor. Point at which the patient settles down to the analytic work involved in the therapeutic experience.

Antianxiety drug. Drug used to reduce pathological anxiety and its related symptoms without influencing cognitive or perceptual disturbance. It is also known as a minor tranquilizer and a psycholeptic drug. Meprobamate derivatives and diazepoxides are typical antianxiety drugs.

Anticholinergic effect. Effect due to a blockade of the cholinergic (parasympathetic and somatic) nerves. It is often seen as a side effect of phenothiazine therapy. Anticholinergic effects include dry mouth and blurred vision. *See also* Paralytic ileus.

Antidepressant drug. Drug used in the treatment of pathological depression. It is also known as a thymoleptic drug and a psychic energizer. The two main classes of antidepressant drugs are the tricyclic drugs and the monoamine oxidase inhibitors. *See also* Hypertensive crisis, Monoamine oxidase inhibitor, Tinnitus, Tricyclic drug.

Antimanic drug. Drug, such as lithium, used to alleviate the symptoms of mania. Lithium is particularly effective in preventing relapses in manic-depressive illness. Other drugs with antimanic effects are haloperidol and chlorpromazine.

Antiparkinsonism drug. Drug used to relieve the symptoms of parkinsonism and the extrapyramidal side effects often induced by antipsychotic drugs. The antiparkinsonism drug acts by diminishing muscle tone and involuntary movements. Antiparkinsonism agents include benztropine, procyclidine, biperiden, and trihexphenidyl. *See also* Cycloplegia, Mydriasis.

Antipsychotic drug. Drug used to treat psychosis, particularly schizophrenia. It is also known as a major tranquilizer and a neuroleptic drug. Phenothiazine derivatives, thioxanthene derivatives, and butyrophenone derivatives are typical antipsychotic drugs. *See also* Autonomic side effect, Dyskinesia, Extrapyramidal effect, Major tranquilizer, Parkinsonismlike effect, Reserpine, Tardive oral dyskinesia.

Antirepression device. Technique used in encounter groups and therapeutic groups to break through the defense of repression. In encounter groups, such techniques are frequently nonverbal and involve physical contact between group members. In therapeutic groups, dream analysis, free association, and role-playing are some antirepression techniques.

Anxiety. Unpleasurable affect consisting of psychophysiological changes in response to an intrapsychic conflict. In contrast to fear, the danger or threat in anxiety is unreal. Physiological changes consist of increased heart rate, disturbed breathing, trembling, sweating, and vasomotor changes. Psychological changes consist of an uncomfortable feeling of impending danger accompanied by overwhelming awareness of being powerless, inability to perceive the unreality of the threat, prolonged feeling of tension, and exhaustive readiness for the expected danger. *See also* Basic anxiety, Fear.

Apathetic withdrawal. *See* Withdrawal.

Apathy. Want of feeling or affect; lack of interest and emotional involvement in one's surroundings. It is observed in certain types of schizophrenia and depression.

Apgar scores. Measurements taken one minute and five minutes after birth to determine physical normality in the neonate. The scores are based on color, respiratory rate, heart beat, reflex action, and muscle tone. Used routinely, they are particularly useful in detecting the effects on the infant of drugs taken by the pregnant mother.

Aphasia. Disturbance in speech due to organic brain disorder. It is characterized by inability to express thoughts verbally. There are several types of aphasia: (1) motor aphasia—inability to speak, although understanding remains; (2) sensory aphasia—inability to comprehend the meaning of words or use of objects; (3) nominal aphasia—difficulty in finding the right name for an object; (4) syntactical aphasia—inability to arrange words in proper sequence.

Apperception. Awareness of the meaning and significance of a particular sensory stimulus as modified by one's own experiences, knowledge, thoughts, and emotions. *See also* Perception.

Archeopsychic function. *See* Child.

Arteriosclerotic cardiovascular disease. A metabolic disturbance characterized by degenerative changes involving the blood vessels of the heart and other arteries, mainly the arterioles. Fatty plaques, deposited within the blood vessels, gradually obstruct the flow of blood. Organic brain syndrome may develop when cerebral arteries are involved in the degenerative process.

Ataractic drug. *See* Major tranquilizer.

Ataxia. Lack of coordination, either physical or mental. In neurology it refers to loss of muscular coordination. In psychiatry the term intrapsychic ataxia refers to lack of coordination between feelings and thoughts; the disturbance is found in schizophrenia.

Atmosphere. *See* Therapeutic atmosphere.

Attention. Concentration; the aspect of consciousness that relates to the amount of effort exerted in focusing on certain aspects of an experience.

Attitude. Preparatory mental posture with which one receives stimuli and reacts to them. Group therapy often involves itself in defining for the group members their attitudes that have unconsciously dominated their reactions.

Auditory hallucination. False auditory sensory perception.

Authenticity. Quality of being authentic, real, and valid. In psychological functioning and personality, it applies to the conscious feelings, perceptions, and thoughts that a person expresses and communicates. It does not apply to the deeper, unconscious layers of the personality. *See also* Honesty.

Authority figure. A real or projected person in a position of power; transferentially, a projected parent.

Authority principle. The idea that each member of an organizational hierarchy tries to comply with the presumed or fantasied wishes of those above him while those below him try to comply with his wishes. *See also* Hierarchical vector, Political therapist, Procedural therapist.

Autism. *See* Autistic thinking.

Autistic thinking. A form of thinking in which the thoughts are largely narcissistic and egocentric, with emphasis on subjectivity rather than objectivity and without regard for reality. The term is used interchangeably with autism and dereism. *See also* Narcissism.

Autoerotism. Sexual arousal of self without the participation of another person. The term, introduced by Havelock Ellis, is at present used interchangeably with masturbation. In psychoanalysis, autoerotism is considered a primitive phase in object-relationship development, preceding the narcissistic stage. In narcissism there is a love object, but there is no love object in autoerotism.

Autonomic side effect. Disturbance of the autonomic nervous system, both central and peripheral. It may be a result of the use of anti-psychotic drugs, particularly the phenothiazine derivatives. The autonomic side effects include hypotension, hypertension, blurred vision, nasal congestion, and dryness of the mouth. *See also* Mydriasis.

Auxiliary ego. In psychodrama, a person, usually a member of the staff, trained to act out different roles during a psychodramatic session to intensify the therapeutic situation. The trained auxiliary ego may represent an important figure in the patient's life. He may express the patient's unconscious wishes and attitudes or portray his unacceptable self. He may represent a delusion, hallucination, symbol, ideal, animal, or object that makes the patient's psychodramatic world real, concrete, and tangible. *See also* Ego model Hallucinatory psychodrama, Mirror, Multiple double.

Auxiliary therapist. Co-therapist. *See also* Co-therapy.

Back-home group. Collection of persons that a patient usually lives with, works with, and socializes with. It does not include the members of his therapy group. *See also* Expanded group.

Bag. Slang for area of classification, interest, or skill. Bringing together members of a group with different bags makes it initially difficult to achieve a feeling of group cohesiveness but later provides the potential for more productive interchange and deeper cohesiveness.

Basic anxiety. As conceptualized by Karen Horney, the mainspring from which neurotic trends get their intensity and pervasiveness. Basic anxiety is characterized by vague feelings of loneliness, helplessness, and fear of a potentially hostile world. *See also* Anxiety, Fear.

Basic skills training. The teaching of leadership functions, communication skills, the use of group processes, and other interpersonal skills. National Training Laboratories' groups include this training as part of the T-group process. *See also* East-Coast-style T-group.

Behavioral group psychotherapy. A type of group therapy that focuses on overt and objectively observable behavior rather than on thoughts and feelings. It aims at symptomatic improvement and the elimination of suffering and maladaptive habits. Various conditioning and anxiety-eliminating techniques derived from learning theory are combined with didactic discussions and techniques adapted from other systems of treatment.

Behind-the-back technique. An encounter group procedure in which a patient talks about himself and then turns his back and listens while the other participants discuss him as if he were physically absent. Later he "returns" to the group to participate in further discussions of his problems.

Bender, Lauretta (1897–). American psychiatrist who has done extensive work in the fields of child psychiatry, neurology, and psychology. She employed group therapy, particularly activity group therapy, with inpatient children in the early 1940's.

Berne, Eric (1910–1970). American psychiatrist. He was the founder of transactional analysis, which is used in both individual and group therapy. *See also* Transactional group psychotherapy.

Bestiality. Sexual deviation in which a person engages in sexual relations with an animal.

Bieber, Irving (1908–). American psychiatrist and psychoanalyst who has done extensive work in the field of homosexuality. He originated the first major scientific study of male homosexuality published as *Homosexuality; A Psychoanalytic Study.*

Bio-energetic group psychotherapy. A type of group therapy developed by Alexander Lowen that directly involves the body and mobilizes energy processes to facilitate the expression of feeling. Verbal interchange and a variety of exercises are designed to improve and coordinate physical functioning with mental functioning.

Bion, Walter R. British psychoanalyst of the Kleinian school. He introduced concepts dealing largely with the group as a whole. He was one of the European workers who demonstrated the use of open wards in mental hospitals and who developed the concept of therapeutic milieu. *See also* Leaderless therapeutic group, Pairing, Therapeutic community.

Bisexuality. Existence of the qualities of both sexes in the same person. Freud postulated that both biologically and psychologically the sexes differentiated from a common core, that differentiation between the two sexes was relative rather than absolute, and that regression to the common core occurs to varying degrees in both normal and abnormal conditions. An adult person who engages in bisexual behavior is one who is sexually attracted to and has contact with members of both sexes. He is also known in lay terms as an AC-DC person. *See also* Heterosexuality, Homosexuality, Latent homosexuality, Overt homosexuality.

Black separatism. Philosophy that blacks, in order to develop a positive identity, must establish cultural, socioeconomic, and political systems that are distinctively black and separate from white systems. *See also* Afro-American.

Blank screen. Neutral backdrop on which the patient projects a gamut of transferential irrationalities. The passivity of the analyst allows him to act as a blank screen.

Blind self. The behavior, feelings, and motivations of a person known to others but not to himself. The blind self is one quadrant of the Johari Window, a diagrammatic concept of human behavior. *See also* Hidden self, Public self, Undeveloped potential.

Blind spot. Area of someone's personality that he is totally unaware of. These unperceived areas are often hidden by repression so that he can avoid painful emotions. In both group and individual therapy, such blind spots often appear obliquely as projected ideas, intentions, and emotions.

Blind walk. A technique used in encounter groups to help a member experience and develop trust. As a group exercise, each member picks a partner; one partner closes his eyes, and the other leads him around, keeping him out of dangerous places. The partners then reverse roles. Later, the group members discuss their reactions to the blind walk.

Blocking. Involuntary cessation of thought processes or speech because of unconscious emotional factors. It is also known as thought deprivation.

Blunted affect. *See* Affect, blunted.

Body-contact-exploration maneuver. Any physical touching of another person for the purpose of becoming more aware of the sensations and emotions aroused by the experience. The technique is used mainly in encounter groups.

Boundary. Physical or psychological factor that separates relevant regions in the group structure. An external boundary separates the group from the external environment. A major internal boundary distinguishes the group leader from the members. A minor internal boundary separates individual members or subgroups from one another.

Brainwashing. Any technique designed to manipulate human thought or action against the desire, will, or knowledge of the person involved. It usually refers to systematic efforts to indoctrinate nonbelievers. *See also* Dog-eat-dog period, Give-up-itis.

Breuer, Josef (1842–1925). Viennese physician with wide scientific and cultural interests. His collaboration with Freud in studies of cathartic therapy were reported in *Studies on Hysteria* (1895). He withdrew as Freud proceeded to introduce psychoanalysis, but he left important imprints on that discipline, such as the concepts of the primary and secondary process.

Brill, A. A. (1874–1948). First American analyst (1908). Freud gave him permission to translate several of his most important works. He was active in the formation of the New York Psychoanalytic Society (1911) and remained in the forefront of propagators of psychoanalysis as a lecturer and writer throughout his life.

Brooding compulsion. *See* Intellectualization.

Bull session. Informal group meeting at which members discuss their opinions, philosophies, and personal feelings about situations and people. Such groups are leaderless, and no attempt is made to perceive group process, but the cathartic value is often great. It is also known as a rap session.

Burned-out anergic schizophrenic. A chronic schizophrenic who is apathetic and withdrawn, with minimal florid psychotic symptoms but with persistent and often severe schizophrenic thought processes.

Burrow, Trigant L. (1875–1951). American student of Freud and Jung who coined the term group analysis and later developed a method called phyloanalysis. Much of Burrow's work was based on his social views and his opinion that individual psychotherapy places the therapist in too authoritarian a role to be therapeutic. He formed groups of patients, students, and colleagues who, living together in a camp, analyzed their interactions.

Catalepsy. *See* Cerea flexibilitas.

Cataphasia. *See* Verbigeration.

Cataplexy. Temporary loss of muscle tone, causing weakness and immobilization. It can be precipitated by a variety of emotional states.

Catecholamine. Monoamine containing a catechol group that has a sympathomimetic property. Norepinephrine, epinephrine, and dopamine are common catecholamines.

Category method. Technique used in structured interactional group psychotherapy. Members are asked to verbally rate one another along a variety of parameters—such as appearance, intelligence, and relatedness.

Catharsis. Release of ideas, thoughts, and repressed materials from the unconscious, accompanied by an affective emotional response and release of tension. Commonly observed in the course of treatment, both individual and group, it can also occur outside therapy. *See also* Abreaction, Bull session, Conversational catharsis.

Cathexis. In psychoanalysis, a conscious or unconscious investment of the psychic energy of a drive in an idea, a concept, or an object.

Cerea flexibilitas. Condition in which a person maintains the body position he is placed into. It is a pathological symptom observed in severe cases of catatonic schizophrenia. It is also known as waxy flexibility or catalepsy.

Chain-reaction phenomenon. Group therapy situation in which information is passed from one group to another, resulting in a loss of confidentiality. This phenomenon is common when members of different groups socialize together.

Chemotherapy. *See* Drug therapy.

Child. In transactional analysis, an ego state that is an archaic relic from an early period of the person's life. It is also known as archeopsychic function. *See also* Adapted Child, Natural Child.

Chlorpromazine. A phenothiazine derivative used primarily as an antipsychotic agent and in the treatment of nausea and vomiting. The drug was synthesized in 1950 and was used in psychiatry for the first time in 1952. At present, chlorpromazine is one of the most widely used drugs in medical practice.

Circumstantiality. Disturbance in the associative thought processes in which the patient digresses into unnecessary details and inappropriate thoughts before communicating the central idea. It is observed in schizophrenia, obsessional disturbances, and certain cases of epileptic dementia. *See also* Tangentiality, Thought process disorder.

Clarification. In transactional analysis, the attainment of Adult control by a patient who understands what he is doing, knows what parts of his personality are involved in what he is doing, and is able to control and decide whether or not to continue his games. Clarification contributes to stability by assuring the patient that his hidden Parent and Child ego states can be monitored by his Adult ego state. *See also* Decontamination, Interpretation.

Class method. Group therapy method that is lecture-centered and designed to enlighten patients as to their condition and provide them with motivations. Joseph Pratt, a Boston physician, first used this method at the turn of the century to help groups of tuberculous patients understand their illness. *See also* Didactic technique, Group bibliotherapy, Mechanical group therapy.

Claustrophobia. Fear of closed places. *See also* Agoraphobia.

Client-centered psychotherapy. A form of psychotherapy, formulated by Carl Rogers, in which the patient or client is believed to possess the ability to improve. The therapist merely helps him clarify his own thinking and feeling. The client-centered approach in both group and individual therapy is democratic, unlike the psychotherapist-centered treatment methods. *See also* Group-centered psychotherapy, Nondirective approach.

Closed group. Treatment group into which no new members are permitted once it has begun the treatment process. *See also* Open group.

Clouding of consciousness. Disturbance of consciousness characterized by unclear sensory perceptions.

Coexistent culture. Alternative system of values, perceptions, and patterns for behavior. The group experience leads to an awareness of other systems as legitimate alternatives to one's own system.

Cognition. Mental process of knowing and becoming aware. One of the ego functions, it is closely associated with judgment. Groups that study their own processes and dynamics use more cognition than do encounter groups, which emphasize emotions. It is also known as thinking.

Cohesion. *See* Group cohesion.

Cold turkey. Abrupt withdrawal from opiates without the benefit of methadone or other drugs. The term was originated by drug addicts to describe their chills and consequent goose flesh. This type of detoxification is generally used by abstinence-oriented therapeutic communities.

Collaborative therapy. A type of marital therapy in which treatment is conducted by two therapists, each of whom sees one spouse. They may confer occasionally or at regular intervals. This form of treatment affords each analyst a double view of his patient—the way in which one patient reports to his analyst and the way in which the patient's mate sees the situation as reported to the analyst's colleague. *See also* Combined therapy, Concurrent therapy, Conjoint therapy, Family therapy, Group marital therapy, Marriage therapy, Quadrangular therapy, Square interview.

Collective experience. The common emotional experiences of a group of people. Identification, mutual support, reduction of ego defenses, sibling transferences, and empathy help integrate the individual member into the group and accelerate the therapeutic process. S. R. Slavson, who coined the phrase, warned against letting the collective experience submerge the individuality of the members or give them an opportunity to escape from their own autonomy and responsibility.

Collective family transference neurosis. A phenomenon observed in a group when a member projects irrational feelings and thoughts onto other members as a result of transferring the family psychopathology from early childhood into the therapeutic group situation. The interpretation and analysis of this phenomenon is one of the cornerstones of psychoanalytic group therapy. *See also* Lateral transference, Multiple transference.

Collective unconscious. Psychic contents outside the realm of awareness that are common to mankind in general, not to one person in particular. Jung, who introduced the term, believed that the collective unconscious is inherited and derived from the collective experience of the species. It transcends cultural differences and explains the analogy between ancient mythological ideas and the primitive archaic projections observed in some patients who have never been exposed to these ideas.

Coma. A profound degree of unconsciousness with minimal or no detectable responsiveness to stimuli. It is seen in conditions involving the brain—such as head injury, cerebral hemorrhage, thrombosis and embolism, and cerebral infection—in such systemic conditions as diabetes, and in drug and alcohol intoxication. In psychiatry, comas may be seen in severe catatonic states.

Coma vigil. A profound degree of unconsciousness in which the patient's eyes remain open but there is minimal or no detectable evidence of responsiveness to stimuli. It is seen in acute brain syndromes secondary to cerebral infection.

Combined therapy. A type of psychotherapy in which the patient is in both individual and group treatment with the same or two different therapists. In marriage therapy, it is the combination of married couples group therapy with either individual sessions with one spouse or conjoint sessions with the marital pair. *See also* Collaborative therapy, Concurrent therapy, Conjoint therapy, Co-therapy, Family therapy, Group marital therapy, Marriage therapy, Quadrangular therapy, Square interview.

Coming on. A colloquial term used in transactional analysis groups to label an emerging ego state. For example, when a patient points his finger and says "should," he is coming on Parent.

Command automation. Condition closely associated with catalepsy in which suggestions are followed automatically.

Command negativism. *See* Negativism.

Common group tension. Common denominator of tension arising out of the dominant unconscious fantasies of all the members in a group.

Each member projects his unconscious fantasy onto the other members and tries to manipulate them accordingly. Interpretation by the group therapist plays a prominent role in bringing about change.

Communion. The union of one living thing with another or the participation of a person in an organization. It is a necessary ingredient in individual and group psychotherapy and in sensitivity training. Both the leader-therapist and the patient-trainee must experience communion for a successful learning experience to occur. *See also* Agency.

Communion-oriented group psychotherapy. A type of group therapy that focuses on developing a spirit of unity and cohesiveness rather than on performing a task.

Community. *See* Therapeutic community.

Community psychiatry. Psychiatry focusing on the detection, prevention, and early treatment of emotional disorders and social deviance as they develop in the community rather than as they are perceived and encountered at large, centralized psychiatric facilities. Particular emphasis is placed on the environmental factors that contribute to mental illness.

Compensation. Conscious or, usually, unconscious defense mechanism by which a person tries to make up for an imagined or real deficiency, physical or psychological or both.

Competition. Struggle for the possession or use of limited goods, concrete or abstract. Gratification for one person largely precludes gratification for another.

Complementarity of interaction. A concept of bipersonal and multipersonal psychology in which behavior is viewed as a response to stimulation and interaction replaces the concept of reaction. Each person in an interactive situation plays both a provocative role and a responsive role.

Complex. A group of inter-related ideas, mainly unconscious, that have a common affective tone. A complex strongly influences the person's attitudes and behavior. *See also* God complex, Inferiority complex, Mother Superior complex, Oedipus complex.

Composition. Make-up of a group according to

sex, age, race, cultural and ethnic background, and psychopathology.

Compulsion. Uncontrollable impulse to perform an act repetitively. It is used as a way to avoid unacceptable ideas and desires. Failure to perform the act leads to anxiety. *See also* Obsession.

Conation. That part of a person's mental life concerned with his strivings, instincts, drives, and wishes as expressed through his behavior.

Concretization of living. As used in psychodrama, the actualization of life in a therapeutic setting, integrating time, space, reality, and cosmos.

Concurrent therapy. A type of family therapy in which one therapist handles two or more members of the same family but sees each member separately. *See also* Collaborative therapy, Combined therapy, Conjoint therapy, Family therapy, Group marital therapy, Marriage therapy, Quadrangular therapy, Square interview.

Conditioning. Procedure designed to alter behavioral potential. There are two main types of conditioning—classical and operant. Classical or Pavlovian conditioning pairs two stimuli—one adequate, such as offering food to a dog to produce salivation, and the other inadequate, such as ringing a bell, which by itself does not have an effect on salivation. After the two stimuli have been paired several times, the dog responds to the inadequate stimulus (ringing of bell) by itself. In operant conditioning, a desired activity is reinforced by giving the subject a reward every time he performs the act. As a result, the activity becomes automatic without the need for further reinforcement.

Confabulation. Unconscious filling of gaps in memory by imagining experiences that have no basis in fact. It is common in organic brain syndromes. *See also* Paramnesia.

Confidentiality. Aspect of medical ethics in which the physician is bound to hold secret all information given him by the patient. Legally, certain states do not recognize confidentiality and can require the physician to divulge such information if needed in a legal proceeding. In group psychotherapy this ethic is adhered to by the members as well as by the therapist.

Confirmation. In transactional analysis, a re-

confrontation that may be undertaken by the patient himself. *See also* Confrontation.

Conflict. Clash of two opposing emotional forces. In a group, the term refers to a clash between group members or between the group members and the leader, a clash that frequently reflects the inner psychic problems of individual members. *See also* Extrapsychic conflict, Intrapsychic conflict.

Conflict-free area. Part of one's personality or ego that is well-integrated and does not cause any conflicts, symptoms, or displeasure. Conflict-free areas are usually not analyzed in individual analysis, but they become obvious in the interaction of an analytic group, where they can then be analyzed.

Confrontation. Act of letting a person know where one stands in relationship to him, what one is experiencing, and how one perceives him. Used in a spirit of deep involvement, this technique is a powerful tool for changing relationships; used as an attempt to destroy another person, it can be harmful. In group and individual therapy, the value of confrontation is likely to be determined by the therapist. *See also* Encounter group, Existential group psychotherapy.

Confusion. Disturbance of consciousness manifested by a disordered orientation in relation to time, place, or person.

Conjoint therapy. A type of marriage therapy in which a therapist sees the partners together in joint sessions. This situation is also called triadic or triangular, since two patients and one therapist work together. *See also* Collaborative therapy, Combined therapy, Concurrent therapy, Family therapy, Group marital therapy, Marriage therapy, Quadrangular therapy, Square interview.

Conscious. One division of Freud's topographical theory of the mind. The content of the conscious is within the realm of awareness at all times. The term is also used to describe a function of organic consciousness. *See also* Preconscious, Unconscious.

Consciousness. *See* Sensorium.

Consensual validation. The continuous comparison of the thoughts and feelings of group members toward one another that tend to modify and correct interpersonal distortions. The term was introduced by Harry Stack Sullivan. Previously, Trigant Burrow referred to consensual observation to describe this process, which results in effective reality-testing.

Contact situation. Encounter between individual persons or groups in which the interaction patterns that develop represent the dynamic interplay of psychological, cultural, and socioeconomic factors.

Contagion. Force that operates in large groups or masses. When the level of psychological functioning has been lowered, some sudden upsurge of anxiety can spread through the group, speeded by a high degree of suggestibility. The anxiety gradually mounts to panic, and the whole group may be simultaneously affected by a primitive emotional upheaval.

Contamination. In transactional analysis, a state in which attitudes, prejudices, and standards that originate in a Parent or Child ego state become part of the Adult ego state's information and are treated as accepted facts. *See also* Clarification, Decontamination.

Contemporaneity. Here-and-now.

Contract. Explicit, bilateral commitment to a well-defined course of action. In group or individual therapy, the therapist-patient contract is to attain the treatment goal.

Conversational catharsis. Release of repressed or suppressed thoughts and feelings in group and individual psychotherapy as a result of verbal interchange.

Conversion. An unconscious defense mechanism by which the anxiety that stems from an intrapsychic conflict is converted and expressed in a symbolic somatic symptom. Seen in a variety of mental disorders, it is particularly common in hysterical neurosis.

Cooperative therapy. *See* Co-therapy.

Co-patients. Members of a treatment group exclusive of the therapist and the recorder or observer. Co-patients are also known as patient peers.

Coprolalia. The use of vulgar, obscene, or dirty words. It is observed in some cases of schizophrenia. The word is derived from the Greek

words *kopros* (excrement) and *lalia* (talking). *See also* Gilles de la Tourette's disease.

Corrective emotional experience. Re-exposure, under favorable circumstances, to an emotional situation that the patient could not handle in the past. As advocated by Franz Alexander, the therapist temporarily assumes a particular role to generate the experience and facilitate reality-testing.

Co-therapy. A form of psychotherapy in which more than one therapist treat the individual patient or the group. It is also known as combined therapy, cooperative therapy, dual leadership, multiple therapy, and three-cornered therapy. *See also* Role-divided therapy, Splitting situation.

Counterdependent person. *See* Nontruster.

Countertransference. Conscious or unconscious emotional response of the therapist to the patient. It is determined by the therapist's inner needs rather than by the patient's needs, and it may reinforce the patient's earlier traumatic history if not checked by the therapist.

Co-worker. Professional or paraprofessional who works in the same clinical or institutional setting.

Creativity. Ability to produce something new. Silvano Arieti describes creativity as the tertiary process, a balanced combination of primary and secondary processes, whereby materials from the id are used in the service of the ego.

Crisis-intervention group psychotherapy. Group therapy aimed at decreasing or eliminating an emotional or situational crisis.

Crisis, therapeutic. *See* Therapeutic crisis.

Crystallization. In transactional analysis, a statement of the patient's position from the Adult of the therapist to the Adult of the patient. *See also* Ego state.

Cultural conserve. The finished product of the creative process; anything that preserves the values of a particular culture. Without this repository of the past, man would be forced to create the same forms to meet the same situations day after day. The cultural conserve also entices new creativity.

Cultural deprivation. Restricted participation in the culture of the larger society.

Current material. Data from present interpersonal experiences. *See also* Genetic material.

Cyclazocine. A narcotic antagonist that blocks the effects of heroin but does not relieve heroin craving. It has been used experimentally with a limited number of drug addicts in research programs.

Cycloplegia. Paralysis of the muscles of accommodation in the eye. It is observed at times as an autonomic side effect of phenothiazine and antiparkinsonism drugs.

Dance therapy. Nonverbal communication through rhythmic body movements, used to rehabilitate people with emotional or physical disorders. Pioneered by Marian Chase in 1940, this method is used in both individual and group therapy.

Data. *See* Current material, Genetic material.

Death instinct. *See* Aggressive drive.

Decision. In transactional analysis, a childhood commitment to a certain existential position and life style. *See also* Script analysis.

Decompensation. In medical science, the failure of normal functioning of an organ, as in cardiac decompensation; in psychiatry, the breakdown of the psychological defense mechanisms that maintain the person's optimal psychic functioning. *See also* Depersonalization.

Decontamination. In transactional analysis, a process whereby a person is freed of Parent or Child contaminations. *See also* Clarification.

Defense mechanism. Unconscious intrapsychic process. Protective in nature, it is used to relieve the anxiety and conflict arising from one's impulses and drives. *See also* Compensation, Conversion, Denial, Displacement, Dissociation, Idealization, Identification, Incorporation, Intellectualization, Introjection, Projection, Rationalization, Reaction formation, Regression, Repression, Sublimation, Substitution, Symbolization, Undoing.

Defensive emotion. Strong feeling that serves as a screen for a less acceptable feeling, one that would cause a person to experience anxiety if it appeared. For example, expressing the emotion of anger is often more acceptable to a group member than expressing the fear that his anger covers up. In this instance, anger is defensive.

Déjà entendu. Illusion of auditory recognition. *See also* Paramnesia.

Déjà vu. Illusion of visual recognition in which a new situation is incorrectly regarded as a repetition of a previous experience. *See also* Paramnesia.

Delirium. A disturbance in the state of consciousness that stems from an acute organic reaction characterized by restlessness, confusion, disorientation, bewilderment, agitation, and affective lability. It is associated with fear, hallucinations, and illusions.

Delusion. A false fixed belief not in accord with one's intelligence and cultural background. Types of delusion include:
Delusion of control. False belief that one is being manipulated by others.
Delusion of grandeur. Exaggerated concept of one's importance.
Delusion of infidelity. False belief that one's lover is unfaithful; it is derived from pathological jealousy.
Delusion of persecution. False belief that one is being harrassed.
Delusion of reference. False belief that the behavior of others refers to oneself; a derivation from ideas of reference in which the patient falsely feels that he is being talked about by others.
Delusion of self-accusation. False feeling of remorse.
Paranoid delusion. Oversuspiciousness leading to false persecutory ideas or beliefs.

Dementia. Organic loss of mental functioning.

Denial. An unconscious defense mechanism in which an aspect of external reality is rejected. At times it is replaced by a more satisfying fantasy or piece of behavior. The term can also refer to the blocking of awareness of internal reality. It is one of the primitive or infantile defenses.

Dependence on therapy. Patient's pathological need for therapy, created out of the belief that he cannot survive without it.

Dependency. A state of reliance on another

for psychological support. It reflects needs for security, love, protection, and mothering.

Dependency phase. *See* Inclusion phase.

Depersonalization. Sensation of unreality concerning oneself, parts of oneself, or one's environment. It is seen in schizophrenics, particularly during the early stages of decompensation. *See also* Decompensation.

Depression. In psychiatry, a morbid state characterized by mood alterations, such as sadness and loneliness; by low self-esteem associated with self-reproach; by psychomotor retardation and, at times, agitation; by withdrawal from interpersonal contact and, at times, a desire to die; and by such vegetative symptoms as insomnia and anorexia. *See also* Grief.

Derailment. *See* Tangentiality.

Derealization. Sensation of distorted spatial relationships. It is seen in certain types of schizophrenia.

Dereism. Mental activity not concordant with logic or experience. This type of thinking is commonly observed in schizophrenic states.

Detoxification. Removal of the toxic effects of a drug. It is also known as detoxication. *See also* Cold turkey, Methadone.

Diagnostic and Statistical Manual of Mental Disorders. A handbook for the classification of mental illnesses. Formulated by the American Psychiatric Association, it was first issued in 1952 (DSM-I). The second edition (DSM-II), issued in 1968, correlates closely with the World Health Organization's *International Classification of Diseases*.

Dialogue. Verbal communication between two or more persons.

Didactic psychodrama. Psychodrama used as a teaching method. It is used with persons involved in the care of psychiatric patients to teach them how to handle typical conflicts.

Didactic technique. Group therapeutic method given prominence by J. M. Klapman that emphasizes the tutorial approach. The group therapist makes use of outlines, texts, and visual aids to teach the group about themselves and their functioning. *See also* Class method, Group bibliotherapy, Mechanical group therapy.

Differentiation. *See* Individuation.

Dilution of transference. Partial projection of irrational feelings and reactions onto various group members and away from the leader. Some therapists do not believe that dilution of transference occurs. *See also* Multiple transference, Transference.

Dipsomania. Morbid, irrepressible compulsion to drink alcoholic beverages.

Directive-didactic approach. Group therapy approach characterized by guided discussions and active direction by the therapist. Various teaching methods and printed materials are used, and autobiographical material may be presented. Such an approach is common with regressed patients in mental institutions.

Discussion model of group psychotherapy. A type of group therapy in which issues, problems, and facts are deliberated, with the major emphasis on rational understanding.

Disinhibition. Withdrawal of inhibition. Chemical substances such as alcohol can remove inhibitions by interfering with functions of the cerebral cortex. In psychiatry, disinhibition leads to the freedom to act on one's own needs rather than to submit to the demands of others.

Displacement. An unconscious defense mechanism by which the affective component of an unacceptable idea or object is transferred to an acceptable one.

Disposition. Sum total of a person's inclinations as determined by his mood.

Dissociation. An unconscious defense mechanism by which an idea is separated from its accompanying affect, as seen in hysterical dissociative states; an unconscious process by which a group of mental processes are split off from the rest of a person's thinking, resulting in an independent functioning of this group of processes and thus a loss of the usual inter-relationships.

Distortion. Misrepresentation of reality. It is based on historically determined motives.

Distractability. Inability to focus one's attention.

Diversified reality. A condition in a treatment situation that provides various real stimuli with which the patient may interact. In a group, the term refers to the variety of personalities of the co-members, in contrast with the one personality of the analyst in the dyadic relationship.

Doctor-patient relationship. Human interchange that exists between the person who is sick and the person who is selected because of training and experience to heal.

Dog-eat-dog period. Early stage of Communist brainwashing of American prisoners during the Korean War. During this period, as described by former Army psychiatrist William Mayer, the Communists encouraged each prisoner to be selfish and to do only what was best for himself. *See also* Give-up-itis.

Dominant member. The patient in a group who tends to monopolize certain group sessions or situations.

Double. *See* Mirror.

Double-bind. Two conflicting communications from another person. One message is usually nonverbal and the other verbal. For example, parents may tell a child that arguments are to be settled peacefully and yet battle with each other constantly. The concept was formulated by Gregory Bateson.

Double-blind study. A study in which one or more drugs and a placebo are compared in such a way that neither the patient nor the persons directly or indirectly involved in the study know which is being given to the patient. The drugs being investigated and the placebo are coded for identification.

Dream. Mental activity during sleep that is experienced as though it were real. A dream has both a psychological and a biological purpose. It provides an outlet for the release of instinctual impulses and wish fulfillment of archaic needs and fantasies unacceptable in the real world. It permits the partial resolution of conflicts and the healing of traumata too overwhelming to be dealt with in the waking state. And it is the guardian of sleep, which is indispensable for the proper functioning of mind and body during the waking state. *See also* Hypnagogic hallucination, Hypnopompic hallucination, Paramnesia.

Dreamy state. Altered state of consciousness likened to a dream situation. It is accompanied by hallucinations—visual, auditory, and olfactory—and is believed to be associated with temporal lobe lesions. *See also* Marijuana.

Drive. A mental constituent, believed to be genetically determined, that produces a state of tension when it is in operation. This tension or state of psychic excitation motivates the person into action to alleviate the tension. Contemporary psychoanalysts prefer to use the term drive rather than Freud's term, instinct. *See also* Aggressive drive, Instinct, Sexual drive.

Drop-out. Patient who leaves group therapy against the therapist's advice.

Drug therapy. The use of chemical substances in the treatment of illness. It is also known as chemotherapy. *See also* Maintenance drug therapy.

DSM. *See* *Diagnostic and Statistical Manual of Mental Disorders.*

Dual leadership. *See* Co-therapy.

Dual therapy. *See* Co-therapy.

Dyad. A pair of persons in an interactional situation—such as husband and wife, mother and father, co-therapists, or patient and therapist.

Dyadic session. Psychotherapeutic session involving only two persons, the therapist and the patient.

Dynamic reasoning. Forming all the clinical evidence gained from free-associative anamnesis into a psychological reconstruction of the patient's development. It is a term used by Franz Alexander.

Dyskinesia. Involuntary, stereotyped, rhythmic muscular activity, such as a tic or a spasm. It is sometimes observed as an extrapyramidal side effect of antipsychotic drugs, particularly the phenothiazine derivatives. *See also* Tardive oral dyskinesia.

Dystonia. Extrapyramidal motor disturbance consisting of uncoordinated and spasmodic movements of the body and limbs, such as arching of the back and twisting of the body and neck. It is observed as a side effect of phenothiazine drugs and other major tranquilizers. *See also* Tardive oral dyskinesia.

East-Coast-style T-group. Group that follows the traditional National Training Laboratories orientation by developing awareness of group process. The first T-groups were held in Bethel, Maine. *See also* Basic skills training, West-Coast-style T-group.

Echolalia. Repetition of another person's words or phrases. It is a psychopathological symptom observed in certain cases of schizophrenia, particularly the catatonic types. Some authors consider this behavior to be an attempt by the patient to maintain a continuity of thought processes. *See also* Gilles de la Tourette's disease.

Echopraxia. Imitation of another person's movements. It is a psychopathological symptom observed in some cases of catatonic schizophrenia.

Ecstasy. Affect of intense rapture.

Ego. One of the three components of the psychic apparatus in the Freudian structural framework. The other two components are the id and the superego. Although the ego has some conscious components, many of its operations are automatic. It occupies a position between the primal instincts and the demands of the outer world, and it therefore serves to mediate between the person and external reality. In so doing, it performs the important functions of perceiving the needs of the self, both physical and psychological, and the qualities and attitudes of the environment. It evaluates, coordinates, and integrates these perceptions so that internal demands can be adjusted to external requirements. It is also responsible for certain defensive functions to protect the person against the demands of the id and the superego. It has a host of functions, but adaptation to reality is perhaps the most important one. *See also* Reality-testing.

Ego-coping skill. Adaptive method or capacity developed by a person to deal with or overcome a psychological or social problem.

Ego defense. *See* Defense mechanism.

Ego ideal. Part of the ego during its development that eventually fuses with the superego. It is a social as well as a psychological concept, reflecting the mutual esteem as well as the disillusionment in child-parent and subsequent relationships.

Egomania. Pathological self-preoccupation or self-centeredness. *See also* Narcissism.

Ego model. A person on whom another person patterns his ego. In a group, the therapist or a healthier member acts as an ego model for members with less healthy egos. In psychodrama, the auxiliary ego may act as the ego model.

Ego state. In Eric Berne's structural analysis, a state of mind and its related set of coherent behavior patterns. It includes a system of feelings directly related to a given subject. There are three ego states—Parent, Adult, and Child.

Eitingon, Max (1881–1943). Austrian psychoanalyst. An emissary of the Zurich school, he gained fame as the first person to be analyzed by Freud—in a few sessions in 1907. Later he became the first chief of the Berlin Psychoanalytic Clinic, a founder of the Berlin Psychoanalytic Institute, and a founder of the Palestine Psychoanalytic Society.

Elation. Affect characterized by euphoria, confidence, and enjoyment. It is associated with increased motor activity.

Electrocardiographic effect. Change seen in recordings of the electrical activity of the heart. It is observed as a side effect of phenothiazine derivatives, particularly thioridazine.

Electroconvulsive treatment. *See* Shock treatment.

Emotion. *See* Affect.

Emotional deprivation. Lack of adequate and appropriate interpersonal or environmental experiences or both, usually in the early developmental years. Emotional deprivation is caused by poor mothering or by separation from the mother.

Emotional insight. *See* Insight.

Emotional support. Encouragement, hope, and inspiration given to one person by another. Members of a treatment group often empathize with a patient who needs such support in order to try a new mode of behavior or to face the truth.

Empathy. Ability to put oneself in another person's place, get into his frame of reference, and understand his feelings and behavior objectively. It is one of the major qualities in a successful therapist, facilitator, or helpful group member. *See also* Sympathy.

Encounter group. A form of sensitivity training that emphasizes the experiencing of individual relationships within the group and minimizes intellectual and didactic input. It is a group that focuses on the present rather than concerning itself with the past or outside problems of its members. J. L. Moreno introduced and developed the idea of the encounter group in 1914. *See also* Here-and-now approach, Intervention laboratory, Nonverbal interaction, Task-oriented group.

Encountertapes. Tape recordings designed to provide a group with guidelines for progressive interaction in the absence of a leader. They are copyrighted by the Bell & Howell Company and are available commercially from their Human Development Institute in Atlanta, Georgia.

Epileptic dementia. A form of epilepsy that is accompanied by progressive mental and intellectual impairment. Some believe that the circulatory disturbances during epileptic attacks cause nerve cell degeneration and lead to dementia.

Epinephrine. A sympathomimetic agent. It is the chief hormone secreted by the adrenal medulla. In a state of fear or anxiety, the physiological changes stem from the release of epinephrine. Also known as adrenaline, it is related to norepinephrine, a substance presently linked with mood disturbances in depression.

Eros. *See* Sexual drive.

Erotomania. Pathological preoccupation with sexual activities or fantasies.

Esalen massage. A particular type of massage taught and practiced at the Esalen Institute, a growth center at Big Sur, California. The massage lasts between one and a half and three hours and is intended to be an intimate, loving communion between the participants. A variation is the massage of one person by a group. The massage is given without words.

Ethnocentrism. Conviction that one's own group is superior to other groups. It impairs one's ability to evaluate members of another group realistically or to communicate with them on an open, equal, and person-to-person basis.

Euphoria. An altered state of consciousness characterized by an exaggerated feeling of well-being that is inappropriate to apparent events. It is often associated with opiate, amphetamine, or alcohol abuse.

Evasion. Act of not facing up to or of strategically eluding something. It consists of suppressing an idea that is next in a thought series and replacing it with another idea closely related to it. Evasion is also known as paralogia and perverted logic.

Exaltation. Affect consisting of intense elation and feelings of grandeur.

Exhibitionism. A form of sexual deviation characterized by a compulsive need to expose one's body, particularly the genitals.

Existential group psychotherapy. A type of group therapy that puts the emphasis on confrontation, primarily in the here-and-now interaction, and on feeling experiences rather than on rational thinking. Less attention is put on patient resistances. The therapist is involved on the same level and to the same degree as the patients. *See also* Encounter group.

Expanded group. The friends, immediate family, and interested relatives of a group therapy patient. They are the people with whom he has to relate outside the formal therapy group. *See also* Back-home group.

Experiencing. Feeling emotions and sensations as opposed to thinking; being involved in what is happening rather than standing back at a distance and theorizing. Encounter groups attempt to bring about this personal involvement.

Experiential group. *See* Encounter group.

Experiential stimulator. Anything that stimulates an emotional or sensory response. Several techniques, many of them nonverbal, have been developed for encounter groups to accomplish this stimulation. *See also* Behind-the-back technique, Blind walk.

Extended family therapy. A type of family therapy that involves family members, beyond the nuclear family, who are closely associated with it and affect it. *See also* **Network, Social** network therapy, Visitor.

Exteropsychic function. *See* Parent.

Extrapsychic conflict. Conflict that arises between the person and his environment. *See also* Intrapsychic conflict.

Extrapyramidal effect. Bizarre, involuntary motor movement. It is a central nervous system side effect sometimes produced by antipsychotic drugs. *See also* Dyskinesia.

Extratherapeutic contact. Contact between group members outside of a regularly scheduled group session.

Facilitator. Group leader. He may be the therapist or a patient who emerges during the course of an encounter and who channels group interaction. He is also known as the session leader.

Fag hag. Slang, derogatory expression often used by homosexuals to describe a woman who has become part of a homosexual social circle and has assumed a central role as a mother figure.

Family neurosis. Emotional maladaptation in which a person's psychopathology is unconsciously inter-related with that of the other members of his family.

Family therapy. Treatment of a family in conflict. The whole family meets as a group with the therapist and explores its relationships and process. The focus is on the resolution of current reactions to one another rather than on individual members. *See also* Collaborative therapy, Combined therapy, Concurrent therapy, Conjoint therapy, Extended family therapy, Group marital therapy, Marriage therapy, Quadrangular therapy, Square interview.

Fantasy. Day dream; fabricated mental picture or chain of events. A form of thinking dominated by unconscious material and primary processes, it seeks wish-fulfillment and immediate solutions to conflicts. Fantasy may serve as the matrix for creativity or for neurotic distortions of reality.

Father surrogate. Father substitute. In psychoanalysis, the patient projects his father image onto another person and responds to that person unconsciously in an inappropriate and unrealistic manner with the feelings and attitudes he had toward the original father.

Fausse reconnaissance. False recognition. *See also* Paramnesia.

Fear. Unpleasurable affect consisting of psychophysiological changes in response to a realistic threat or danger to one's existence. *See also* Anxiety.

Federn, Paul (1871–1950). Austrian psychoanalyst, one of Freud's earliest followers, and the last survivor of the original Wednesday Evening Society. He made important original contributions to psychoanalysis—such as the concepts of flying dreams and ego feeling—and was instrumental in saving the minutes of the Vienna Psychoanalytic Society for subsequent publication.

Feedback. Expressed response by one person or a group to another person's behavior. *See also* Sociometric feedback, Transaction.

Feeling-driven group. A group in which little or no attention is paid to rational processes, thinking, or cognition and where the expression of all kinds of emotion is rewarded. *See also* Affectualizing, Encounter group, Existential group psychotherapy.

Ferenczi, Sandor (1873–1933). Hungarian psychoanalyst, one of Freud's early followers, and a brilliant contributor to all aspects of psychoanalysis. His temperament was more romantic than Freud's, and he came to favor more active and personal techniques, to the point that his adherence to psychoanalysis during his last years was questioned.

Field theory. Concept postulated by Kurt Lewin that a person is a complex energy field in which all behavior can be conceived of as a change in some state of the field during a given unit of time. Lewin also postulated the presence within the field of psychological tensions—states of readiness or preparation for action. The field theory is concerned essentially with the present field, the here-and-now. The theory has been applied by various group psychotherapists.

Fliess, Wilhelm (1858–1928). Berlin nose and throat specialist. He shared an early interest with Freud in the physiology of sex and entered into a prolonged correspondence that figures importantly in the records of Freud's self-analysis. Freud was influenced by Fliess's concept of bisexuality and his theory of the periodicity of the sex functions.

Focal-conflict theory. Theory elaborated by Thomas French in 1952 that explains the current behavior of a person as an expression of his method of solving currently experienced personality conflicts that originated very early in his life. He constantly resonates to these early-life conflicts.

Focused exercise. Technique used particularly in encounter groups to help participants break through their defensive behavior and express such specific emotional reactions as anger, affection, and joy. A psychodrama, for instance, may focus on a specific problem that a group member is having with his wife. In playing out both his part and her part, he becomes aware of the emotion he has been blocking.

Folie à deux. Emotional illness shared by two persons. If it involves three persons, it is referred to as *folie à trois*, etc.

Forced interaction. Relationship that occurs in a group when the therapist or other members demand that a particular patient respond, react, and be active. *See also* Structured interactional group psychotherapy.

Ford negative personal contacts with Negroes scale. A scale that measures whites' negative social contacts with blacks. *See also* Kelley desegregation scale, Rosander anti-Negro behavior scale, Steckler anti-Negro scale, Steckler anti-white scale.

Ford negative personal contacts with whites scale. A scale that measures blacks' negative personal contacts with whites. It helps assess the extent to which negative social contacts influence prejudiced attitudes, thus contributing to the theoretical basis for the employment of interracial group experiences to reduce prejudice. *See also* Kelley desegregation scale, Rosander anti-Negro behavior scale, Steckler anti-Negro scale, Steckler anti-white scale.

Formal operations. Jean Piaget's label for the complete development of a person's logical thinking capacities.

Foulkes, S. H. (1923–). English psychiatrist and one of the organizers of the group therapy movement in Great Britain. His work combines Moreno's ideas—the here-and-now, the socio-genesis, the social atom, the psychological network—with psychoanalytic views. He stresses the importance of group-as-a-whole phenomena. *See also* Group analytic psychotherapy, Network.

Free association. Investigative psychoanalytic technique devised by Freud in which the patient seeks to verbalize, without reservation or censor, the passing contents of his mind. The conflicts that emerge while fulfilling this task constitute resistances that are the basis of the analyst's interpretations. *See also* Antirepression device, Conflict.

Free-floating anxiety. Pervasive, unrealistic fear that is not attached to any idea or alleviated by symptom substitution. It is observed particularly in anxiety neurosis, although it may be seen in some cases of latent schizophrenia.

Freud, Sigmund (1856–1939). Austrian psychiatrist and the founder of psychoanalysis. With Josef Breuer, he explored the potentialities of cathartic therapy, then went on to develop the analytic technique and such fundamental concepts of mental phenomena as the unconscious, infantile sexuality, repression, sublimation, superego, ego, and id formation and their applications throughout all spheres of human behavior.

Fulfillment. Satisfaction of needs that may be either real or illusory.

Future projection. Psychodrama technique wherein the patient shows in action how he thinks his future will shape itself. He, sometimes with the assistance of the director, picks the point in time, the place, and the people, if any, he expects to be involved with at that time.

Galactorrhea. Excessive or spontaneous flow of milk from the breast. It may be a result of the endocrine influence of phenothiazine drugs.

Gallows transaction. A transaction in which a person with a self-destructive script smiles while narrating or engaging in a self-destructive act. His smile evokes a smile in the listener, which is in essence an encouragement for self-destruction. *See also* Hamartic script.

Game. Technique that resembles a traditional game in being physical or mental competition conducted according to rules but that is used in the group situation as an experiential learning device. The emphasis is on the process of the game rather than on the objective of the game. A game in Eric Berne's transactional analysis refers to an orderly sequence of social maneuvers with an ulterior motive and resulting in a psychological payoff for the players. *See also* Hit-and-run game, Million-dollar game, Pastime, Survival, Transactional group psychotherapy.

Game analysis. In transactional analysis, the analysis of a person's social interactions that are not honest and straightforward but are contaminated with pretenses for personal gain. *See also* Script analysis, Structural analysis.

Genetic material. Data out of the personal history of the patient that are useful in developing an understanding of the psychodynamics of his present adaptation. *See also* Current material.

Genital phase. The final stage of psychosexual development. It occurs during puberty. In this stage the person's psychosexual development is so organized that he can achieve sexual gratification from genital-to-genital contact and has the capacity for a mature, affectionate relationship with someone of the opposite sex. *See also* Anal phase, Infantile sexuality, Latency phase, Oral phase, Phallic phase.

Gestalt therapy. Type of psychotherapy that emphasizes the treatment of the person as a whole—his biological component parts and their organic functioning, his perceptual configuration, and his inter-relationships with the outside world. Gestalt therapy, developed by Frederic S. Perls, can be used in either an individual or a group therapy setting. It focuses on the sensory awareness of the person's here-and-now experiences rather than on past recollections or future expectations. Gestalt therapy employs role-playing and other techniques to promote the patient's growth process and to develop his full potential. *See also* Nonverbal interaction.

Gilles de la Tourette's disease. A rare illness that has its onset in childhood. The illness, first described by a Paris physician, Gilles de la Tourette, is characterized by involuntary muscular movements and motor incoordination accompanied by echolalia and coprolalia. It is considered by some to be a schizophrenic condition.

Give-up-itis. Syndrome characterized by a giving up of the desire to live. The alienation, isolation, withdrawal, and eventual death associated with this disease syndrome were experienced by many American prisoners during the Korean War, particularly in the early stages of Communist brainwashing. *See also* Dog-eat-dog period.

Go-around. Technique used in group therapy, particularly in structured interactional group psychotherapy, in which the therapist requires that each member of the group respond to another member, a theme, an association, etc. This procedure encourages participation of all members in the group.

God complex. A belief, sometimes seen in therapists, that one can accomplish more than is humanly possible or that one's word should not be doubted. The God complex of the aging psychoanalyst was first discussed by Ernest Jones, Freud's biographer. *See also* Mother Superior complex.

Gould Academy. Private preparatory school in Bethel, Maine, that has been used during summers as the site of the human relations laboratories run by the National Educational Association.

Grief. Alteration in mood and affect consisting of sadness appropriate to a real loss. *See also* Depression.

Group. *See* Therapeutic group.

Group action technique. Technique used in group work to help the participants achieve skills in interpersonal relations and improve their capacity to perform certain tasks better on the job or at home; technique, often involving physical interaction, aimed at enhancing involvement or communion within a new group.

Group analysand. A person in treatment in a psychoanalytically oriented group.

Group analytic psychotherapy. A type of group therapy in which the group is used as the principal therapeutic agent and all communications and relationships are viewed as part of a total field of interaction. Interventions deal primarily with group forces rather than with individual forces. S. H. Foulkes applied the term to his treatment procedure in 1948. It is also known as therapeutic group analysis. *See also* Phyloanalysis, Psychoanalytic group psychotherapy.

Group apparatus. Those people who preserve order and ensure the survival of a group. The internal apparatus deals with members' proclivities in order to maintain the structure of the group and strengthen cohesion. The therapist usually serves as his own apparatus in a small therapy group; in a courtroom, a bailiff ensures internal order. The external apparatus deals with the environment in order to minimize the threat of external pressure. The therapist usually acts as his own external apparatus by setting the time and place for the meetings and making sure that outsiders do not interfere; in a war, combat forces act as the external apparatus.

Group bibliotherapy. A form of group therapy that focuses on the use of selected readings as stimulus material. Outside readings and oral presentations of printed matter by therapist and patients are designed to encourage verbal interchange in the sessions and to hold the attention of severely regressed patients. This approach is used in the treatment of large groups of institutionalized patients. *See also* Class method, Didactic technique, Mechanical group therapy.

Group-centered psychotherapy. A short-term, nonclinical form of group therapy developed by followers of Carl Rogers and based on his client-centered method of individual treatment. The therapist maintains a nonjudgmental attitude, clarifies the feelings expressed in the sessions, and communicates empathic understanding and respect. The participants are not diagnosed, and uncovering techniques are not employed.

Group climate. Atmosphere and emotional tone of a group therapy session.

Group cohesion. Effect of the mutual bonds between members of a group as a result of their concerted effort for a common interest and purpose. Until cohesiveness is achieved, the group cannot concentrate its full energy on a common task. *See also* Group growth.

Group dynamics. Phenomena that occur in groups; the movement of a group from its inception to its termination. Interactions and interrelations among members and between the members and the therapist create tension, which maintains a constantly changing group equilibrium. The interactions and the tension they create are highly influenced by individual members' psychological make-up, unconscious instinctual drives, motives, wishes, and fantasies. The understanding and effective use of group dynamics is essential in group treatment. It is also known as group process. *See also* Group mobility, Psychodynamics.

Group grope. Belittling reference to procedures used in certain encounter groups. The procedures are aimed at providing emotional release through physical contact.

Group growth. Gradual development of trust and cohesiveness in a group. It leads to awareness of self and of other group process and to more effective coping with conflict and intimacy problems. *See also* Group cohesion.

Group history. Chronology of the experiences of a group, including group rituals, group traditions, and group themes.

Group inhibition. *See* Group resistance.

Group marathon. Group meeting that usually lasts from eight to 72 hours, although some sessions last for a week. The session is interrupted only for eating and sleeping. The leader works for the development of intimacy and the open expression of feelings. The time-extended group experience culminates in intense feelings of excitement and elation. Group marathon was developed by George Bach and Frederick Stoller. *See also* Accelerated interaction, Nude marathon, Too-tired-to-be-polite phenomenon.

Group marital therapy. A type of marriage therapy that makes use of a group. There are two basic techniques: (1) Inviting the marital partner of a group member to a group session. The other group members are confronted with the neurotic marriage pattern, which gives them new insights and awareness. (2) Placing a husband and wife together in a traditional group of patients. This method seems indicated if the spouses are unable to achieve meaningful intimacy because they fear the loss of their individual identity at an early phase of the marriage, before a neurotic equilibrium is established. *See also* Collaborative therapy, Combined therapy, Concurrent therapy, Conjoint therapy, Family therapy, Quadrangular therapy, Square interview.

Group mind. Autonomous and unified mental life in an assemblage of people bound together by mutual interests. It is a concept used by group therapists who focus on the group as a unit rather than on the individual members.

Group mobility. Spontaneity and movement in

the group brought about by changes in the functions and roles of individual members, relative to their progress. *See also* Group dynamics.

Group-on-group technique. Device used in T-groups wherein one group watches another group in action and then gives feedback to the observed group. Frequently, one group breaks into two sections, each taking turns in observing the other. The technique is intended to sharpen the participants' observation of individual behavior and group process.

Group phenomenon. *See* Group dynamics.

Group pressure. Demand by group members that individual members submit and conform to group standards, values, and behavior.

Group process. *See* Group dynamics.

Group psychotherapy. A type of psychiatric treatment that involves two or more patients participating together in the presence of one or more psychotherapists, who facilitate both emotional and rational cognitive interaction to effect changes in the maladaptive behavior of the members. *See also* Behavioral group psychotherapy, Bio-energetic group psychotherapy, Client-centered psychotherapy, Communion-oriented group psychotherapy, Crisis-intervention group psychotherapy, Existential group psychotherapy, Group analytic psychotherapy, Group bibliotherapy, Group-centered psychotherapy, Individual therapy, Inspirational-supportive group psychotherapy, Psychoanalytic group psychotherapy, Repressive-inspirational group psychotherapy, Social network therapy, Structured interactional group psychotherapy, Traditional group therapy, Transactional group psychotherapy.

Group resistance. Collective natural aversion of the group members toward dealing with unconscious material, emotions, or old patterns of defense.

Group ritual. Tradition or activity that any group establishes to mechanize some of its activities.

Group stimulus. Effect of several group members' communicating together. Each member has a stimulating effect on every other member, and the total stimulation is studied for therapeutic purposes. *See also* Transactions.

Group therapy. *See* Group psychotherapy.

Group tradition. Activity or value established historically by a group. It determines in part the group's manifest behavior.

Group value. Relative worth or standard developed by and agreed on by the members of a group.

Guilt. Affect associated with self-reproach and need for punishment. In psychoanalysis, guilt refers to a neurotic feeling of culpability that stems from a conflict between the ego and the superego. It begins developmentally with parental disapproval and becomes internalized as conscience in the course of superego formation. Guilt has normal psychological and social functions, but special intensity or absence of guilt characterizes many mental disorders, such as depression and antisocial personality. Some psychiatrists distinguish shame as a less internalized form of guilt.

Gustatory hallucination. False sense of taste.

Hallucination. A false sensory perception without a concrete external stimulus. It can be induced by emotional and by organic factors, such as drugs and alcohol. Common hallucinations involve sights or sounds, although any of the senses may be involved. *See also* Auditory hallucination, Gustatory hallucination, Hypnagogic hallucination, Hypnopompic hallucination, Kinesthetic hallucination, Lilliputian hallucination, Tactile hallucination, Visual hallucination.

Hallucinatory psychodrama. A type of psychodrama wherein the patient portrays the voices he hears and the visions he sees. Auxiliary egos are often called on to enact the various phenomena expressed by the patient and to involve him in interaction with them, so as to put them to a reality test. The intended effect on the patient is called psychodramatic shock.

Hallucinogenic drug. *See* Psychotomimetic drug.

Hamartic script. In transactional analysis, a life script that is self-destructive and tragic in character. *See also* Gallows transaction, Script, Script antithesis, Script matrix.

Healthy identification. Modeling of oneself, consciously or unconsciously, on another person who has sound psychic make-up. The identification has constructive purposes. *See also* Imitation.

Herd instinct. Desire to belong to a group and to participate in social activities. Wilfred Trotter used the term to indicate the presence of a hypothetical social instinct in man. In psychoanalysis, herd instinct is viewed as a social phenomenon rather than as an instinct. *See also* Aggressive drive, Sexual drive.

Here-and-now. Contemporaneity. *See also* There-and-then.

Here-and-now approach. A technique that focuses on understanding the interpersonal and intrapersonal responses and reactions as they occur in the on-going treatment session. Little or no emphasis is put on past history and experiences. *See also* Encounter group, Existential group psychotherapy.

Heterogeneous group. A group that consists of patients from both sexes, a wide age range, differing psychopathologies, and divergent socioeconomic, racial, ethnic, and cultural backgrounds. *See also* Homogeneous group.

Heterosexuality. Sexual attraction or contact between opposite-sex persons. The capacity for heterosexual arousal is probably innate, biologically programmed, and triggered in very early life, perhaps by olfactory modalities, as seen in lower animals. *See also* Bisexuality, Homosexuality.

Hidden self. The behavior, feelings, and motivations of a person known to himself but not to others. It is a quadrant of the Johari Window, a diagrammatic concept of human behavior. *See also* Blind self, Public self, Undeveloped potential.

Hierarchical vector. Thrust of relating to the other members of a group or to the therapist in a supraordinate or subordinate way. It is the opposite of relating as peers. It is also known as vertical vector. *See also* Authority principle, Horizontal vector, Political therapist.

Hit-and-run game. Hostile or nonconstructive aggressive activity indiscriminately and irresponsibly carried out against others. *See also* Game, Million dollar game, Survival.

Homogeneous group. A group that consists of patients of the same sex, with similarities in

their psychopathology, and from the same age range and socioeconomic, racial, ethnic, and cultural background. *See also* Heterogeneous group.

Homosexuality. Sexual attraction or contact between same-sex persons. Some authors distinguish two types: overt homosexuality and latent homosexuality. *See also* Bisexuality, Heterosexuality, Inversion, Lesbianism.

Homosexual panic. Sudden, acute onset of severe anxiety, precipitated by the unconscious fear or conflict that one may be a homosexual or act out homosexual impulses. *See also* Homosexuality.

Honesty. Forthrightness of conduct and uprightness of character; truthfulness. In therapy, honesty is a value manifested by the ability to communicate one's immediate experience, including inconsistent, conflicting, or ambivalent feelings and perceptions. *See also* Authenticity.

Hook. In transactional analysis, to switch one's transactions to a new ego state. For example, a patient's Adult ego state is hooked when he goes to the blackboard and draws a diagram.

Horizontal vector. Thrust of relating to the therapist or other members of the group as equals. It is also known as peer vector. *See also* Authority principle, Hierarchical vector, Political therapist.

House encounter. Group meeting of all the persons in a treatment facility. Such a meeting is designed to deal with specific problems within the therapeutic community that affect its functioning, such as poor morale and poor job performances.

Hydrotherapy. External or internal use of water in the treatment of disease. In psychiatry, the use of wet packs to calm an agitated psychotic patient was formerly a popular treatment modality.

Hyperactivity. Increased muscular activity. The term is commonly used to describe a disturbance found in children that is manifested by constant restlessness and movements executed at a rapid rate. The disturbance is believed to be due to brain damage, mental retardation, emotional disturbance, or physiological disturbance. It is also known as hyperkinesis.

Hyperkinesis. *See* Hyperactivity.

Hypermnesia. Exaggerated degree of retention and recall. It is observed in schizophrenia, the manic phase of manic-depressive illness, organic brain syndrome, drug intoxication induced by amphetamines and hallucinogens, hypnosis, and febrile conditions. *See also* Memory.

Hypertensive crisis. Severe rise in blood pressure that can lead to intracranial hemorrhage. It is occasionally seen as a side effect of certain antidepressant drugs.

Hypnagogic hallucination. False sensory perception that occurs just before falling asleep. *See also* Hypnopompic hallucination.

Hypnodrama. Psychodrama under hypnotic trance. The patient is first put into a hypnotic trance. During the trance he is encouraged to act out the various experiences that torment him.

Hypnopompic hallucination. False sensory perception that occurs just before full wakefulness. *See also* Hypnagogic hallucination.

Hypnosis. Artificially induced alteration of consciousness of one person by another. The subject responds with a high degree of suggestibility, both mental and physical, during the trancelike state.

Hypochondriasis. Exaggerated concern with one's physical health. The concern is not based on real organic pathology.

Hypotension, orthostatic. *See* Orthostatic hypotension.

Hysterical anesthesia. Disturbance in sensory perception characterized by absence of sense of feeling in certain areas of the body. It is observed in certain cases of hysterical neurosis, particularly the conversion type, and it is believed to be a defense mechanism.

Id. Part of Freud's concept of the psychic apparatus. According to his structural theory of mental functioning, the id harbors the energy that stems from the instinctual drives and desires of a person. The id is completely in the unconscious realm, unorganized and under the influence of the primary processes. *See also* Conscious, Ego, Preconscious, Primary process, Superego, Unconscious.

Idealization. A defense mechanism in which a person consciously or, usually, unconsciously overestimates an attribute or an aspect of another person.

Ideas of reference. Misinterpretation of incidents and events in the outside world as having a direct personal reference to oneself. Occasionally observed in normal persons, ideas of reference are frequently seen in paranoid patients. *See also* Projection.

Ideational shield. An intellectual, rational defense against the anxiety a person would feel if he became vulnerable to the criticisms and rejection of others. As a result of his fear of being rejected, he may feel threatened if he criticizes another person—an act that is unacceptable to him. In both group and individual therapy, conditions are set up that allow the participants to lower this ideational shield.

Identification. An unconscious defense mechanism in which a person incorporates into himself the mental picture of an object and then patterns himself after this object; seeing oneself as like the person used as a pattern. It is distinguished from imitation, a conscious process. *See also* Healthy identification, Imitation, Role.

Identification with the aggressor. An unconscious process by which a person incorporates within himself the mental image of a person who represents a source of frustration from the outside world. A primitive defense, it operates in the interest and service of the developing ego. The classical example of this defense occurs toward the end of the oedipal stage, when the male child, whose main source of love and gratification is the mother, identifies with his father. The father represents the source of frustration, being the powerful rival for the mother; the child cannot master or run away from his father, so he is obliged to identify with him. *See also* Psychosexual development.

Idiot. *See* Mental retardation.

I-It. Philosopher Martin Buber's description of damaging interpersonal relationships. If a person treats himself or another person exclusively as an object, he prevents mutuality, trust, and growth. When pervasive in a group, I-It relationships prevent human warmth, destroy cohesiveness, and retard group process. *See also* I-Thou.

Ileus, paralytic. *See* Paralytic ileus.

Illusion. False perception and misinterpretation of an actual sensory stimulus.

Illustration. In transactional analysis, an anecdote, simile, or comparison that reinforces a confrontation or softens its potentially undesirable effects. The illustration may be immediate or remote in time and may refer to the external environment or to the internal situation in the group.

Imbecile. *See* Mental retardation.

Imitation. In psychiatry, a conscious act of mimicking another person's behavior pattern. *See also* Healthy identification, Identification.

Impasse. *See* Therapeutic impasse.

Improvement scale. In transactional analysis, a quantitative specification of a patient's position in terms of improvement in the course of therapy.

Improvisation. In psychodrama, the acting out of problems without prior preparation.

Impulse. Unexpected, instinctive urge motivated by conscious and unconscious feelings over which the person has little or no control. *See also* Drive, Instinct.

Inappropriate affect. Emotional tone that is out of harmony with the idea, object, or thought accompanying it.

Inclusion phase. Early stage of group treatment. In this phase, each group member's concern focuses primarily on belonging and being accepted and recognized, particularly by the therapist. It is also known as the dependency stage. *See also* Affection phase, Power phase.

Incorporation. An unconscious defense mechanism in which an object representation is assimilated into oneself through symbolic oral ingestion. One of the primitive defenses, incorporation is a special form of introjection and is the primary mechanism in identification.

Individual psychology. Holistic theory of personality developed by Alfred Adler. Personality development is explained in terms of adaptation to the social milieu (life style), strivings toward perfection motivated by feelings of inferiority, and the interpersonal nature of the person's problems. Individual psychology is applied in

group psychotherapy and counseling by Adlerian practitioners.

Individual therapy. A type of psychotherapy in which a professionally trained psychotherapist treats one patient who either wants relief from disturbing symptoms or improvement in his ability to cope with his problems. This one therapist-one patient relationship, the traditional dyadic therapeutic technique, is opposed to other techniques that deal with more than one patient. *See also* Group psychotherapy, Psychotherapy.

Individuation. Differentiation; the process of molding and developing the individual personality so that it is different from the rest of the group. *See also* Actualization.

Infantile dynamics. Psychodynamic integrations, such as the Oedipus complex, that are organized during childhood and continue to exert unconsciously experienced influences on adult personality.

Infantile sexuality. Freudian concept regarding the erotic life of infants and children. Freud observed that, from birth, infants are capable of erotic activities. Infantile sexuality encompasses the overlapping phases of psychosexual development during the first five years of life and includes the oral phase (birth to 18 months), when erotic activity centers around the mouth; the anal phase (ages one to three), when erotic activity centers around the rectum; and the phallic phase (ages two to six), when erotic activity centers around the genital region. *See also* Psychosexual development.

Inferiority complex. Concept, originated by Alfred Adler, that everyone is born with inferiority or a feeling of inferiority secondary to real or fantasied organic or psychological inadequacies. How this inferiority or feeling of inferiority is handled determines a person's behavior in life. *See also* Masculine protest.

Infra reality. Reduced actuality that is observed in certain therapeutic settings. For example, according to J. L. Moreno, who coined the term, the contact between doctor and patient is not a genuine dialogue but is an interview, research situation, or projective test.

Injunction. In transactional analysis, the instructions given by one ego state to another, usually the Parent ego state to the Child ego state, that become the basis of the person's life script decisions. *See also* Permission, Program, Role, Script analysis.

Inner-directed person. A person who is self-motivated and autonomous and is not easily guided or influenced by the opinions and values of other people. *See also* Other-directed person.

Insight. Conscious awareness and understanding of one's own psychodynamics and symptoms of maladaptive behavior. It is highly important in effecting changes in the personality and behavior of a person. Most therapists distinguish two types: (1) intellectual insight—knowledge and awareness without any change of maladaptive behavior; (2) emotional or visceral insight—awareness, knowledge, and understanding of one's own maladaptive behavior, leading to positive changes in personality and behavior.

Inspirational-supportive group psychotherapy. A type of group therapy that focuses on the positive potential of members and stresses reinforcement for accomplishments or achievements. *See also* Alcoholics Anonymous.

Instinct. A biological, species-specific, genetically determined drive to respond in an automatic, complex, but organized way to a particular stimulus. *See also* Drive, Impulse.

Institute of Industrial Relations. A department of the Graduate School of Business Administration at the University of California at Los Angeles. It has conducted sensitivity training laboratories for business and professional people for nearly 20 years.

Insulin coma therapy. A form of psychiatric treatment originated by Manfred Sakel in which insulin is administered to the patient to produce coma. It is used in certain types of schizophrenia. *See also* Shock treatment.

Intellectual insight. *See* Insight.

Intellectualization. An unconscious defense mechanism in which reasoning or logic is used in an attempt to avoid confrontation with an objectionable impulse or affect. It is also known as brooding or thinking compulsion.

Intelligence. Capacity for understanding, recalling, mobilizing, and integrating constructively what one has learned and for using it to meet new situations.

Intensive group process. Group process designed to evoke a high degree of personal interaction and involvement, often accompanied by the expression of strong or deep feelings.

Interaction. *See* Transaction.

Interpersonal conflict. *See* Extrapsychic conflict.

Interpersonal psychiatry. Dynamic-cultural system of psychoanalytic therapy based on Harry Stack Sullivan's interpersonal theory. Sullivan's formulations were couched in terms of a person's interactions with other people. In group psychotherapy conducted by practitioners of this school, the focus is on the patients' transactions with one another.

Interpersonal skill. Ability of a person in relationship with others to express his feelings appropriately, to be socially responsible, to change and influence, and to work and create. *See also* Socialization.

Interpretation. A psychotherapeutic technique used in psychoanalysis, both individual and group. The therapist conveys to the patient the significance and meaning of his behavior, constructing into a more meaningful form the patient's resistances, defenses, transferences, and symbols (dreams). *See also* Clarification.

Interpretation of Dreams, The. Title of a book by Freud. Published in 1899, this work was a major presentation not only of Freud's discoveries about the meaning of dreams—hitherto regarded as outside scientific interest—but also of his concept of a mental apparatus that is topographically divided into unconscious, preconscious, and conscious areas.

Interracial group. *See* Heterogeneous group.

Intervention laboratory. Human relations laboratory, such as an encounter group or training group, especially designed to intervene and resolve some group conflict or crisis.

Intrapersonal conflict. *See* Intrapsychic conflict.

Intrapsychic ataxia. *See* Ataxia.

Intrapsychic conflict. Conflict that arises from the clash of two opposing forces within oneself.

It is also known as intrapersonal conflict. *See also* Extrapsychic conflict.

Introjection. An unconscious defense mechanism in which a psychic representation of a loved or hated object is taken into one's ego system. In depression, for example, the emotional feelings related to the loss of a loved one are directed toward the introjected mental representation of the loved one. *See also* Identification, Incorporation.

Inversion. Synonym for homosexuality. Inversion was the term used by Freud and his predecessors. There are three types: absolute, amphigenous, and occasional. *See also* Homosexuality, Latent homosexuality, Overt homosexuality.

I-Thou. Philosopher Martin Buber's conception that man's identity develops from true sharing by persons. Basic trust can occur in a living partnership in which each member identifies the particular real personality of the other in his wholeness, unity, and uniqueness. In groups, I-Thou relationships promote warmth, cohesiveness, and constructive group process. *See also* I-It.

Jamais vu. False feeling of unfamiliarity with a real situation one has experienced. *See also* Paramnesia.

Jaundice, allergic. Yellowish staining of the skin and deeper tissues accompanied by bile in the urine secondary to a hypersensitivity reaction. An obstructive type of jaundice, it is occasionally detected during the second to fourth week of phenothiazine therapy.

Johari Window. A schematic diagram used to conceptualize human behavior. It was developed by Joseph (Jo) Luft and Harry (Hari) Ingham at the University of California at Los Angeles in 1955. The diagram is composed of quadrants, each representing some aspect of a person's behavior, feelings, and motivations. *See also* Blind self, Hidden self, Public self, Undeveloped potential.

Jones, Ernest (1879–1958). Welsh psychoanalyst and one of Freud's early followers. He was an organizer of the American Psychoanalytic Association in 1911 and the British Psychoanalytical Society in 1919 and a founder and longtime editor of the journal of the International Psychoanalytical Association. He was the author of many valuable works, the most important of which is his three-volume biography of Freud.

Judgment. Mental act of comparing or evaluating choices within the framework of a given set of values for the purpose of electing a course of action. Judgment is said to be intact if the course of action chosen is consistent with reality; judgment is said to be impaired if the chosen course of action is not consistent with reality.

Jung, Carl Gustav (1875–1961). Swiss psychiatrist and psychoanalyst. He founded the school of analytic psychology. *See also* Collective unconscious.

Karate-chop experience. A technique used in encounter groups to elicit aggression in timid or inhibited participants in a humorous way. The timid one stands facing a more aggressive member. Both make violent pseudokarate motions at each other, without making physical contact but yelling "Hai!" as loudly as possible at each stroke. After this exercise, the group members discuss the experience.

Kelley desegregation scale. A scale designed to measure the attitudes of whites toward blacks in the area of school integration. The scale provides a rough measure of racial prejudice and may be of help in ascertaining the effects on prejudice of participation in an interracial group. *See also* Ford negative personal contacts with Negroes scale, Ford negative personal contacts with whites scale, Rosander anti-Negro behavior scale, Steckler anti-Negro scale, Steckler anti-white scale.

Kinesthetic hallucination. False perception of muscular movement. An amputee may feel movement in his missing limb; this phenomenon is also known as phantom limb.

Kinesthetic sense. Sensation in the muscles as differentiated from the senses that receive stimulation from outside the body.

Kleptomania. Pathological compulsion to steal. In psychoanalytic theory, it originates in the infantile stage of psychosexual development.

Latency phase. Stage of psychosexual development extending from age five to the beginning of adolescence at age 12. Freud's work on ego psychology showed that the apparent cessation of sexual preoccupation during this period stems from a strong, aggressive blockade of libidinal and sexual impulses in an effort to avoid the dangers of the oedipal relationships. During the latency period, boys and girls are inclined to choose friends and join groups of their own sex. *See also* Identification with the aggressor, Psychosexual development.

Latent homosexuality. Unexpressed conscious or unconscious homoerotic wishes that are held in check. Freud's theory of bisexuality postulated the existence of a constitutionally determined, though experientially influenced, instinctual masculine-feminine duality. Normally, the opposite-sex component is dormant, but a breakdown in the defenses of repression and sublimation may activate latent instincts and result in overt homoeroticism. Many writers have questioned the validity of a universal latent homoeroticism. *See also* Bisexuality, Homosexuality, Overt homosexuality.

Lateral transference. Projection of long-range attitudes, values, and emotions onto the other members of the treatment group rather than onto the therapist. The patient sees other members of the group, co-patients, and peers in terms of his experiences in his original family. *See also* Collective family transference neurosis, Multiple transference.

Leaderless therapeutic group. An extreme form of nondirective group, conducted primarily for research purposes, such as the investigations of intragroup tensions by Walter R. Bion. On occasion, the therapist interacts verbally in a nonauthoritarian manner, but he generally functions as a silent observer—withholding explanations, directions, and support.

Leadership function. *See* Leadership role.

Leadership role. Stance adopted by the therapist in conducting a group. There are three main leadership roles: authoritarian, democratic, and laissez-faire. Any group—social, therapeutic, training, or task-oriented—is primarily influenced by the role practiced by the leader.

Leadership style. *See* Leadership role.

Lesbianism. Female homosexuality. About 600 B.C. on the island of Lesbos in the Aegean Sea, the poetess Sappho encouraged young women to engage in mutual sex practices. Lesbianism is also known as Sapphism. *See also* Bisexuality, Homosexuality, Latent homosexuality, Overt homosexuality.

Lewin, Kurt (1890–1946). German psychologist who emigrated to the United States in 1933. His work on the field theory has been useful in the experimental study of human behavior in a social situation. He was one of the early workers who helped develop the National Training Laboratories.

Libido theory. Freudian theory of sexual instinct, its complex process of development, and its accompanying physical and mental manifestations. Before Freud's introduction and completion of the dual-instinct theory (sexual and aggressive) in 1920, all instinctual manifestations were related to the sexual instinct, making for some confusion at that time. Current psychoanalytic practice assumes the existence of two instincts: sexual (libido) and aggressive (death). *See also* Aggressive drive, Sexual drive.

Life instinct. *See* Sexual drive.

Life lie. A contrary-to-fact conviction around which a person structures his life philosophy and attitudes.

Life line. A group technique in which each member is asked to draw a line representing his life, beginning with birth and ending with death. Comparison and discussion usually reveal that the shape and slope of the lines are based on a variety of personally meaningful parameters, such as maturity and academic achievement.

Lifwynn Foundation. Organization established by Trigant Burrow in 1927 as a social community in which the participants examined their interactions in the daily activities in which they were engaged. Lifwynn is currently under the direction of Hans Syz, M.D., in Westport, Conn.

Lilliputian hallucination. False perception that persons are reduced in size. *See also* Micropsia.

Lobotomy. Neurosurgical procedure in which one or more nerve tracts in a lobe of the cerebrum are severed. Prefrontal lobotomy is the ablation of one or more nerve tracts in the prefrontal area of the brain. It is used in the treatment of certain severe mental disorders that do not respond to other treatments.

Locus. Place of origin.

Logorrhea. Copious, pressured, coherent speech. It is observed in manic-depressive illness, manic type. Logorrhea is also known as tachylogia, verbomania, and volubility.

LSD (lysergic acid diethylamide). A potent psychotogenic drug discovered in 1942. LSD produces psychoticlike symptoms and behavior changes—including hallucinations, delusions, and time-space distortions.

Lysergic acid diethylamide. *See* LSD.

Macropsia. False perception that objects are larger than they really are. *See also* Micropsia.

Maintenance drug therapy. A stage in the course of chemotherapy. After the drug has reached its maximal efficacy, the dosage is reduced and sustained at the minimal therapeutic level that will prevent a relapse or exacerbation.

Major tranquilizer. Drug that has antipsychotic properties. The phenothiazines, thioxanthenes, butyrophenones, and reserpine derivatives are typical major tranquilizers, which are also known as ataractics, neuroleptics, and antipsychotics. *See also* Dystonia, Minor tranquilizer.

Maladaptive way. Poorly adjusted or pathological behavior pattern.

Mannerism. Stereotyped involuntary activity that is peculiar to a person.

MAO inhibitor. *See* Monoamine oxidase inhibitor.

Marathon. *See* Group marathon.

Marijuana. Dried leaves and flowers of *Cannabis sativa* (Indian hemp). It induces somatic and psychic changes in man when smoked or ingested in sufficient quantity. The somatic changes include increased heart rate, rise in blood pressure, dryness of the mouth, increased appetite, and occasional nausea, vomiting, and diarrhea. The psychic changes include dreamy-state level of consciousness, disruptive chain of ideas, perceptual disturbances of time and space, and alterations of mood. In strong doses, marijuana can produce hallucinations and, at times, paranoid ideas and suspiciousness. It is also known as pot, grass, weed, tea, and Mary Jane.

Marital counseling. Process whereby a trained counselor helps married couples resolve problems that arise and trouble them in their relationship. The theory and techniques of this approach were first developed in social agencies as part of family casework. Husband and wife are seen by the same worker in separate and joint counseling sessions, which focus on immediate family problems.

Marital therapy. *See* Marriage therapy.

Marriage therapy. A type of family therapy that involves the husband and the wife and focuses on the marital relationship, which affects the individual psychopathology of the partners. The rationale for this method is the assumption that psychopathological processes within the family structure and in the social matrix of the marriage perpetuate individual pathological personality structures, which find expression in the disturbed marriage and are aggravated by the feedback between partners. *See also* Collaborative therapy, Combined therapy, Concurrent therapy, Conjoint therapy, Family therapy, Group marital therapy, Marital counseling, Quadrangular therapy, Square interview.

Masculine identity. Well-developed sense of gender affiliation with males.

Masculine protest. Adlerian doctrine that depicts a universal human tendency to move from a passive and feminine role to a masculine and active role. This doctrine is an extension of his ideas about organic inferiority. It became the prime motivational force in normal and neurotic behavior in the Adlerian system. *See also* Adler, Alfred; Inferiority complex.

Masculinity-femininity scale. Any scale on a psychological test that assesses the relative masculinity or femininity of the testee. Scales vary and may focus, for example, on basic identification with either sex or preference for a particular sex role.

Masochism. A sexual deviation in which sexual gratification is derived from being maltreated by the partner or oneself. It was first described by an Austrian novelist, Leopold von Sacher-Masoch (1836–1895). *See also* Sadism, Sadomasochistic relationship.

Masturbation. *See* Autoerotism.

Mattress-pounding. A technique used in encounter groups to mobilize repressed or suppressed anger. A group member vents his resentments by beating the mattress with his fists and yelling. Frequently, the mattress becomes in fantasy a hated parent, sibling, or spouse. After this exercise, the group members discuss their reactions. *See also* Pillow-beating.

Maximal expression. Utmost communication. In psychodrama, it is the outcome of an involved sharing by the group of the three portions of the session: the warm-up, the action, and the post-action. During the action period the patient is encouraged to express all action and verbal communication to the limit. To this end, delusions, hallucinations, soliloquies, thoughts, and fantasies are allowed to be part of the production.

Mechanical group therapy. A form of group therapy that makes use of mechanical devices. As applied in the early 1950's, it required neither a group nor a therapist. An example of this form of therapy is the playing of brief recorded messages over the loudspeaker system of a mental hospital; the same statement, bearing on some elementary principle of mental health, is frequently repeated to secure general acceptance. *See also* Class method, Didactic technique, Group bibliotherapy.

Megalomania. Morbid preoccupation with expansive delusions of power and wealth.

Melancholia. Old term for depression that is rarely used at the present time. As used in the term involutional melancholia, it refers to a morbid state of depression and not to a symptom.

Memory. Ability to revive past sensory impressions, experiences, and learned ideas. Memory includes three basic mental processes: registration—the ability to perceive, recognize, and establish information in the central nervous system; retention—the ability to retain registered information; and recall—the ability to retrieve stored information at will. *See also* Amnesia, Hypermnesia, Paramnesia.

Mental aberration. *See* Aberration, mental.

Mental illness. Psychiatric disease included in the list of mental disorders in the *Diagnostic and Statistical Manual of Mental Disorders* published by the American Psychiatric Association and in the *Standard Nomenclature of Diseases and Operations* approved by the American Medical Association.

Mental retardation. Subnormal general intellectual functioning, which may be evident at birth or may develop during childhood. Learning, social adjustment, and maturation are impaired, and emotional disturbance is often present. The degree of retardation is commonly measured in terms of I.Q.: borderline (68–85), mild (52–67), moderate (36–51), severe (20–35), and profound (under 20). Obsolescent terms that are still used occasionally are idiot (mental age of less than three years), imbecile (mental age of three to seven years), and moron (mental age of eight years).

Methadone. Methadone hydrochloride, a long-acting synthetic narcotic developed in Germany as a substitute for morphine. It is used as an analgesic and in detoxification and maintenance treatment of opiate addicts.

Methadone maintenance treatment. Long-term use of methadone on a daily basis to relieve narcotic craving and avert the effects of narcotic drugs.

Micropsia. False perception that objects are smaller than they really are. *See also* Lilliputian hallucination, Macropsia.

Milieu therapy. Treatment that emphasizes appropriate socioenvironmental manipulation for the benefit of the patient. The setting for milieu therapy is usually the psychiatric hospital.

Million-dollar game. Group game designed to explore the psychological meaning of money and to encourage free, creative thinking. The group is told that it has a million dollars, which is to be used productively in any way, as long as the endeavor actively involves all members of the group. *See also* Game, Hit-and-run game, Survival.

Minnesota Multiphasic Personality Inventory. Questionnaire type of psychological test for ages 16 and over with 550 true-false statements that are coded in 14 scales, ranging from a social scale to a schizophrenia scale. Group and individual forms are available.

Minor tranquilizer. Drug that diminishes tension, restlessness, and pathological anxiety without any antipsychotic effect. Meprobamate and diazepoxides are typical minor tranquilizers, which are also known as psycholeptics. *See also* Major tranquilizer.

Minutes of the Vienna Psychoanalytic Society. Diary of Freud's Wednesday Evening Society (after 1910, the Vienna Psychoanalytic Society) as recorded by Otto Rank, the paid secretary between 1906 and 1915.

Mirror. In psychodrama, the person who represents the patient, copying his behavior and trying to express his feelings in word and movement, showing the patient as if in a mirror how other people experience him. The mirror may exaggerate, employing techniques of deliberate distortion in order to arouse the patient to come forth and change from a passive spectator into an active participant. The mirror is also known as the double. *See also* Auxiliary ego.

Mirroring. A group process by which a person sees himself in the group by the reflections that come back to him in response to the way he presents himself. The image may be true or distorted, depending on the level of truth at which the group is functioning at the time. Mirroring has been used as an exercise in encounter group therapy and as a laboratory procedure in the warming-up period of the psychodrama approach.

Mixed-gender group. *See* Heterogeneous group.

MMPI. *See* Minnesota Multiphasic Personality Inventory.

Mobility. *See* Group mobility.

Monoamine oxidase inhibitor. Agent that inhibits the enzyme monoamine oxidase (MAO), which oxidizes such monoamines as norepinephrine and serotonin. Some of the MAO inhibitors are highly effective as antidepressants. *See also* Tricyclic drug.

Monomania. Morbid mental state characterized by preoccupation with one subject. It is also known as partial insanity.

Mood. Feeling tone that is experienced by a person internally. Mood does not include the external expression of the internal feeling tone. *See also* Affect.

Mood swing. Oscillation of a person's emotional feeling tone between periods of euphoria and depression.

Moron. *See* Mental retardation.

Moses and Monotheism. Title of a book by Freud published in 1939. In this book, Freud undertook a historical but frankly speculative reconstruction of the personality of Moses and examined the concept of monotheism and the abiding effect of the patriarch on the character of the Jews. One of Freud's last works, it bears the imprint of his latter-day outlook and problems.

Mother Superior complex. Tendency of a therapist to play the role of the mother in his relations with his patients. The complex often leads to interference with the therapeutic process. *See also* God complex.

Mother surrogate. Mother substitute. In psychoanalysis, the patient projects his mother image onto another person and responds to that person unconsciously in an inappropriate and unrealistic manner with the feelings and attitudes he had toward the original mother.

Motivation. Force that pushes a person to act to satisfy a need. It implies an incentive or desire that influences the will and causes the person to act.

Mourning. *See* Grief.

Multibody situation. Group situation. The term was originally used in the description of the evolution of social interaction in human beings from narcissism through the dyadic relationship to the three-body constellation of the Oedipus complex to the multibody situation prevailing in groups.

Multiple double. Several representations of the patient, each portraying a part of him—one as he is now, another as he was (for instance, five years ago), another at a crucial moment in his life (for example, when his mother died), a fourth how he may be 20 years hence. The multiple representations of the patient are presented in sequence, each continuing where the last left off. *See also* Auxiliary ego.

Multiple ego states. Many psychological stages, relating to different periods of one's life or to different depths of experience. These states may be of varying degrees of organization and complexity, and they may or may not be capable of being called to awareness consecutively or simultaneously.

Multiple interaction. Group behavior in which many members participate in the transactions, both verbal and nonverbal, at any one moment in the session.

Multiple intragroup transference. *See* Multiple transference.

Multiple reactivity. A phenomenon in which many group members respond in a variety of ways to the provocative role or stimulation afforded by one patient's behavior.

Multiple therapy. *See* Co-therapy.

Multiple transferences. Feelings and attitudes originally held toward members of one's family that become irrationally attached to the therapist and various group members simultaneously. *See also* Collective family transference neurosis, Lateral transference.

Mutism. *See* Stupor.

Mutual support. Expressions of sympathy, understanding, and affection that group members give to one another. *See also* Pairing.

Mydriasis. Dilatation of the pupil. The condition sometimes occurs as an autonomic side effect of phenothiazine and antiparkinsonism drugs.

Nalline test. The use of Nalline, a narcotic antagonist, to determine abstinence from opiates. An injection of Nalline precipitates withdrawal symptoms if opiates have been used recently. The most important use for Nalline, however, is as an antidote in the treatment of opiate overdose.

Narcissism. Self-love. It is linked to autoerotism but is devoid of genitality. The word is derived from Narcissus, a Greek mythology figure who fell in love with his own reflected image. In psychoanalytic theory, it is divided into primary narcissism and secondary narcissism. Primary narcissism refers to the early infantile phase of object relationship development, when the child has not differentiated himself from the outside world. All sources of pleasure are unrealistically recognized as coming from within himself, giving him a false sense of omnipotence.

Secondary narcissism is the type of narcissism that results when the libido once attached to external love objects is redirected back to the self. *See also* Autistic thinking, Autoerotism.

Narcotic hunger. A physiological craving for a drug. It appears in abstinent narcotic addicts.

National Training Laboratories. Organization started in 1947 at Bethel, Maine, to train professionals who work with groups. Interest in personal development eventually led to sensitivity training and encounter groups. The organization is now called the NTL Institute for Applied Behavioral Science. *See also* Basic skills training, East Coast style T-group.

Natural Child. In transactional analysis, the autonomous, expressive, archaic Child ego state that is free from parental influence. *Se also* Adapted Child.

Natural group. Group that tends to evolve spontaneously in human civilization, such as a kinship, tribal, or religious group. In contrast are various contrived groups or aggregates of people who meet for a relatively brief time to achieve some goal.

Negativism. Verbal or nonverbal opposition to outside suggestions and advice. It is also known as command negativism.

Neologism. New word or condensation of several words formed by patient in an effort to express a highly complex idea. It is often seen in schizophrenia.

Neopsychic function. *See* Adult.

Network. The persons in the patient's environment with whom he is most intimately connected. It frequently includes the nuclear family, the extended family, the orbit of relatives and friends, and work and recreational contacts. S. H. Foulkes believes that this dynamically interacting network has a fundamental significance in the production of illness in the patient. *See also* Extended family therapy, Social network therapy, Visitor.

Neuroleptic. *See* Antipsychotic drug, Major tranquilizer.

Neurosis. Mental disorder characterized by anxiety. The anxiety may be experienced and expressed directly, or, through an unconscious psychic process, it may be converted, displaced, or somatized. Although neuroses do not manifest depersonalization or overt distortion of reality, they can be severe enough to impair a person's functioning. The neuroses, also known as psychoneuroses, include the following types: anxiety neurosis, hysterical neurosis, phobic neurosis, obsessive-compulsive neurosis, depressive neurosis, neurasthenic neurosis, depersonalization neurosis, and hypochondriacal neurosis.

Nondirective approach. Technique in which the therapist follows the lead of the patient in the interview rather than introducing his own theories and directing the course of the interview. This method is applied in both individual and group therapy, such as Carl Rogers' client-centered and group-centered therapy. *See also* Passive therapist.

Nontruster. A person who has a strong unfilled need to be nurtured but whose early experience was one of rejection or overprotection. As a defense against repetition of this experience, he develops an overly strong show of independence. Sometimes this independence is manifested in group therapy by a member's constant rejection of support and of attempts by other members to get close to him. *See also* Outsider.

Nonverbal interaction. Technique used without the aid of words in encounter groups to promote communication and intimacy and to bypass verbal defenses. Many exercises of this sort are carried out in complete silence; in others, the participants emit grunts, groans, yells, cries, or sighs. Gestalt therapy pays particular attention to nonverbal expression.

Norepinephrine. A catecholamine that functions as a neurohumoral mediator liberated by postganglionic adrenergic nerves. It is also present in the adrenal medulla and in many areas in the brain, with the highest concentration in the hypothalamus. A disturbance in the metabolism of norepinephrine is considered to be an important factor in the etiology of depression. *See also* Serotonin.

Nuclear family. Immediate members of a family, including the parents and the children. *See also* Extended family therapy, Network, Social network therapy, Visitor.

Nuclear group member. *See* Therapist surrogate.

Nude marathon. Encounter group in which members assemble for an emotional experience of prolonged duration (from a minimum of eight hours to a couple of days), with the added factor of physical nakedness as members go about their activities. The theory is that clothes are themselves defenses against openness, that they connote limiting roles and result in stereotyped responses from others, and that they allow participants to avoid facing conflicts about their own bodies. *See also* Group marathon, Sensory-experiential group.

Nymphomania. Morbid, insatiable need in women for sexual intercourse. *See also* Satyriasis.

Observer. Person who is included but is generally not an active participant in therapy sessions. His observations are later discussed in posttherapy meetings with the staff or supervisor. *See also* Recorder.

Observer therapist. *See* Passive therapist.

Obsession. Persistent idea, thought, or impulse that cannot be eliminated from consciousness by logical effort. *See also* Compulsion.

Oedipus complex. A distinct group of associated ideas, aims, instinctual drives, and fears that are generally observed in children when they are from three to six years of age. During this period, which coincides with the peak of the phallic phase of psychosexual development, the child's sexual interest is attached chiefly to the parent of the opposite sex and is accompanied by aggressive feelings and wishes for the parent of the same sex. One of Freud's most important concepts, the Oedipus complex was discovered in 1897 as a result of his self-analysis. *See also* *Totem and Taboo.*

Ogre. In structural analysis, the Child ego state in the father that supersedes the nurturing Parent and becomes a pseudo-Parent.

One-gender group. *See* Homogeneous group.

Open group. Treatment group in which new members are continuously added as other members leave. *See also* Closed group.

Oral dyskinesia, tardive. *See* Tardive oral dyskinesia.

Oral phase. The earliest stage in psychosexual development. It lasts through the first 18 months of life. During this period, the oral zone is the center of the infant's needs, expression, and pleasurable erotic experiences. It has a strong influence on the organization and development of the child's psyche. *See also* Anal phase, Genital phase, Infantile sexuality, Latency phase, Phallic phase.

Orientation. State of awareness of one's relationships and surroundings in terms of time, place, and person.

Orthostatic hypotension. Reduction in blood pressure brought about by a shift from a recumbent to an upright position. It is observed as a side effect of several psychotropic drugs.

Other-directed person. A person who is readily influenced and guided by the attitudes and values of other people. *See also* Inner-directed person.

Outsider. In group therapy, a member who feels alienated and isolated from the group. Such a person has usually experienced repetitive rejection in his early life and is wary of trusting people in the present. Often much effort is required by the group and the therapist before the outsider trusts someone. *See also* Nontruster.

Overt homosexuality. Behaviorally expressed homoeroticism as distinct from unconsciously held homosexual wishes or conscious wishes that are held in check. *See also* Homosexuality, Latent homosexuality.

Pairing. Term coined by Walter R. Bion to denote mutual support between two or more group members who wish to avoid the solution of their problems. The term is often used more loosely to denote an attraction between two group members.

Panic. An acute, intense attack of anxiety associated with personality disorganization. Some writers use the term exclusively for psychotic episodes of overwhelming anxiety. *See also* Homosexual panic.

Pantomime. Gesticulation; psychodrama without the use of words.

Paralogia. *See* Evasion.

Paralytic ileus. Intestinal obstruction of the nonmechanical type, secondary to paralysis of the bowel wall, that may lead to fecal retention.

It is a rare anticholinergic side effect of phenothiazine therapy.

Paramnesia. Disturbance of memory in which reality and fantasy are confused. It is observed in dreams and in certain types of schizophrenia and organic brain syndromes. *See also* Confabulation, Déjà entendu, Déjà vu, Fausse reconnaissance, Jamais vu, Retrospective falsification.

Paranoid delusion. *See* Delusion.

Parent. In transactional analysis, an ego state borrowed from a parental figure. It is also known as exteropsychic function.

Parental rejection. Denial of affection and attention to a child by one or both parents. The child in turn develops great affect hunger and hostility, which is directed either outwardly in the form of tantrums, etc., or inwardly toward himself in the form of allergies, etc.

Parkinsonism. Syndrome characterized by rhythmical muscular tremors known as pill rolling accompanied by spasticity and rigidity of movement, propulsive gait, droopy posture, and masklike facies. It is usually seen in later life as a result of arteriosclerotic changes in the basal ganglia.

Parkinsonismlike effect. Symptom that is a frequent side effect of antipsychotic drugs. Typical symptoms are motor retardation, muscular rigidity, alterations of posture, tremor, and autonomic nervous system disturbances. *See also* Phenothiazine derivative.

Partial insanity. *See* Monomania.

Passive therapist. Type of therapist who remains inactive but whose presence serves as a stimulus for the patient in the group or individual treatment setting. *See also* Active therapist, Leaderless therapeutic group, Nondirective approach.

Pastime. In transactional analysis, semistereotyped set of transactions dealing with a certain topic. Unlike Berne's term game, a pastime has no ulterior motive and no psychological payoff.

Patient peers. *See* Co-patients.

Patty-cake exercise. An encounter group technique that involves the palm-to-palm contact made by children in the game of patty-cake. This type of contact is familiar and does not usually arouse much anxiety in participants, yet it allows people to bypass verbal defenses in getting to know each other. After this exercise, the group members discuss their reactions. Also called Hand-dance.

Pecking order. Sequence of hierarchy or authority in an organization or social group. *See also* Hierarchical vector.

Peer co-therapist. Therapist who is equal in status to the other therapist treating a group and who relates to him on an equal level.

Peer-group phenomenon. Interaction or reaction of a person with a group of equals. These phenomena include activities he does within the group that he would probably not do individually outside the group.

Peer identification. Unconscious process that occurs in a group when one member incorporates within himself the qualities and attributes of another member. It usually occurs in members with low self-esteem who would like to feel at one with members who have improved.

Peer vector. *See* Horizontal vector.

Perception. Mental process by which data—intellectual, sensory, and emotional—are organized meaningfully. Through perception, a person makes sense out of the many stimuli that bombard him. It is one of the many ego functions. Therapy groups and T-groups aim to expand and alter perception in ways conducive to the development of the potential of each participant. *See also* Agnosia, Apperception, Clouding of consciousness, Ego, Hallucination, Hysterical anesthesia, Memory.

Perceptual expansion. Development of one's ability to recognize and interpret the meaning of sensory stimuli through associations with past experiences with similar stimuli. Perceptual expansion through the relaxation of defenses is one of the goals in both individual and group therapy.

Permission. In transactional analysis, a therapeutic transaction designed to permanently neutralize the parental injunctions.

Personal growth laboratory. A sensitivity training laboratory in which the primary emphasis is on each participant's potentialities for creativity, empathy, and leadership. In such a laboratory the facilitator encourages most modalities of experience and expression—such as art, sensory stimulation, and intellectual, emotional, written, oral, verbal, and nonverbal expression. *See also* National Training Laboratories.

Personality. Habitual configuration of behavior of a person, reflecting his physical and mental activities, attitudes, and interests and corresponding to the sum total of his adjustment to life.

Personality disorder. Mental disorder characterized by maladaptive patterns of adjustment to life. There is no subjective anxiety, as seen in neurosis, and no disturbance in the capacity to recognize reality, as seen in psychosis. The types of personality disorders include passive-aggressive, antisocial, schizoid, hysterical, paranoid, cyclothymic, explosive, obsessive-compulsive, asthenic, and inadequate.

Perversion. Deviation from the expected norm. In psychiatry it commonly signifies sexual perversion. *See also* Sexual deviation.

Perverted logic. *See* Evasion.

Peter Principle. Theory that man tends to advance to his level of incompetence. The idea was popularized in a book of the same name by Laurence J. Peter and Raymond Hull.

Phallic overbearance. Domination of another person by aggressive means. It is generally associated with masculinity in its negative aspects.

Phallic phase. The third stage in psychosexual development. It occurs when the child is from two to six years of age. During this period, the child's interest, curiosity, and pleasurable experiences are centered around the penis in boys and the clitoris in girls. *See also* Anal phase, Genital phase, Infantile sexuality, Latency phase, Oral phase.

Phantasy. *See* Fantasy.

Phantom limb. *See* Kinesthetic hallucination.

Phenothiazine derivative. Compound derived from phenothiazine. It is particularly known for its antipsychotic property. As a class, the phenothiazine derivatives are among the most widely used drugs in medical practice, particularly in psychiatry. Chlorpromazine, triflupromazine, fluphenazine, perphenazine, and thioridazine are some examples of phenothiazine derivatives. *See also* Anticholinergic effect, Autonomic side effect, Electrocardiographic effect, Mydriasis, Paralytic ileus, Parkinsonismlike effect.

Phobia. Pathological fear associated with some specific type of stimulus or situation. *See also* Acrophobia, Agoraphobia, Algophobia, Claustrophobia, Xenophobia, Zoophobia.

Phyloanalysis. A means of investigating disorders of human behavior, both individual and collective, resulting from impaired tensional processes that affected the organism's internal reaction as a whole. Trigant Burrow adopted the word to replace his earlier term, group analysis, which he first used in 1927 to describe the social participation of many persons in their common analysis. Because group analysis was confused with group psychotherapy of the analytic type, Burrow changed his nomenclature to phylo-analysis.

Pillow-beating. A technique used in encounter groups to elicit pent-up rage in a group member who needs to release it in a physical way. The member beats the pillow and yells angry words until he gets tired. The acceptance of his anger by the group is considered therapeutic. After this exercise, the group members discuss their reactions. *See also* Mattress-pounding.

Placebo. Inert substance prepared to resemble the active drug being tested in experimental research. It is sometimes used in clinical practice for a psychotherapeutic effect. The response to the placebo may represent the response due to the psychological effect of taking a pill and not to any pharmacological property.

Play therapy. Type of therapy used with children, usually of preschool and early latency ages. The patient reveals his problems on a fantasy level with dolls, clay, and other toys. The therapist intervenes opportunely with helpful explanations about the patient's responses and behavior in language geared to the child's comprehension. *See also* Activity group therapy.

Political therapist. A therapist who gives strong weight to the personalities of those above him as far as they impinge on his professional activities. He pays particular attention to the personal and historical aspects of authority. *See also* Authority principle, Hierarchical vector, Procedural therapist.

Popular mind. The primitive, fickle, suggestible, impulsive, uncritical type of mind that Le Bon felt was characteristic of the mass. He was referring to the unorganized crowds who lack leadership.

Postsession. *See* After-session.

Power phase. Second stage in group treatment. In this phase members start expressing anger and hostility—usually directed at the leader, sometimes directed at other members—in an attempt to achieve individuation and autonomy. *See also* Affection phase, Inclusion phase.

Pratt, Joseph H. Boston physician born in 1842 generally considered to be the first pioneer in group psychotherapy in America. He is known for his work with tuberculous patients (1900–1906). He formed discussion groups to deal with the physical aspects of tuberculosis. Later, these groups began discussing the emotional problems that stemmed from the illness. *See also* Class method.

Preconscious. In psychoanalysis, one of the three divisions of the psyche according to Freud's topographical psychology. The preconscious includes all ideas, thoughts, past experiences, and other memory impressions that can be consciously recalled with effort. *See also* Conscious, Unconscious.

Prefrontal lobotomy. *See* Lobotomy.

Prejudice. Adverse judgment or opinion formed without factual knowledge. Elements of irrational suspicion or hatred are often involved, as in racial prejudice.

Premeeting. Group meeting of patients without the therapist. It is held immediately before the regular therapist-led session and is also referred to as warming-up session and presession. *See also* After-session, Alternate session.

Preoccupation of thought. *See* Trend of thought.

Pressure cooker. Slang phrase to describe the high degree of group involvement and emotional pitch sought by certain intensive groups, such as marathon groups.

Primal father. Hypothetical head of the tribe. He is depicted by Freud in *Totem and Taboo* as slain by his sons, who subsequently devour him in a cannibalistic rite. Later, he is promoted to a god. The son who murders him is the prototype of the tragic hero, and the memory of the crime is perpetuated in the conscience of the individual and of the culture.

Primal scene. In psychoanalysis, the real or fantasied observation by a child of sexual intercourse, particularly between his parents.

Primary process. In psychoanalysis, the mental process directly related to the functions of the id and characteristic of unconscious mental activity. The primary process is marked by unorganized, illogical thinking and by the tendency to seek immediate discharge and gratification of instinctual demands. *See also* Secondary process.

Probe. An encounter technique designed for a specific purpose—for instance, to determine motivation for admission to treatment. The technique is commonly used in such drug rehabilitation centers as Odyssey House.

Procedural therapist. A therapist who places the most weight on the written word, on formal rules and regulations, and on the hierarchical system. *See also* Authority principle, Political therapist.

Process-centered group. Group whose main purpose is to study the dynamics of the group itself—how it operates and through what stages it progresses. Such groups often ask the question, "What's going on here?" rather than the encounter group question, "What are you experiencing or feeling?" *See also* Group analytic psychotherapy, Group-centered psychotherapy.

Program. In transactional analysis, the teaching by one of the parents of how best to comply with the script injunction.

Projection. Unconscious defense mechanism in which a person attributes to another the ideas, thoughts, feelings, and impulses that are part of his inner perceptions but that are unacceptable to him. Projection protects the person from anxiety arising from an inner conflict. By externalizing whatever is unacceptable, the person deals with it as a situation apart from himself. *See also* Blind spot, Future projection.

Projective method. Group treatment procedure that uses the spontaneous creative work of the patients. For example, group members make and analyze drawings, which are often expressions of their underlying emotional problems.

Protagonist. In psychodrama, the patient who is the focal point of a psychodramatic session. He is asked to be himself, to portray his own private world on the stage.

Pseudoauthenticity. False or copied expression of thoughts and feelings.

Pseudocollusion. Sense of closeness, relationship, or cooperation that is not real but is based on transference.

Psychic determinism. Freudian adaptation of the concept of causality. It states that all phenomena or events have antecedent causes that operate on an unconscious level, beyond the control of the person involved.

Psychoactive drug. Drug that alters thoughts, feelings, or perceptions. Such a drug may help a person in either individual or group therapy overcome depression, anxiety, or rigidity of thought and behavior while he learns new methods of perceiving and responding.

Psychoanalysis. Freud's method of psychic investigation and form of psychotherapy. As a technique for exploring the mental processes, psychoanalysis includes the use of free association and the analysis and interpretation of dreams, resistances, and transferences. As a form of psychotherapy, it uses the investigative technique, guided by Freud's libido and instinct theories and by ego psychology, to gain insight into a person's unconscious motivations, conflicts, and symbols and thus to effect a change in his maladaptive behavior. Several schools of thought are loosely referred to as psychoanalytic at present. Psychoanalysis is also known as analysis in depth.

Psychoanalytically oriented group psychotherapy. *See* Psychoanalytic group psychotherapy.

Psychoanalytic group psychotherapy. A major method of group psychotherapy, pioneered by Alexander Wolf and based on the operational principles of individual psychoanalytic therapy. Analysis and interpretation of a patient's transferences, resistances, and defenses are modified to take place in a group setting. Although strictly designating treatment structured to produce significant character change, the term encompasses the same approach in groups conducted at more superficial levels for lesser goals. *See also* Collective family transference neurosis, Discussion model of group psychotherapy, Verbal-deep approach.

Psychoanalytic treatment. *See* Psychoanalysis.

Psychodrama. Psychotherapy method originated by J. L. Moreno in which personality make-up, interpersonal relationships, conflicts, and emotional problems are explored by means of dramatic methods. The therapeutic dramatization of emotional problems includes: (1) protagonist or patient, the person who presents and acts out his emotional problems with the help of (2) auxiliary egos, persons trained to act and dramatize the different aspects of the patient that are called for in a particular scene in order to help him express his feelings, and (3) director, leader, or therapist, the person who guides those involved in the drama for a fruitful and therapeutic session. *See also* Actional-deep approach, Analytic psychodrama, Concretization of living, Didactic psychodrama, Hallucinatory psychodrama, Hypnodrama, Improvisation, Maximal expression, Mirror, Re-enactment, Regressive-reconstructive approach, Role-playing, Role reversal, Self-realization.

Psychodramatic director. Leader of a psychodrama session. The director has three functions: producer, therapist, and analyst. As producer, he turns every clue the patient offers into dramatic action. As therapist, he attacks and shocks the patient at times, laughs and jokes with him at times, and becomes indirect and passive at times. As analyst, he interprets and elicits responses from the audience.

Psychodramatic shock. *See* Hallucinatory psychodrama.

Psychodynamics. Science of the mind, its mental processes, and affective components that influence human behavior and motivations. *See also* Group dynamics, Infantile dynamics.

Psychological defense system. *See* Defense mechanism.

Psychological procedure. Any technique intended to alter a person's attitude toward and

perception of himself and others. *See also* Group psychotherapy, Psychoanalysis, Psychotherapy.

Psychomotor stimulant. Drug that arouses the patient through its central excitatory and analeptic properties. Amphetamine and methylphenidate are drugs in this class.

Psychopathology. Branch of science that deals with morbidity of the mind.

Psychophysiological disorder. Mental disorder characterized by physical symptoms of psychic origin. It usually involves a single organ system innervated by the autonomic nervous system. The physiological and organic changes stem from a sustained emotional disturbance.

Psychosexual development. Maturation and development of the psychic phase of sexuality from birth to adult life. Its phases are oral, anal, phallic, latency, and genital. *See also* Identification with the aggressor, Infantile sexuality.

Psychosis. Mental disorder in which a person's mental capacity, affective response, and capacity to recognize reality, communicate, and relate to others are impaired enough to interfere with his capacity to deal with the ordinary demands of life. The psychoses are subdivided into two major classifications according to their origin—psychoses associated with organic brain syndromes and functional psychoses.

Psychosomatic illness. *See* Psychophysiological disorder.

Psychosurgery. *See* Lobotomy.

Psychotherapy. Form of treatment for mental illness and behavioral disturbances in which a trained person establishes a professional contract with the patient and through definite therapeutic communication, both verbal and nonverbal, attempts to alleviate the emotional disturbance, reverse or change maladaptive patterns of behavior, and encourage personality growth and development. Psychotherapy is distinguished from such other forms of psychiatric treatment as the use of drugs, surgery, electric shock treatment, and insulin coma treatment. *See also* Growth psychotherapy, Individual therapy, Psychoanalysis.

Psychotomimetic drug. Drug that produces psychic and behavioral changes that resemble psychosis. Unlike other drugs that can produce organic psychosis as a reaction, a psychotomimetic drug does not produce overt memory impairment. It is also known as a hallucinogenic drug. Lysergic acid diethylamide (LSD), tetrahydrocannabinol, and mescaline are examples of psychotomimetic drugs.

Psychotropic drug. Drug that affects psychic function and behavior. Also known as a phrenotropic drug, it may be classified as an antipsychotic drug, antidepressant drug, antimanic drug, antianxiety drug, or hallucinogenic drug. *See also* Agranulocytosis, Orthostatic hypotension.

Public self. The behavior, feelings, and motivations of a person known both to himself and to others. It is a quadrant of the Johari Window, a diagrammatic concept of human behavior. *See also* Blind self, Hidden self, Undeveloped potential.

Quadrangular therapy. A type of marital therapy that involves four people: the married pair and each spouse's therapist. *See also* Collaborative therapy, Combined therapy, Concurrent therapy, Conjoint therapy, Family therapy, Group marital therapy, Marriage therapy, Square interview.

Rank, Otto (1884–1939). Austrian psychoanalyst. He was one of Freud's earliest followers and the long-time secretary and recorder of the minutes of the Vienna Psychoanalytic Society. He wrote such fundamental works as *The Myth of the Birth of the Hero.* He split with Freud on the significance of the birth trauma, which he used as a basis of brief psychotherapy.

Rapport. Conscious, harmonious accord that usually reflects a good relationship between two persons. In a group, rapport is the presence of mutual responsiveness, as evidenced by spontaneous and sympathetic reaction to each other's needs, sentiments, and attitudes. *See also* Countertransference, Transference.

Rap session. *See* Bull session.

Rationalization. An unconscious defense mechanism in which an irrational behavior, motive, or feeling is made to appear reasonable. Ernest Jones introduced the term.

Reaction formation. An unconscious defense mechanism in which a person develops a socialized attitude or interest that is the direct antithesis of some infantile wish or impulse in the

unconscious. One of the earliest and most unstable defense mechanisms, it is closely related to repression; both are defenses against impulses or urges that are unacceptable to the ego.

Reality. The totality of objective things and factual events. Reality includes everything that is perceived by a person's special senses and is validated by other people.

Reality-testing. Fundamental ego function that consists of the objective evaluation and judgment of the world outside the self. By interacting with his animate and inanimate environment, a person tests its real nature as well as his own relation to it. How the person evaluates reality and his attitudes toward it are determined by early experiences with the significant persons in his life. *See also* Ego.

Recall. Process of remembering thoughts, words, and actions of a past event in an attempt to recapture what actually happened. It is part of a complex mental function known as memory. *See also* Amnesia, Hypermnesia.

Recathexis. In transactional analysis, the experiencing of different ego states.

Recognition. *See* Memory.

Reconstructive psychotherapy. A form of therapy that seeks not only to alleviate symptoms but to produce alterations in maladaptive character structures and to expedite new adaptive potentials. This aim is achieved by bringing into consciousness an awareness of and insight into conflicts, fears, inhibitions, and their derivatives. *See also* Psychoanalysis.

Recorder. Person who takes notes during the group or individual therapy session. Also referred to as the recorder-observer, he generally does not participate in therapy. *See also* Observer.

Re-enactment. In psychodrama, the acting out of a past experience as if it were happening in the present so that a person can feel, perceive, and act as he did the first time.

Registration. *See* Memory.

Regression. Unconscious defense mechanism in which a person undergoes a partial or total return to earlier patterns of adaptation. Regression is observed in many psychiatric conditions, particularly schizophrenia.

Regressive-reconstructive approach. A psychotherapeutic procedure in which regression is made an integral element of the treatment process. The original traumatic situation is reproduced to gain new insight and to effect significant personality change and emotional maturation. *See also* Psychoanalysis, Reconstructive psychotherapy.

Reik, Theodor (1888–1969). Psychoanalyst and early follower of Freud, who considered him one of his most brilliant pupils. Freud's book, *The Question of Lay Analysis* was written to defend Reik's ability to practice psychoanalysis without medical training. Reik made many valuable contributions to psychoanalysis on the subjects of religion, masochism, and technique. *See also* Third ear.

Relatedness. Sense of sympathy and empathy with regard to others; sense of oneness with others. It is the opposite of isolation and alienation.

Reparenting. A technique evolved in transactional analysis for the treatment of schizophrenia. The patient is first regressed to a Child ego state, and then missing Parent transactions are supplied and contaminations corrected.

Repeater. Group member who has had experience in another group.

Repetitive pattern. Continual attitude or mode of behavior characteristic of a person and performed mechanically or unconsciously.

Repression. An unconscious defense mechanism in which a person removes from consciousness those ideas, impulses, and affects that are unacceptable to him. A term introduced by Freud, it is important in both normal psychological development and in neurotic and psychotic symptom formation. Freud recognized two kinds of repression: (1) repression proper—the repressed material was once in the conscious domain; (2) primal repression—the repressed material was never in the conscious realm. *See also* Suppression.

Repressive-inspirational group psychotherapy. A type of group therapy in which discussion is intended to bolster patients' morale and help them avoid undesired feelings. It is used primarily with large groups of seriously regressed patients in institutional settings.

Reserpine. An alkaloid extracted from the root of the *Rauwolfia serpentina* plant. It is used primarily as an antihypertensive agent. It was formerly used as an antipsychotic agent because of its sedative effect.

Residential treatment facility. A center where the patient lives and receives treatment appropriate for his particular needs. A children's residential treatment facility ideally furnishes both educational and therapeutic experiences for the emotionally disturbed child.

Resistance. A conscious or unconscious opposition to the uncovering of the unconscious. Resistance is linked to underlying psychological defense mechanisms against impulses from the id that are threatening to the ego. *See also* Group resistance.

Resonance. Unconscious response determined by early life experiences. In a group, a member may respond by fantasizing at a particular level of psychosexual development when another member functions regressively at that level. The unconscious sounding board is constructed in the first five years of life. *See also* Focal-conflict theory.

Retardation. Slowness of development or progress. In psychiatry there are two types, mental retardation and psychomotor retardation. Mental retardation refers to slowness or arrest of intellectual maturation. Psychomotor retardation refers to slowness or slackened psychic activity or motor activity or both; it is observed in pathological depression.

Retention. *See* Memory.

Retrospective falsification. Recollection of false memory. *See also* Paramnesia.

Review session. Meeting in which each member reviews with the group his goals and progress in treatment. It is a technique used in structured interactional group psychotherapy.

Ritual. Automatic activity of psychogenic or cultural origin. *See also* Group ritual.

Role. Pattern of behavior that a person takes. It has its roots in childhood and is influenced by significant people with whom the person had primary relationships. When the behavior pattern conforms with the expectations and demands of other people, it is said to be a complementary role. If it does not conform with the demands and expectation of others, it is known as noncomplementary role. *See also* Identification, Injunction, Therapeutic role.

Role-divided therapy. Therapeutic arrangement in a co-therapy situation when each therapist takes on a specific function in treatment. For example, one therapist may take the role of a provocateur, while the other takes the role of a passive observer and interpreter. *See also* Splitting situation.

Role limit. Boundary placed on the therapist or the patient by virtue of his conscious position in the therapy group. The patient plays the patient, and the therapist plays the therapist; there is no reversal of roles.

Role model. In a therapeutic community or methadone program, an ex-addict who, because of his successful adjustment and similarity of experience with the patient population, becomes a source of positive identification and a tangible proof of success. *See also* Ego model.

Role-playing. Psychodrama technique in which a person is trained to function more effectively in his reality roles—such as employer, employee, student, and instructor. In the therapeutic setting of psychodrama, the protagonist is free to try and to fail in his role, for he is given the opportunity to try again until he finally learns new approaches to the situation he fears, approaches that he can then apply outside. *See also* Antirepression device.

Role reversal. Technique used in psychodrama whereby an auxiliary ego plays the role of the patient, and the patient plays the role of the other person. Distortions of interpersonal perception are thereby brought to the surface, explored, and corrected.

Role-training. *See* Role-playing.

Roll and rock. An encounter group technique that is used to develop trust in a participant. A person stands, with eyes closed, in a tight circle of group members and is passed around (rolled) from member to member. Then he is placed on his back on the floor, gently lifted by the group members, and rocked back and forth. He is then put back on the floor. After this exercise, the group members discuss their reactions.

Rosander anti-Negro behavior scale. A scale that measures white attitudes toward blacks by asking respondents what their behavior would be in various hypothetical situations involving black participants. The scale can be of aid in determining the degree of prejudice held by whites toward blacks and the influence of a group experience on such prejudices. *See also* Ford negative personal contacts with Negroes scale, Ford negative personal contacts with whites scale, Kelley desegregation scale, Steckler anti-Negro scale, Steckler anti-white scale.

Rosenberg self-esteem scale. A scale designed to measure a person's opinion of himself. Use of this scale gives the therapist a means of evaluating the effect a group experience has on a member's self-esteem.

Saboteur. One who obstructs progress within a group, either deliberately or unconsciously.

Sadism. A sexual deviation in which sexual gratification is achieved by inflicting pain and humiliation on the partner. Donatien Alphonse François de Sade (1740–1814), a French writer, was the first person to describe this condition. *See also* Masochism, Sadomasochistic relationship.

Sadomasochistic relationship. Relationship in which the enjoyment of suffering by one person and the enjoyment of inflicting pain by the other person are important and complementary attractions in their on-going relationship. *See also* Masochism, Sadism.

Satyriasis. Morbid, insatiable sexual needs or desires in men. It may be caused by organic or psychiatric factors. *See also* Nymphomania.

Schilder, Paul (1886–1940). American neuropsychiatrist. He started the use of group psychotherapy at New York's Bellevue Hospital, combining social and psychoanalytic principles.

Schizophrenia. Mental disorder of psychotic level characterized by disturbances in thinking, mood, and behavior. The thinking disturbance is manifested by a distortion of reality, especially by delusions and hallucinations, accompanied by fragmentation of associations that results in incoherent speech. The mood disturbance is manifested by inappropriate affective responses. The behavior disturbance is manifested by ambivalence, apathetic withdrawal, and bizarre activity. Formerly known as dementia praecox, schizophrenia as a term was introduced by Eugen Bleuler. The causes of schizophrenia remain unknown. The types of schizophrenia include simple type, hebephrenic type, catatonic type, paranoid type, schizo-affective type, childhood type, residual type, latent type, acute schizophrenic episode, and chronic undifferentiated type.

Schreber case. One of Freud's cases. It involved the analysis in 1911 of Daniel Paul Shreber's autobiographical account, *Memoirs of a Neurotic,* published in 1903. Analysis of these memoirs permitted Freud to decipher the fundamental meaning of paranoid processes and ideas, especially the relationship between repressed homosexuality and projective defenses.

Screening. Initial patient evaluation that includes medical and psychiatric history, mental status evaluation, and diagnostic formulation to determine the patient's suitability for a particular treatment modality.

Script. In transactional analysis, a complex set of transactions that are adaptations of infantile responses and experiences. The script is recurrent and operates on an unconscious level. It is the mold on which a person's life adaptation is based. *See also* Hamartic script.

Script analysis. The analysis of a person's life adaption—that is, his injunctions, decisions, and life scripts—and the therapeutic process that helps reverse the maladaptive behavior. It is the last phase in transactional analysis. *See also* Game analysis, Structural analysis.

Script antithesis. In transactional analysis, a therapeutic transaction designed to avert temporarily a tragic event in a script. *See also* Script, Script matrix.

Script matrix. Diagram used in transactional analysis to represent two parents and an offspring. It is useful in representing the genesis of life scripts. *See also* Script, Script antithesis.

Secondary process. In psychoanalysis, the mental process directly related to the functions of the ego and characteristic of conscious and preconscious mental activities. The secondary process is marked by logical thinking and by the tendency to delay gratification by regulation of discharge of instinctual demands. *See also* Primary process.

Sedative. Drug that produces a calming or relaxing effect through central nervous system depression. Some drugs with sedative properties are barbiturates, chloral hydrate, paraldehyde, and bromide.

Selective inattention. An aspect of attentiveness in which a person blocks out those areas that generate anxiety.

Self-analysis. Investigation of one's own psychic components. It plays a part in all analysis, although to a limited extent, since few are capable of sustaining independent and detached attitudes for it to be therapeutic.

Self-awareness. Sense of knowing what one is experiencing. For example, realizing that one has just responded with anger to another group member as a substitute for the anxiety felt when he attacked a vital part of one's self concept. Self-awareness is a major goal of all therapy, individual and group.

Self-discovery. In psychoanalysis, the freeing of the repressed ego in a person who has been brought up to submit to the wishes of the significant others around him.

Self-presentation. Psychodrama technique in which the patient plays the role of himself and of related persons (father, mother, brother, etc.) as he perceives them in a completely subjective manner.

Self-realization. Psychodrama technique in which the protagonist enacts, with the aid of a few auxiliary egos, the plan of his life, no matter how remote it may be from his present situation. For instance, an accountant who has been taking singing lessons, hoping to try out for a musical comedy part in summer stock, and planning to make the theatre his life's work can explore the effects of success in this venture and of possible failure and return to his old livelihood.

Sensation. Feeling or impression when the sensory nerve endings of any of the six senses—taste, touch, smell, sight, kinesthesia, and sound —are stimulated.

Sensitivity training group. Group in which members seek to develop self-awareness and an understanding of group processes rather than gain relief from an emotional disturbance. *See also* Encounter group, Personal growth laboratory, T-group.

Sensorium. Theoretical sensory center located in the brain that is involved with a person's awareness about his surroundings. In psychiatry, it is often referred to as consciousness.

Sensory-experiential group. An encounter group that is primarily concerned with the emotional and physical interaction of the participants. The experience itself, not the examination of the group process, is considered the *raison d'être* for the group.

Serotonin. A monoamine that is believed to be a neurohumoral transmitter. It is found in the serum and, in high concentrations, in the hypothalamus of the brain. Recent pharmacological investigations link depression to disorders in the metabolism of serotonin and other biogenic amines, such as norepinephrine.

Session leader. *See* Facilitator.

Sexual deviation. Mental disorder characterized by sexual interests and behavior other than what is culturally accepted. Sexual deviation includes sexual interest in objects other than a person of the opposite sex, such as homosexuality or bestiality; bizarre sexual practices, such as necrophilia; and other sexual activities that are not accompanied by copulation. *See also* Bestiality, Exhibitionism, Homosexuality, Masochism, Sadism.

Sexual drive. One of the two primal instincts (the other is the aggressive drive) according to Freud's dual-instinct theory of 1920. It is also known as eros and life instinct. Its main goal is to preserve and maintain life. It operates under the influence of the pleasure-unpleasure principle. *See also* Aggressive drive, Libido theory.

Shifting attention. A characteristic of group therapy in which the focus changes from one patient to another so that no one patient remains continuously in the spotlight. It is also known as alternating scrutiny. *See also* Structured interactional group psychotherapy.

Shock treatment. A form of psychiatric treatment with a chemical substance (ingested, inhaled, or injected) or sufficient electric current to produce a convulsive seizure and unconsciousness. It is used in certain types of schizophrenia and mood disorders. Shock treatment's mechanism of action is still unknown.

Sibling rivalry. Competition among children for the attention, affection, and esteem of their parents. The children's jealousy is accompanied by hatred and death wishes toward each other. The rivalry need not be limited to actual siblings; it is a factor in both normal and abnormal competitiveness throughout life.

Slavson, S. R. (1890–   ). American theoretician who pioneered in group psychotherapy based on psychoanalytic principles. In his work with children, from which he derived most of his concepts, he introduced and developed activity group therapy. *See also* Collective experience.

Sleep. A temporary physiological state of unconsciousness characterized by a reversible cessation of the person's waking sensorimotor activity. A biological need, sleep recurs periodically to rest the whole body and to regenerate neuromuscular tissue. *See also* Dream.

Social adaptation. Adjustment to the whole complex of interpersonal relationships; the ability to live and express oneself in accordance with society's restrictions and cultural demands. *See also* Adaptational approach.

Social configuration. Arrangement of interpersonal interactions. *See also* Hierarchical vector, Horizontal vector.

Social instinct. *See* Herd instinct.

Socialization. Process of learning interpersonal and interactional skills according to and in conformity with one's society. In a group therapy setting, it includes a member's way of participating both mentally and physically in the group. *See also* Interpersonal skill.

Social network therapy. A type of group therapy in which the therapist assembles all the persons—relatives, friends, social relations, work relations—who have emotional or functional significance in the patient's life. Some or all of the social network may be assembled at any given time. *See also* Extended family therapy, Visitor.

Social psychiatry. Branch of psychiatry interested in ecological, sociological, and cultural variables that engender. intensify, or complicate maladaptive patterns of behavior and their treatment.

Social therapy. A rehabilitative form of therapy with psychiatric patients. The aim is to improve social functioning. Occupational therapy, therapeutic community, recreational therapy, milieu therapy, and attitude therapy are forms of social therapy.

Sociogram. Diagrammatic portrayal of choices, rejections, and indifferences of a number of persons involved in a life situation.

Sociometric distance. The measurable degree of perception one person has for another. It can be hypothesized that the greater the sociometric distance between persons, the more inaccurate will be their social evaluation of their relationship.

Sociometric feedback. Information that people give each other about how much closeness or distance they desire between them. It is a measure of how social one would like to be with another. An example of sociometric feedback would be the answer by a group member to the question, "With what three members of this group would you prefer to spend six months on a desert island?"

Sociometrist. Social investigator engaged in measuring the interpersonal relations and social structures in a community.

Soliloquy. *See* Therapeutic soliloquy.

Somnambulism. Sleepwalking; motor activity during sleep. It is commonly seen in children. In adults, it is observed in persons with schizoid personality disorders and certain types of schizophrenia.

Splitting situation. Condition in a co-therapy group. A patient is often unable to express opposite feelings toward one therapist. The splitting situation allows him to express contrasting feelings—positive-love feeling and negative-hostile feeling—by directing one feeling at one co-therapist and the opposite feeling at the other co-therapist. *See also* Role-divided therapy.

Splitting transference. Breaking of an irrational feeling or attitude into its component parts, which are then assigned to different persons. For example, ambivalence toward a mother may be expressed in a group by reacting to one member as to a good mother and reacting to another member as to a bad mother.

Square interview. Occasional session in marriage therapy in which both spouses and each spouse's therapist are present. The therapists and sometimes the patients are able to observe, experience, and respond to the transactional dynamics among the four of them, thus encouraging a common viewpoint by all four people involved in marital therapy. *See also* Collaborative therapy, Combined therapy, Concurrent therapy, Conjoint therapy, Group marital therapy, Marriage therapy, Quadrangular therapy.

Square situation. *See* Quadrangular therapy, Square interview.

Squeaky wheel. Person who is continually calling attention to himself. Because of his style of interacting, he is likely to get more than his share of a group's effort and energy.

Status value. Worth of a person in terms of such criteria as income, social prestige, intelligence, and education. It is considered an important parameter of one's position in the society.

Steckler anti-Negro scale. A scale designed to measure the attitude of Negroes toward Negroes. It can be of use in ascertaining the degree of prejudice blacks have against their own race and in evaluating the corrective efficacy of group experience. *See also* Ford negative personal contacts with Negroes scale, Ford negative personal contacts with whites scale, Kelley desegregation scale, Rosander anti-Negro behavior scale.

Steckler anti-white scale. A scale designed to measure the attitudes of Negroes toward whites. It can be used to ascertain the amount of prejudice blacks have against whites and to evaluate the influence of a group experience. *See also* Ford negative personal contacts with Negroes scale, Ford negative personal contacts with whites scale, Kelley desegregation scale.

Stegreiftheater. *See* Theatre of Spontaneity.

Stekel, Wilhelm (1868–1940). Viennese psychoanalyst. He suggested the formation of the first Freudian group, the Wednesday Evening Society, which later became the Vienna Psychoanalytic Society. A man given to intuition rather than to systematic research, his insight into dreams proved stimulating and added to the knowledge of symbols. Nevertheless, his superficial wild analysis proved incompatible with the Freudian school. He introduced the word thanatos to signify death wish.

Stereotypy. Continuous repetition of speech or physical activities. It is observed in cases of catatonic schizophrenia.

Stimulant. Drug that affects one or more organ systems to produce an exciting or arousing effect, increase physical activity and vivacity, and promote a sense of well-being. There are, for example, central nervous system stimulants, cardiac stimulants, respiratory stimulants, and psychomotor stimulants.

Stress immunity. Failure to react to emotional stress.

Stroke. In transactional analysis, a unit of human recognition. Early in life, strokes must involve physical contact; later in life, strokes can be symbolic—such as, "Glad to see you!"

Structural analysis. Analysis of the personality into its constituent ego states. The goal of structural analysis is to establish and maintain the predominance of reality-testing ego states, free from contamination. It is considered the first phase of transactional analysis. *See also* Contamination, Ego state, Game analysis, Ogre, Script analysis, Transactional analysis.

Structured interactional group psychotherapy. A type of group psychotherapy, developed by Harold Kaplan and Benjamin Sadock, in which the therapist provides a structural matrix for the group's interactions. The important part of the structure is that a different member of the group is the focus of the interaction in each session. *See also* Forced interaction, Go-around, Up.

Studies on Hysteria. Title of a book by Josef Breuer and Sigmund Freud. Published in 1895, it described the cathartic method of treatment and the beginnings of psychoanalysis. It demonstrated the psychological origins of hysterical symptoms and the possibility of effecting a cure through psychotherapy.

Stupor. Disturbance of consciousness in which the patient is nonreactive to and unaware of his surroundings. Organically, it is synonymous with unconsciousness. In psychiatry, it is referred to as mutism and is commonly found in catatonia and psychotic depression.

Subjectivity. Qualitative appraisal and interpretation of an object or experience as influenced by one's own feelings and thinking.

Subject session. Group technique, used particularly in structured interactional group psychotherapy, in which a topic is introduced by the therapist or a group member and is then explored by the whole group.

Sublimation. An unconscious defense mechanism in which unacceptable instinctual drives are diverted into personally and socially acceptable channels. Unlike other defense mechanisms, sublimation offers some minimal gratification of the instinctual drive or impulse.

Substituting. Providing a nonverbal alternate for something a patient missed in his early life. Crossing the room to sit beside a group member who needs support is an example of substituting.

Substitution. An unconscious defense mechanism in which a person replaces an unacceptable wish, drive, emotion, or goal with one that is more acceptable.

Suggestibility. State of compliant responsiveness to an idea or influence. It is commonly observed among persons with hysterical traits.

Sullivan, Harry Stack (1892–1949). American psychiatrist. He is best known for his interpersonal theory of psychiatry. *See also* Consensual validation.

Summer session. In structured interactional group psychotherapy, regularly scheduled group session during the therapist's vacation.

Superego. One of the three component parts of the psychic apparatus. The other two are the ego and the id. Freud created the theoretical concept of the superego to describe the psychic functions that are expressed in moral attitudes, conscience, and a sense of guilt. The superego results from the internalization of the ethical standards of the society in which the person lives, and it develops by identification with the attitudes of his parents. It is mainly unconscious and is believed to develop as a reaction to the Oedipus complex. It has a protective and rewarding function, referred to as the ego ideal, and a critical and punishing function, which evokes the sense of guilt.

Support. *See* Mutual support.

Suppression. Conscious act of controlling and inhibiting an unacceptable impulse, emotion, or idea. Suppression is differentiated from repression in that the latter is an unconscious process.

Surplus reality. The intangible, invisible dimensions of intrapsychic and extrapsychic life. The term was coined by J. L. Moreno.

Survival. Game used in a professionally homogeneous group. It is designed to create awareness of one another's talents. An imaginary situation is created in which the members are no longer permitted to continue in their particular professions and must, as a group, find some other activity in which to work together meaningfully and profitably. *See also* Game, Hit-and-run game, Million-dollar game.

Symbolization. An unconscious defense mechanism whereby one idea or object comes to stand for another because of some common aspect or quality in both. Symbolization is based on similarity and association. The symbols formed protect the person from the anxiety that may be attached to the original idea or object. *See also* Defense mechanism.

Sympathomimetic drug. Drug that mimics the actions of the sympathetic nervous system. Examples of these drugs are amphetamine and epinephrine.

Sympathy. Sharing of another person's feelings, ideas, and experiences. As opposed to empathy, sympathy is not objective. *See also* Identification, Imitation.

Symptom formation. *See* Symptom substitution.

Symptom substitution. Unconscious psychic process in which a repressed impulse is indirectly released and manifested through a symptom. Such symptoms as obsession, compulsion, phobia, dissociation, anxiety, depression, hallucination, and delusion are examples of symptom substitution. It is also known as symptom formation.

Tachylogia. *See* Logorrhea.

Tactile hallucination. False sense of touch.

Tangentiality. Disturbance in the associative thought processes in which the patient is unable to express his idea. In contrast to circumstantiality, the digression in tangentiality is such that the central idea is not communicated. It is observed in schizophrenia and certain types of or-

ganic brain disorders. Tangentiality is also known as derailment. *See also* Circumstantiality.

Tardive oral dyskinesia. A syndrome characterized by involuntary movements of the lips and jaw and by other bizarre involuntary dystonic movements. It is an extrapyramidal effect occurring late in the course of antipsychotic drug therapy.

Target patient. Group member who is perceptively analyzed by another member. It is a term used in the process of going around in psychoanalytically oriented groups.

Task-oriented group. Group whose main energy is devoted to reaching a goal, finding a solution to a problem, or building a product. Distinguished from this type of group is the experiential group, which is mainly concerned with sharing whatever happens. *See also* Action group.

Tele. In psychodrama, an objective social process that strengthens association and promotes cohesiveness in groups. It is believed to function on the basis of transference and empathy.

Tension. An unpleasurable alteration of affect characterized by a strenuous increase in mental and physical activity.

Termination. Orderly conclusion of a group member's therapy or of the whole group's treatment as contrasted with a drop-out that is not advised by the therapist.

T-group (training group). A type of group that emphasizes training in self-awareness and group dynamics. *See also* Action group, Intervention laboratory, National Training Laboratories, Sensitivity training.

Thanatos. Death wish. *See also* Stekel, Wilhelm.

Theatre of Spontaneity (Stegreiftheater). Theatre in Vienna which improvised group processes and which was developed by J. L. Moreno, M.D.

Theoretical orientation. Alignment with a hypothetical point of view already espoused by a person or group.

Therapeutic agent. Anything—people and/or drugs—that causes healing in a maladaptive person. In group therapy, it refers mainly to people who help others.

Therapeutic alliance. Conscious relationship between therapist and patient in which each implicitly agrees that they need to work together by means of insight and control to help the patient with his conflicts. It involves a therapeutic splitting of the patient's ego into observing and experiencing parts. A good therapeutic alliance is especially necessary during phases of strong negative transference in order to keep the treatment going. It is as important in group as in dyadic psychotherapy. *See also* Working alliance.

Therapeutic atmosphere. All therapeutic, maturational, and growth-supporting agents—cultural, social, and medical.

Therapeutic community. Ward or hospital treatment setting that provides an effective environment for behavioral changes in patients through resocialization and rehabilitation.

Therapeutic crisis. Turning point in the treatment process. An example is acting out, which, depending on how it is dealt with, may or may not lead to a therapeutic change in the patient's behavior. *See also* Therapeutic impasse.

Therapeutic group. Group of patients joined together under the leadership of a therapist for the purpose of working together for psychotherapeutic ends—specifically, for the treatment of each patient's emotional disorders.

Therapeutic group analysis. *See* Group analytic psychotherapy.

Therapeutic impasse. Deadlock in the treatment process. Therapy is in a state of imminent failure when there is no further insight or awareness and sessions are reduced to routine meetings of patient and therapist. Unresolved resistances and transference and countertransference conflicts are among the common causes of this phenomenon. *See also* Therapeutic crisis.

Therapeutic role. Position in which one aims to treat, bring about an improvement, or provide alleviation of a distressing condition or state.

Therapeutic soliloquy. Psychodrama technique that involves a patient's portrayal—by side dialogues and side actions—of his hidden thoughts and feelings that parallel his overt thoughts and actions.

Therapeutic transaction. Interplay between therapist and patient or among group members that is intended to improve the patient.

Therapist surrogate. Group member who—by virtue of experience, intuition, or training—is able to be an effective group leader in the absence of or in concert with the group therapist. He is also known as a nuclear group member. *See also* Leaderless therapeutic group.

There-and-then. Past experience rather than immediate experience. *See also* Here-and-now.

Thinking. *See* Cognition.

Thinking compulsion. *See* Intellectualization.

Thinking through. The mental process that occurs in an attempt to understand one's own behavior and gain insight from it.

Third ear. Ability to make use of intuition, sensitivity, and awareness of subliminal cues to interpret clinical observations of individual and group patients. First introduced by the German philosopher Frederic Nietzsche, it was later used in analytic psychotherapy by Theodor Reik.

Thought deprivation. *See* Blocking.

Thought process disorder. A symptom of schizophrenia that involves the intellectual functions. It is manifested by irrelevance and incoherence of the patient's verbal productions. It ranges from simple blocking and mild circumstantiality to total loosening of associations, as in word salad.

Three-cornered therapy. *See* Co-therapy.

Three Essays on the Theory of Sexuality. Title of a book by Freud. Published in 1905, it applied the libido theory to the successive phases of sex instinct maturation in the infant, child, and adolescent. It made possible the integration of a vast diversity of clinical observations and promoted the direct observation of child development.

Tic. Involuntary, spasmodic, repetitive motor movement of a small segment of the body. Mainly psychogenic, it may be seen in certain cases of chronic encephalitis.

Timidity. Inability to assert oneself for fear of some fancied reprisal, even though there is no objective evidence of potential harm. In a therapy group, the timid person may make others fear the destructiveness of their normal aggression.

Tinnitus. Noises in one or both ears, such as ringing and whistling. It is an occasional side effect of some of the antidepressant drugs.

Tolerance. In group therapy, the willingness to put up with disordered behavior by co-patients in the group.

Too-tired-to-be-polite phenomenon. Phenomenon in a marathon group that stems from fatigue and results in the relaxation of the social facades of politeness. Some proponents of marathon groups have stressed the helpfulness of fatigue in breaking through the social games that participants play in the early stages of the group. *See also* Group marathon.

Totem and Taboo. Title of a book by Freud. Published in 1913, it applied his concepts to the data of anthropology. He was able to afford much insight into the meaning of tribal organizations and customs, especially by invoking the Oedipus complex and the characteristics of magical thought as he had discovered them from studies of the unconscious. *See also* Oedipus complex, Primal father.

Toucher. Someone who enjoys touching another person. When the touching is not of the clinging type, such a person in an encounter group usually helps inhibited people lose their anxiety about physical contact and closeness.

Traditional group therapy. Group therapy of a conventional type in which the role of the therapist is clearly delineated and the other participants are understood to be clients or patients who are attending the group meetings to overcome or resolve some definite emotional problems. *See also* Encounter group, Group psychotherapy, Sensitivity training.

Trainer. Professional leader or facilitator of a sensitivity training or T-group; teacher or supervisor of a person learning the science and practice of group therapy.

Training group. *See* T-group.

Tranquilizer. Psychotropic drug that induces tranquility by calming, soothing, quieting, or pacifying without clouding the conscious. The major tranquilizers are antipsychotic drugs, and the minor tranquilizers are antianxiety drugs.

Transaction. Interaction that arises when two or more persons have an encounter. In transactional analysis, it is considered the unit of social interaction. It involves a stimulus and a response. *See also* Complementarity of interaction, Forced interaction, Group stimulus, Structured interactional group psychotherapy, Therapeutic transaction.

Transactional analysis. A system introduced by Eric Berne that centers on the study of interactions going on in the treatment sessions. The system includes four components: (1) structural analysis of intrapsychic phenomena; (2) transactional analysis proper, the determination of the currently dominant ego state (Parent, Child, or Adult) of each participant; (3) game analysis, identification of the games played in their interactions and of the gratifications provided; and (4) script analysis, uncovering of the causes of the patient's emotional problems.

Transactional group psychotherapy. A system of therapy founded by Eric Berne. It is based on the analysis of interactions and on the understanding of patterns of transactions as they occur during treatment sessions. Social control is the main goal of therapy.

Transference. Unconscious phenomenon in which the feelings, attitudes, and wishes originally linked with important figures in one's early life are projected onto others who have come to represent them in current life. *See also* Countertransference, Lateral transference, Multiple transference, Rapport, Transference neurosis.

Transference neurosis. A phenomenon occurring in psychoanalysis in which the patient develops a strong emotional attachment to the therapist as a symbolized nuclear familial figure. The repetition and depth of this misperception or symbolization characterize it as a transference neurosis. In transference analysis, a major therapeutic technique in both individual and group therapy, the therapist uses transference to help the patient understand and gain insight into his behavior. *See also* Collective family transference neurosis, Dilution of transference.

Trend of thought. Thinking that centers on a particular idea associated with an affective tone.

Triad. Father, mother, and child relationship projectively experienced in group therapy. *See also* Nuclear family.

Trichotillomania. Morbid compulsion to pull out one's hair.

Tricyclic drug. Antidepressant drug believed by some to be more effective than monoamine oxidase inhibitors. The tricyclic drugs (imipramine and amitriptyline) are presently the most popular drugs in the treatment of pathological depression.

Tyramine. A sympathomimetic amine that is believed to influence the release of stored norepinephrine. Its degradation is inhibited by monoamine oxidase. The use of monoamine oxidase inhibitors in the treatment of depression prevents the degradation of tyramine. The ingestion of food containing tyramine, such as cheese, may cause a sympathomimetic effect, such as an increase in blood pressure, that could be fatal.

Unconscious. 1. (Noun) Structural division of the mind in which the psychic material—primitive drives, repressed desires, and memories—is not directly accessible to awareness. 2. (Adjective) In a state of insensibility, with absence of orientation and perception. *See also* Conscious, Preconscious.

Underachievement. Failure to reach a biopsychological, age-adequate level.

Underachiever. Person who manifestly does not function up to his capacity. The term usually refers to a bright child whose school test grades fall below expected levels.

Undeveloped potential. The behavior, feelings, and motivations of a person known neither to himself nor to others. It is the unknown quadrant of the Johari Window, a diagrammatic concept of human behavior. *See also* Blind self, Hidden self, Public self.

Undoing. An unconscious defense mechanism by which a person symbolically acts out in reverse something unacceptable that has already been done. A primitive defense mechanism, undoing is a form of magical expiatory action. Repetitive in nature, it is commonly observed in obsessive-compulsive neurosis.

Unisexual group. *See* Homogeneous group.

Universality. Total effect produced when all group members share specific symptoms or problems.

Up. The member who is the focus of discussion in group therapy, particularly in structured interactional group psychotherapy.

Up-tight. Slang term that describes defensive, rigid behavior on the part of a person whose values are threatened or who is afraid of becoming vulnerable and of experiencing painful emotions. Such a person frequently becomes a target for pressure in a therapy group.

Urine-testing. Thin-layer chromatography-testing for the presence of opiates, quinine, barbiturates, and amphetamines. Addict treatment programs use such testing to verify abstinence from illicit drug use.

Vector. An engineering term used to imply a pointed force being felt by the group. *See also* Hierarchical vector, Horizontal vector.

Verbal-deep approach. Procedure used in small groups in which communication is conducted exclusively through verbal means and is oriented to major goals. It is a technique used in analytical group therapy. *See also* Actional-deep approach, Actional-superficial approach, Verbal-superficial approach.

Verbal-superficial approach. Group therapy procedure in which language is the sole medium of communication and the therapeutic process is structured to attain limited objectives. It is a technique traditionally used in the treatment of large groups. *See also* Actional-deep approach, Actional-superficial approach, Verbal-deep approach.

Verbal technique. Any method of group or individual therapy in which words are used. The major part of most psychotherapy is verbal.

Verbigeration. Meaningless repetition of words or phrases. Also known as cataphasia, it is a morbid symptom seen in schizophrenia.

Verbomania. *See* Logorrhea.

Vertical vector. *See* Hierarchical vector.

Vienna Psychoanalytic Society. An outgrowth of the Wednesday Evening Society, an informal group of Freud's earliest followers. The new name was acquired and a reorganization took place in 1910, when the Society became a component of the newly formed International Psychoanalytical Society. Alfred Adler was president from 1910 to 1911, and Freud was president from 1911 until it was disbanded by the Nazis in 1938.

Visceral insight. *See* Insight.

Visitor. Guest who participates in discussions with patients in group therapy. In family therapy, members outside the nuclear family who are invited to the session are considered visitors. *See also* Extended family therapy, Social network therapy.

Visual hallucination. False visual perception.

Volubility. *See* Logorrhea.

Warming-up session. *See* Premeeting.

Waxy flexibility. *See* Cerea flexibilitas.

Wednesday Evening Society. A small group of Freud's followers who in 1902 started meeting with him informally on Wednesday evenings to receive instruction in psychoanalysis. As the society grew in numbers and importance, it evolved in 1910 into the Vienna Psychoanalytic Society.

West-Coast-style T-group. Sensitivity training or encounter group that is oriented toward the experience of union, intimacy, and personal awareness, with relative disregard for the study of group process. It is a style popular in California. *See also* East-Coast-style T-group.

Wild therapy. Group therapy conducted by a leader whose background may not be professional or whose theoretical formulations include widely deviant procedures when compared with conventional techniques.

Withdrawal. Act of retreating or going away from. Observed in schizophrenia and depression, it is characterized by a pathological retreat from interpersonal contact and social involvement, leading to self-preoccupation. In a group setting, this disorder creates a barrier for therapeutic progress.

Wittels, Fritz (1880–1950). Austrian psychoanalyst. One of Freud's early followers, he wrote a biography of him in 1924, during a period of estrangement, when he was under the influence of Wilhelm Stekel. Later, a reconciliation took place, and Freud conceded that some of Wittels' interpretations were probably correct.

Wolf-pack phenomenon. Group process in which a member or the therapist is the scapegoat.

Word salad. An incoherent mixture of words and phrases. This type of speech results from a disturbance in thinking. It is commonly observed in far-advanced states of schizophrenia.

Working alliance. Collaboration between the group as a whole and each patient who is willing to strive for health, growth, and maturation with the help of the therapist. *See also* Therapeutic alliance.

Working out. Stage in the treatment process in which the personal history and psychodynamics of a patient are discovered.

Working through. Process of obtaining more and more insight and personality changes through repeated and varied examination of a conflict or problem. The interactions between free association, resistance, interpretation, and working through constitute the fundamental facets of the analytic process.

Xenophobia. Fear of strangers.

Zoophobia. Fear of animals.

Contributors

E. James Anthony, M.D.
Ittleson Professor of Child Psychiatry and Director, Division of Child Psychiatry, Washington University School of Medicine; Supervising Psychoanalyst, Chicago Institute for Psychoanalysis; Professorial Lecturer, University of Chicago School of Medicine, Chicago, Illinois; Physician, Barnes and Allied Hospitals and The Jewish Hospital, St. Louis, Missouri.

Edrita Fried, Ph.D.
Associate Clinical Professor of Psychiatry, New York Medical College; Training Psychoanalyst and Senior Supervisor, Postgraduate Center for Mental Health, New York, New York

Harold I. Kaplan, M.D.
Professor of Psychiatry and Director of Psychiatric Education and Training, New York Medical College; Attending Psychiatrist, Flower and Fifth Avenue Hospitals; Visiting Psychiatrist, Metropolitan Hospital and Bird S. Coler Memorial Hospital and Home, New York, New York

Benjamin J. Sadock, M.D.
Associate Professor of Psychiatry and Director, Division of Group Process, New York Medical College; Associate Attending Psychiatrist, Flower and Fifth Avenue Hospitals; Associate Visiting Psychiatrist, Metropolitan Hospital; Assistant Attending Psychiatrist, New York State Psychiatric Institute, New York, New York

Hyman Spotnitz, M.D., Med. Sc.D.
Author: *The Couch and the Circle: A Story of Group Psychotherapy* and *Modern Psychoanalysis of the Schizophrenic Patient*